MY SON TOM

MY SON TOM

THE LIFE AND TRAGIC DEATH OF TOM HURNDALL

JOCELYN HURNDALL

WITH HAZEL WOOD

BLOOMSBURY

First published 2007 under the title *Defy the Stars*
This paperback edition published 2008

Copyright © 2007 by Jocelyn Hurndall

Map © John Gilkes

Lyrics of 'Hotel California' (Felder/Henley/Frey) courtesy of Warner Chappell Ltd

The moral right of the author has been asserted

Bloomsbury Publishing Plc, 36 Soho Square, London WID 3QY

A CIP catalogue record is available from the British Library

ISBN 978 0 7475 9288 4
10 9 8 7 6 5 4 3 2 1

All papers used by Bloomsbury Publishing are natural,
recyclable products made from wood grown in well-managed
forests. The manufacturing processes conform to the
environmental regulations of the country of origin.

Typeset by Hewer Text UK Ltd, Edinburgh
Printed in Great Britain by Clays Ltd, St Ives plc

www.bloomsbury.com

for Sophie, Bill and Fred

We did not travel for adventures, nor for company,
but to see with our eyes and to measure with our hearts.

John Ruskin, *Praeterita*

Abbreviations

IDF   Israeli Defence Force
ISM   International Solidarity Movement
FCO   Foreign Commonwealth Office

CONTENTS

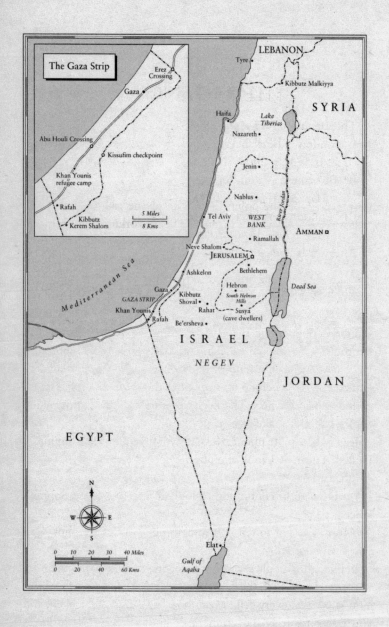

The Gaza Strip

Erez
Crossing
Gaza
Abu Houli Crossing
Kissufim checkpoint
Khan Younis
refugee camp
Rafah
Kibbutz
Kerem Shalom

5 Miles
8 Kms

LEBANON
Tyre
Kibbutz Malkiyya
SYRIA
Haifa
Lake
Tiberias
Nazareth
Jenin
Nablus
River Jordan
WEST
Tel Aviv
BANK
AMMAN
Ramallah
Neve Shalom
JERUSALEM
Ashkelon
Bethlehem
Gaza
Hebron
Dead Sea
Kibbutz
Shoval
South Hebron
Hills
Khan Younis
Rahat
Susya
GAZA STRIP
(cave dwellers)
Rafah
Be'ersheva
ISRAEL
Mediterranean Sea
NEGEV
JORDAN
EGYPT
N
W   E
S
Elat
0   10   20   30   40 Miles
Gulf of
Aqaba
0   20   40   60 Kms

THE BEGINNING

'Joss, can you come down? There's a phone call for you, Joss.'

It was the last day of term, and I'd been working that afternoon to finish a report for the educational psychologist on a child who had been diagnosed with Asperger's syndrome. I'd just printed it out and was making my way downstairs to the photocopying machine in the main office when I heard the call on the tannoy. Jean, the school's warm and efficient admin officer, always sounded definite, and there was nothing particularly unusual in her tone. As I crossed the hall my mind was still on the report, but I was also aware of a kind of question mark, a wordless anxiety that had hovered behind my conscious thoughts all week, while I considered now who would need to see the report . . . how many copies I should make . . .

Jean held out the phone: 'Joss, it's your daughter. It's Sophie.' I looked at Jean as I took the phone.

'Hi, darling.'

I was aware of continuing to look at Jean as I heard Sophie's voice.

'Mum, I've got to tell you something. Tom's been shot. Can you come home?'

Between the single second of receiving bad news and the next in comprehending it, there is a silent space like the eye of a storm. You know that every cell in your body is going to be shaken, and you freeze to delay the moment of impact. Your whole life is concertinaed into the still space between the blow and the pain. I remember sitting down, and I remember Jean reaching for my hand. Although she had no idea why Sophie was phoning, she must have heard the anxiety in her voice and seen the look on my face.

'Who told you?' I tried to sound calm.

'I think it was a paper. I can't remember. I think it was the *Daily Mirror*. They were asking me all these questions, what I knew about the shooting. That's how I found out. They said it was on Reuters, that he was helping a woman and child across a road. The phone keeps on ringing. Please, Mum, can you come home?'

'Darling, it's OK, I'm coming, straight away,' I said, aware that Jean was still looking at me, still holding my hand. 'Did they tell you anything else?'

'The Foreign Office called and they're going to phone back. They don't know where Tom is. Nobody knows where he is. But I think they said he was shot in a place called Rafah, in the Gaza Strip. There's a number for you to ring.'

Strangely, when I'd put the phone down, like an automaton I photocopied the report, wrote the initials of the recipients at the top of it, systematically distributed copies to the various trays and addressed a copy to the educational psychologist. I suppose I was trying to delay discovering the truth, to convince myself that this was some melodrama stirred up by the media, that Tom's was only a minor injury, though in my heart I knew that it was something really serious. I was aware of Jean beside me in the office, of people leaving, getting their things together for the Easter break. Someone came up to me and said, 'I hear Tom's been shot', and I could only nod and say 'Yes'.

It was the kind of news I had been dreading ever since my twenty-one-year-old son had left for Baghdad two months before with a group who had volunteered themselves as human shields against the threat of Anglo-American attack. He had been relatively conscientious about keeping in touch, e-mailing us from internet cafés and phoning when he could. We knew that he

had left Iraq after it had become clear that the authorities intended
to use the volunteers to protect power stations and other installations rather than schools and hospitals. Tom wanted to
prevent loss of life, but he wasn't prepared to be a sitting target,
and there were many other reasons for this journey. The last we
had heard he was in a refugee camp in Jordan, helping to put up
tents.

But then the e-mails had stopped and for ten days we'd heard
nothing. The previous evening Sophie and I had discussed
whether we should get in touch with my former husband
Anthony, who was away in Russia. It was quite possible, Sophie
and I thought, that he would have heard from Tom.

So I'd phoned Anthony that morning soon after our regular
7.40 senior management team meeting. Standing in the school's
inspiring, purpose-built learning support unit of which I was
manager, looking out of its wide, roof-level windows at the
dappled April sky behind the dark London buildings, I had heard
Anthony's voice, strangely clear from St Petersburg. No, he'd
heard nothing from Tom either, he said. Yes, it was a bit
worrying. But he'd be home tomorrow, and we'd decide then
what to do.

I picked up the phone again now and dialled the number I had
presumed was for the Foreign Office. But it was the *Sunday Times*
news desk. As I started asking questions, I could hear a change in
the voice of the journalist at the other end as he began to grasp the
situation and who it was he was talking to. 'Look,' he said, 'I'm
terribly sorry. I'll look on Reuters for you. But just be aware –
when things first come through they're not always accurate.'

There was a pause, during which I could hear the click of the
computer keys and the sound of my own uneven breathing.

'What's coming up,' he said slowly, 'is that peace activist Tom
Hurndall has been shot, and that he's brain dead.' And then, as if
to cancel out the brutal words, 'But as I said, you really mustn't
believe everything you first hear.'

I

LONDON – BE'ERSHEVA

APRIL–MAY 2003

ONE

Tom had left London for Baghdad on 21 February 2003. I had important meetings at school that day, but even if I'd been able to I wouldn't have gone to the airport to see him off. This journey didn't – couldn't – have my blessing, though I understood why Tom felt he must go.

So our last and final hug was outside Tom's bedroom the night before he left. How often in the past, hearing him moving around in the early hours of the morning, I'd tiptoed into that untidy room to bring him a cup of cocoa and found him sitting on the low chair in front of the window, feet up on the ledge, long legs stretched out, notepad on his knees, pencil in hand. Tom was always writing; he wanted to record every moment, to forget nothing. He wrote slowly because, though he had an exceptionally quick intelligence, he had a minor condition which affected his fine motor control. During his early days at Winchester College, a highly academic school, it had caused no particular problem, and as he grew older it began to work in his favour, the slight physical effort required for writing chiming with his unusual depth of thought and concise use of words. I worried about Tom's insomnia, but he'd always refused to see the doctor. 'There's nothing he can do,' he'd say. 'There's no point.' I understood. Rather than take pills, you might as well do something useful.

Over the previous months, particularly since the huge 'Stop the War' protest in central London on 15 February, we'd all noticed a change in Tom. He'd come down for the march from Manchester

Metropolitan University, where he had recently changed his course from criminology to photography, and though he was clearly ill with flu he'd insisted on going, taking his camera with him – Tom photographed wherever he went. It was on that march, as his girlfriend Kay told me later, that he had been handed a leaflet by the group who were volunteering to go out to Iraq as human shields.

Though Tom did go through the motions of consulting his family and friends – most of whom were, of course, appalled – I think that from the moment he was given that leaflet his mind was made up. Nothing any of us said could change it. A deep chord had been struck. As he was to say in a television interview, he didn't see why, by a mere accident of geography, other twenty-one-year-olds should be living in a state of conflict while he wasn't, and he wanted to show solidarity. He wanted to record the risks they were facing.

Anthony and I went over those risks with him, but he knew what we were going to say before we said it. I realised, as we talked, that even if I had not quite accepted it before, he was no longer a child, but a thoughtful young man who had made it his business to understand the main issues and was determined to try to make a difference. It was clear that while he was away at university he'd done a lot of research into the Middle East – its geography, its political history, even its religions – and now the walls of his room were covered with a series of eerie aerial pictures of the region that I suppose he must have found on the internet. They seemed to have been taken from a great height, almost from space. He had even written in the scale.

Now Tom, adventurous Tom, who even as a toddler was forever wanting to see over walls, down drains and round corners, was going to this unforgiving terrain. I was shocked, yet somehow resigned. We'd been here before – Tom was always challenging, always questioning. As I hugged him that last evening I could feel the nervous tension. I knew he was scared – he was too well informed not to be – and that when he'd had lunch with Kay that

day he had still been questioning his real motives for going. Tom
wasn't offering himself simply as a human shield, though he was
angry about the war in Iraq. The reporter in him wanted to see, to
photograph and record for himself what the human shields were
doing. As I held him I was almost unable to speak. All I could do
was repeat, over and over, 'Take care, Tom. Take care. Keep
safe.'

I had driven barely two hundred yards out of the school car park
when my mobile rang. I pulled in to the curb outside the
headquarters of my own union, the National Union of Teachers,
and opposite another, UNISON, two organisations that were to
play a supportive role in what was to come, though of course I
had no idea of it then. It was the journalist from the *Sunday Times*.

'Are you're all right?' he said. 'Please do drive carefully. How
far do you have to go? Look, I live just near you, in Tufnell Park.
Please let me know if there's anything I can do to help.' He was
no longer wearing his journalist's hat but speaking simply as one
human being to another, and I could hear that he was genuinely
concerned.

As I put my key in the front door I could hear the phone
ringing. It stopped briefly, then started again. I put my bag down
on the black and white tiled hall floor – everything so comfort-
ingly familiar, yet an entirely different place now from the one I
had left that morning. Sophie came up the stairs from the kitchen
and for a long moment we just held one another. 'Where's Billy?'
I said.

Apparently after hearing the news, my middle son, eighteen-
year-old Billy, had sat for some time at the kitchen table, silently,
with his head in his hands, and had then gone out for a walk on his
own: thinking things through, working things out quietly, as Billy
always does.

As the phone continued ringing – the national newspapers,
London Tonight, all wanting to come round and interview us – I
was thankful that Fred, our youngest, who was just twelve, was

out with friends. He and Tom adored one another and Tom's first thought was always for Fred. As soon as Tom came through the front door he'd always yell for him, and Fred would come running. They'd smack hands with a 'Gimme Five!', and Tom would pick his brother up and sling him over his shoulder while Fred laughed and struggled, pretending to hate it, shouting to be put down. Fred looked up to Tom. How could I tell him now?

When finally I heard the car and Fred hopped out, muddy and cheerful from quad-biking, I stood with him at the gate for longer than we needed to, waving our friends goodbye. 'Let him have these last few minutes of happiness,' I kept thinking.

Like all of us, Fred was barely able to absorb the news. 'Shot?' he said, blank, gazing out at the blossom trees. 'Shot? Where was he shot?'

Still we didn't know, despite a call from the Foreign Office. All the duty officer could tell me was that Tom had been flown by helicopter to a hospital in Israel, but they didn't know which one. They would call me when they knew more.

Between interviews and phone calls from the press, and from concerned friends who had now heard the news, I tried desperately to get hold of Anthony, but his phone was switched off. At 11.30 p.m. an acquaintance of Anthony's finally managed to reach him – that very evening his mobile had been stolen – and he rang immediately. It was 3 a.m. Russian time, and he had been woken by the phone call. We had some minutes of desperate conversation: What had Tom been doing in the Gaza Strip? How could we discover what his condition really was, and which hospital he had been taken to? Anthony said he'd be on the earliest flight the next day.

Afterwards I simply stood for a moment holding the phone, shaking my head, unable to believe what was happening. *Brain dead* – I had been pushing the fearful words to the back of my mind ever since my conversation with the journalist at the *Sunday Times*, and I hadn't used them to the children who, by this time, had finally gone upstairs, though I could still hear them moving about. Now I knew without question that I must discover every detail of what had happened to Tom. As his mother, I had an absolute compulsion to know. Around midnight I began phoning Israeli hospitals until finally I got through to the main hospital in Jerusalem.

As with the previous calls, a voice answered in Hebrew, then hearing my question switched quickly to English. No, I was told yet again, he wasn't there.

'So he was in Rafah? Then he would have been taken to the Soroka Hospital in Be'ersheva,' said the voice on the other end of the phone.

'The Soroka Hospital?'

'Yes. That serves the whole of southern Israel, the Negev. This is the number.'

'I'm trying to discover the whereabouts of my son, Tom Hurndall, who was shot today in Rafah, in the Gaza Strip. I'm told he would have been brought to your hospital,' I said when the phone was answered at the Soroka Hospital.

There was a perceptible pause. 'One moment.' Then, 'I'm putting you through to the Director.'

Another voice. 'Hello.' The same question. Another pause. 'Yes, your son is here.'

'Please tell me his condition.'

'It's not good news, I'm afraid. He has a very, very serious head wound.'

'A gunshot wound?'

'Yes.'

'Is he conscious?'

'No. I have to tell you, Mrs Hurndall, the situation is very bad. The bullet entered the left frontal lobe and exited at the back. It has done extensive damage and he has lost a great deal of blood. I'm sorry to have to tell you this when you are so far away, but I'm doubtful Tom is going to make it. He could last until tomorrow, or he could go in half an hour.'

Tom had arrived a few hours before by helicopter, the Director told me, and had been taken immediately to the emergency room next to the helicopter pad, where they had attempted to stop the bleeding and had given him blood transfusions. He was now in the Intensive Care Unit but still bleeding heavily. He was in a critical state.

'I'm coming,' I said. 'I'll be on a plane in the morning.'

'Really,' said the even voice, 'I must emphasise how serious his condition is, Mrs Hurndall. Is it really necessary for you to come? If Tom dies your journey may be for nothing . . . And you know, he can be sent back.'

Sent back? I was conscious that though he hadn't actually said so in as many words, the Director was telling me it wasn't worth my while to fly to Israel. That they could fly Tom's body back to England and spare me the journey. But whether Tom lasted the night or not, there was no doubt whatever that I was going to him. Nothing was going to stop me reaching my son.

'There's absolutely no question, I shall be coming tomorrow,' I said.

An hour later the Director phoned to tell me they had decided to operate, to clear the detritus from around the wound in Tom's head, and to stop the bleeding. It was the smallest ray of hope, but I clung on to it through a sleepless night. As I lay there I was so tense I felt dizzy, almost disembodied, as if my head was no longer mine. There was a humming in my ears, and my mind raced with anxieties about Billy and Sophie and Fred and how they would cope. Pictures of Tom lying injured and alone in a foreign hospital bed were overlaid with other images: Tom as a baby, full of curiosity, his feet running in the air, his arms waving like propellers as I held him up to see, touch or smell something that had caught his attention; skinny six-year-old Tom, tipping out of the car as we arrived from London at his grandmother's cottage in the country, throwing his clothes off to run laughing round the croquet lawn, stark naked in the pouring rain; Tom with blackberry-stained face and chest and hands . . . Tom . . . Tom . . .

At eight o'clock the next morning the Director phoned again to tell me that the operation had been completed. They had removed much of the detritus from around the wound, managed to stop most of the bleeding and given Tom further huge quantities of blood. He had made it through the night.

As I came out of my room into the arid greyness of the morning, I saw two figures on the landing. Sophie and Billy stood hugging one another and quietly weeping. I hesitated for a moment, not wanting to intrude, to break the comfort they were giving each another: Billy, so tall and gentle and thoughtful, Sophie, so strong and extreme yet vulnerable too, and frightened. All of us frightened. I went up to them and gently put my arms round them, but knew there was nothing I could do to help. I think it was then that I began to understand something of the isolation of grief. Also a flickering premonition of the anger that comes with it. How could they know that grieving is lonely, something you have to do on your own?

Anthony arrived back in England that morning, and at about twelve o'clock I saw his familiar figure walking down the road, carrying his briefcase, and I sensed his numbness. I felt the same huge sadness I had felt for Sophie and Billy at the thought at what he would have to face. Anthony had worked hard at his relationship with Tom – we'd both had to at different times. Unlike me, he had been able to be supportive of Tom's decision to go to Iraq, believing that he should be given his head. It was Anthony who had taken him to the airport, discussed with him yet again the dangers of taking photographs, and how careful he must be to respect the local culture and customs. Anthony was the last member of the family to have seen Tom before this terrible thing happened. He told me later how much he regretted not giving him a hug at the airport. Instead he'd given him a Swiss Army knife which Tom had stowed away in his main rucksack, and then waved him goodbye at the barrier, man to man. Now all we could do was hold one another in silence in our hallway. For those moments there was nothing to say.

We sat at the kitchen table, trying to work out the best thing to do, one or other of us reaching out from time to time to answer the ceaselessly ringing phone. Every cell in my body demanded that I should be with Tom, but I also knew that the other children needed me, particularly Fred. I knew, too, that Anthony's analytical mind and lawyer's training, his objectivity and assertiveness, would be vital when it came to gathering information in Israel. I knew we had to be strictly practical. So we agreed that Anthony would fly to Tel Aviv that night. Billy quietly decided that he was going with him. He knew he had to be there. Billy had made up his own mind and I respected him for it.

How can I begin to describe this weekend that changed our lives? Close friends came round, bringing us food and consolation and making practical arrangements, booking the flight to Tel Aviv, taking Anthony and Billy to the airport, doing their best to fill the hours for Fred, who was a lost soul, like the rest of us. By Saturday evening, Sophie and I were left in the echoing house to answer the doorbell and take calls from the media, all eager to have the Hurndall 'take' on the story and to find out about Tom – what had made him volunteer to be a human shield, was he a 'peace activist', why had he been in the Gaza Strip? The interest from the media was overwhelming, and Anthony had already seen that this was an opportunity to draw attention to what was happening in Gaza. Often they asked questions I couldn't answer – we did not know then that Tom had sent Anthony a series of e-mails explaining his decision to go to Gaza, which Anthony was unable to access for a week. But they made me search my heart again about what had impelled Tom to go. Shortly before he left, a remark he had made to a journalist from the *Independent* had been picked up by the paper as one of its 'Quotes of the Week': 'I want to put a real face on the situation, instead of what most people think. That we are tree-hugging hippies.' Even then Tom was creating waves.

Now it came to me that he had always been a kind of human shield. 'Tom was the sort of person,' I overheard Sophie saying to a journalist, 'who used to help schoolchildren at Tufnell Park tube when the older kids were trying to pinch their mobiles. Tom's always stuck up for people who were at a disadvantage.' She was right. The headmaster of his prep school had told us that it was always Tom who protected the younger boys from bullies. Tom's impulse to go to Iraq hadn't been simply a kind of aberration, but an extension of who he was.

Gradually, through Reuters and the other news media, more information was emerging. The first official Israeli version was that a Palestinian gunman wearing fatigues had been shooting a pistol at a watchtower and had been targeted by a member of the Israeli Defence Force. But the story now coming to us from all quarters was that Tom, unarmed and wearing an internationally recognised peaceworker's fluorescent jacket, had been rescuing some Palestinian children from Israeli sniper fire and had been gunned down himself. This was soon endorsed by such responsible foreign correspondents as James Reynolds of the BBC and Chris McGreal of the *Guardian*, both of whom had a deep knowledge of the situation in the area.

Talking to the press was draining, but also a relief. There really seemed nothing else to talk about, and Sophie and I both felt passionately that we wanted to speak out, to tell the world of this terrible wrong that had been committed. I watched Sophie as she answered the phone and dealt with the media in her usual clear and assertive way. Now twenty-three, Sophie, the first of my children, was protective of all her brothers. Tom was the closest to her in age, and even at five she was keeping an anxious eye on him as he wandered off to explore, always wanting to know, to test the boundaries, to see what was going on *out there*. For Tom, Sophie was a very solid presence and they confided in one another. She had tried to dissuade him from going to Iraq, and now under her warm, larger-than-life exterior I sensed she was frozen with grief. Once too often Tom's need to see what was happening had taken him off 'out there', and she hadn't managed to stop him. It was a trait of Tom's we all recognised.

Anthony phoned early on Sunday morning from the hotel in Be'ersheva where he and Billy were staying. His voice was bleak, and what he had to tell me of the situation was bleaker. My impulse was to go, *now*, but how could I leave Sophie and Fred? During the day several good friends who lived nearby and whose children knew ours arrived, and I remember that we all sat in my bedroom, going over and over the situation. I shall be eternally grateful that they understood my need to be with Tom and strongly endorsed my decision to go. When they reassured me that they would watch over Sophie and Fred I knew I could trust them absolutely, and Sophie and Fred bravely convinced me they could cope.

On Monday night I was on a flight to Tel Aviv.

TWO

I dozed uneasily during the long, dark, fearful flight, glad that I had a row of seats to myself, for I don't think I could have spoken to anyone sitting next to me. By now I was so exhausted I felt quite unconnected to what was happening around me. It was as if I was seeing everything through glass. All past life seemed to have been erased. It had ceased to matter. Time and space were mangled into a meaningless mass. Walls closed around me one minute and didn't seem to be there the next. It was possible only to think of the next few seconds, or of what was immediately around me. My head was filled with terrible images of Tom and of the distress of our other children.

A friend had driven me to Heathrow and I'd gone through the formalities in a daze. When the girl behind the check-in desk asked me the usual questions – whether I'd packed my own bag, left it unattended, or been given anything by anyone – I answered automatically. I'd brought very few clothes and hadn't even thought to find out what the temperature would be in Israel. My overwhelming thought was of getting to Tom. It was the beginning of a feeling that was to become familiar, of functioning on many different levels. I wondered, was this normal?

Fortunately the night flight was fairly empty, and I was grateful for somewhere quiet where I could sit and wait. Huddled in an armchair in a corner of the departure lounge I'd phoned a close friend, Vicky, and it was reassuring to hear her voice. I could see her, standing in the kitchen of the warm north London home I knew so well, cradling the phone as she waved to one of her teenage children on his way out, checking when he'd be back. It gave me a glimmer of comfort to think of ordinary life continuing – of blinds being lowered, of people clearing supper tables, homework being done – as I waited for the plane that would fly me eastwards into this grim and uncertain future. Only last week we had been a relatively 'normal' family, but now, it seemed, the whole world was focused in outrage on Tom's shooting. I don't think it was the natural reaction of a protective mother that made me feel this. There was a deep and genuine sense of public shock in Britain.

I think my state must have been obvious, or perhaps the airline staff had been warned, because one of them came up to me and said kindly, 'Why don't you go to sleep? I'll wake you when they call your flight.' I tried to close my eyes but my thoughts took off into the past, to happy family times at the cottage on the Essex/ Suffolk border – days of wood chopping and evenings in front of the log fire as a storm blew up across the mud flats from the Harwich Estuary. And always at the centre of these memories, Tom – tall, skinny and strong, a lovely sight as he ran across the grass or down the lane beside the cottage, completely single-minded and full of verve and mischief. It dawned on me that Tom, at twenty-one, was exactly the same age as I had been when I first went to Israel.

I tried to reconcile in my mind this place where he was lying at death's door with the place in which my father had developed a passionate interest and where I had spent a couple of months of carefree work and travel. My father had been a scientist with a mission – the generation of energy from wave power – and had been decorated for his pioneering contribution to engineering projects in the Middle East. Before the Six-Day War in 1967 he had spent time in Jordan as a consultant with what was then the Ministry of Overseas Development. I loved him dearly, although he was a somewhat remote figure in my childhood. But in later life, when we came to know each other better, he often spoke to me of his time there. I remembered his telling me how, one day when he was walking beside the Dead Sea, King Hussein's helicopter had landed not far away. My father, who respected this leader who had shown himself to be a man of vision with a well-known interest in alternative energy, had strolled over and struck up a conversation on this topic of mutual interest. It was to be the first of many meetings during which they shared this concern. I remember the signed photograph of the King in my father's study, alongside some carved camels and other bits of Middle Eastern memorabilia.

Just like Tom, I thought. It was the issue that counted. Not much regard for formalities – just straight to the matter in hand. I knew, too, how painfully my father had struggled to reconcile his passionate interest in engineering with his Christian beliefs. It was something that troubled him. A family friend once told me that he had gone through the entire Bible, New and Old Testaments, highlighting every reference to the sea. Was this his effort to resolve an internal conflict between science and religion? It was a search I had respected. That seemed like Tom, too – the idealism, the questioning, the independence – and the aloneness. Even when Tom was a little boy I had sensed a restless streak in him.

Sometimes, when I saw him sitting at the kitchen table or at the desk in his room, forehead on hand, shoulders hunched, I would come and sit quietly beside him. He didn't always want to talk. He just needed to know I was there. He was never short of friends, who were profoundly important to him, but I sensed there were times when he felt in some way separate, different. People didn't always understand his thinking, and this was certainly true when he made up his mind to go to Iraq with the human shields. But Tom kept his own counsel.

At about five in the morning, as the plane began its descent into Tel Aviv, I looked down at the harsh outlines of the modern city, the arterial roads and roundabouts, the high-rise blocks all touched with gold by the rising sun. Although it was so early I could already sense the heat of the day, bringing with it that feeling of being in a foreign country which I'd found so exciting as a student, arriving all those years ago to work on a kibbutz. As the plane taxied along the runway, I remembered landing at Lod airport, as it was then called, and even more vividly leaving it on my way back to London. I could see myself, wearing sawn-off jeans, a tank top, and carrying a smelly white Afghan coat I'd bargained for in a Jerusalem market, bundled up in a sheet from my sleeping bag.

I was thrilled with this ankle-length Dr Zhivago-style coat that looked as though it had been freshly shorn, and just as pleased with the empty cartridge hipster belt I was wearing, all the rage back in London in the 1970s. Even in those days Lod airport was bristling with young soldiers and within minutes one of them had motioned me over with a blank, impersonal look and, without a word or a glance directly at me, indicated that I should take the belt off. He raised it to eye level to let the daylight shine in and looked slowly and purposefully inside every cartridge case before handing it back. Then, seeing my strangely shaped bundle, he showed me into a cubicle, where a female soldier unwrapped and searched the coat laboriously. Little did I realise then that this was routine, for I had never before witnessed such treatment, let alone experienced it first-hand. Unused to being considered a suspicious character, I found this brush with the military distinctly thought-provoking, and I boarded the plane rather relieved to be on board a British flight home. That had been the summer of 1972.

As the plane juddered to a halt now and I began to unwind my cramped and painful limbs, a stewardess appeared beside me.

'There's an Embassy car waiting for you on the tarmac,' she said. 'As soon as the steps are down, follow me. Just bring your hand luggage, don't worry about anything else. The driver will deal with all that.'

The plane doors opened and a wave of heat hit me as I followed her down the steps to where an official looking car and a driver were waiting. It was a huge relief to sink into the comfortable anonymity of the back seat as we drove off across the airport. I suppose we must have gone through passport control, must have collected my luggage. I don't remember. I felt drained, and glad to be guided through the formalities, glad that everything was being taken care of.

In a car parking space reserved for diplomatic vehicles behind the Arrivals terminal we drew up behind a Range Rover flying a Union Jack. Someone with a friendly face was standing waiting.

'Mrs Hurndall? Tom Fitzalan Howard. I'm the Defence Attaché, British Embassy. Extremely good to meet you, but I'm sorry it's in these circumstances. I hope you had a reasonable flight.'

I heard myself uttering the usual pleasantries as my hand was taken in a firm and reassuring grasp by a rather military looking man with a kind and humorous expression. 'I'm so very sorry about Tom,' he said in the direct way I would come to know. 'Let me tell you what the arrangements are today. We're going to drive straight down to Be'ersheva to the hospital now so that you can see Tom, and we'll collect Anthony from the hotel on the way. Here, let me take your things. Do get into the front.'

I clambered up into the Range Rover but I felt I hadn't a muscle in my body. My legs were leaden and I had the sense of being outside my physical self that comes with extreme shock. Tom Fitzalan Howard took my arm sympathetically, helped me in and got into the driving seat beside me; the heavy door closed with a resounding clunk. Shut away from the loud airport noises, there was an immediate silence. It felt like being in an armoured car – which, of course, I soon realised it was.

As we left Ben Gurion airport through various guard posts and checkpoints, I became aware that they were all manned by uniformed soldiers carrying rifles. I was struck by how small and wiry these soldiers were, and how young – most of them looked no more than eighteen. The way their rifles were slung so casually across their shoulders, swinging around like menacing toys, shocked me. Ordinary to Israeli culture, obviously, but not to a Brit. Further on I saw groups of young soldiers standing at bus stops, hitching lifts, talking on their mobiles, just gathering in groups waiting to move on. What was the point of carrying these guns around? There seemed to be people in military uniform everywhere, men and women. I did not yet fully understand how profoundly militarised Israeli society is, how deeply this runs through the whole cultural fabric, but I knew immediately I was in a country permanently geared for war. And I sensed a challenge in this degree of alertness, almost a provocation.

We drove out through the Tel Aviv suburbs, along streets where the bougainvillea was in flower and past roundabouts filled with great succulent sharp-leaved aloe vera plants. At first I had the impression that the outside of every apartment block, every roof, terrace and balcony, was studded with industrial-sized refrigerators, but soon realised these must be air-conditioning units. Before long we hit the motorway south. On long stretches of it the jacaranda trees were coming into bloom, and suddenly it seemed that everything was enveloped in a cloud of luminescent lilac. I realised then that I could not allow myself to feel the beauty of that exquisite sight. If I did, my heart would break. The consciousness of what Tom might have lost came over me in waves and my eyes filled with tears.

As we drove Colonel Fitzalan Howard, or TFH as we would come to know him, steered the conversation with all the ease of the practised diplomat; we found we had a number of acquaintances in common, including an old friend of mine I had not seen for years, now a general in the Royal Green Jackets who had served in Northern Ireland. It was an odd sensation to find myself able to converse at this polite and social level while my mind was filled with thoughts of how soon we would reach the hospital and dread at what I would find. I heard myself thanking TFH for collecting me from the airport and apologising for the early start he must have had to make.

'Oh, no trouble at all,' he said warmly. 'I'm quite used to it. We've had a number of diplomats arriving recently and this is the flight we usually meet.'

It was a curious split feeling to continue to smile, to exchange ordinary civilities, not to reveal that my body felt as if it had been hurled against a brick wall and my mind had gone missing. But I knew I must not fall apart. Yet even though we were talking at this superficial level I very quickly became aware that I was not talking to a superficial man. Though it was clear that TFH was a practical person and not one for getting bogged down in senti- mentality, I sensed that here was someone I could trust absolutely, who understood every aspect of the situation. During the one- and-a-half-hour journey he impressed me as intelligent, knowl- edgeable and confident – someone who said exactly what he thought but only after he had given it much consideration and had gathered all the information. A straight talker, who brooked no nonsense and was wholly unafraid to challenge immorality and untruth in any given situation. Someone who would want to do the right thing for the greater good and not just for his own country. I also sensed a mischievous wit to which, in different circumstances, I knew I would have been able to respond.

'You realise, don't you,' he said, looking at me very directly, 'that we're not going to get anywhere with the Israelis.'

At first I didn't understand. 'All we want is to get at the truth. Doesn't everyone?'

'It's not quite as simple as that,' said TFH. 'They're a hard- bitten lot. They're not going to admit to anything. A lot of people have tried to call them to account, but I'm afraid they haven't succeeded.'

I was too tired and terrified for Tom to say much, but I tried to take in everything he was telling me, though I found it hard to concentrate. But as TFH talked on, I came to understand that we were going to get no cooperation whatever from the Israeli authorities. Worse, there would probably be obstruction. When the IDF's propaganda about Tom's shooting had appeared in the Israeli press we had certainly been deeply suspicious, but to have the position stated so starkly now by someone so well informed was something of a shock.

'Most people living outside the Middle East have no idea what the Israeli Defence Force is like,' TFH said.

I realised he was trying to brief me, to prepare me for the reality of what I would be seeing and hearing.

'When we travel down into the Gaza Strip later today and pass through UN refugee camps,' he went on, 'you'll see for yourself the destruction that's taken place.'

What did he mean? Destruction of homes? Destruction of land? Thinking back to my last visit to Israel, I remembered how even then, in the early 1970s, it was not advisable to enter Gaza. I now began to wonder why. When I was twenty-one I hadn't been drawn there by political anger, and, therefore, hadn't asked the questions. I recall learning that the Israeli government had declared that theirs was 'the most moral army in the world'. I remember thinking then that it was a strange way to describe your army. What reason could there be for making such a declaration? What Israeli general had come up with such an idea? If you were a moral army, why would you have to say it? Thinking in terms of a scale of military morality, with 'moral' at one end and 'immoral' at the other, I wondered where you would place other world armies? Who was convincing whom?

That statement had left me uneasy. It didn't ring true. I could relate to a motto such as that of the SAS: 'Who dares wins'. Mottos helped to build morale, self-belief, and act as an inspiration. But 'a moral army' – was it an indoctrination of the young or a statement designed to boost public image? A suggestion to the outside world to view it in that way? I did not know much about the young state of Israel. I had put my unease, then, down to my own lack of political awareness and of historical knowledge about the region, and pushed this unresolved feeling on to the back burner.

I focused my thoughts back on what TFH was saying. 'Have I understood you correctly?' I asked. 'I thought the Israeli army was supposed to be a moral army.'

'You know an Israeli soldier is not like a British soldier,' said TFH.

What exactly was he getting at, I wondered.

'The concept of minimum force is central to a British soldier who is trained, absolutely, to be accountable for his actions,' he went on. 'The British rules of engagement are very strict on this, and they are always applied. It's quite different with the IDF. For a start their soldiers are very young – conscripts, mainly, though there are professional soldiers. The soldiers are invariably backed up by their commander and the chain of command. Jocelyn, I have to tell you' – here he spoke slowly as if for emphasis – 'that the investigations are invariably a sham. This will be difficult for you and Anthony to deal with. A soldier is rarely held to account, and whatever he's done he would never face a murder or manslaughter charge – he'd only be on a lesser charge, perhaps failing to carry out the correct drills. I really don't want you to expect too much.'

So we had been warned. Though I had a feeling of blankness, at the same time I knew, with burning certainty, that we were going to use every possible means to get at the truth. I was sure the family would want to keep an open mind until we'd seen for ourselves everything there was to see. It was not that I didn't believe what this experienced military man was saying. It was just that we needed first-hand evidence before coming to any conclusions, and I suspected there would be a long way to go before any of us made up our minds. Anthony, as a lawyer, would be adamant about retaining objectivity and I knew he would not be hurried. His personality and training picked up on every detail, and he would insist on thoroughness. He would not settle for half measures.

The closer we came to the Negev, the more parched the land became. Strings of camels appeared on the skyline – that sure and magical sign of the East. They were cropping the scorched grass in small enclosures beside the motorway, tethered near groups of makeshift corrugated–iron shacks surrounded by a few olive trees. The contrast between the raggedness of the dwellings and the care with which the olive trees were clearly tended was striking. TFH told me these were Bedouin settlements.

'The Bedouin have a hard time of it,' he said. 'From time to time the Israelis simply come along and bulldoze these huts because they claim they're illegal. In the Negev they've herded the Bedouin together in seven shanty towns – you'll see the largest of them, Rahat, when we reach the Negev.'

It was impossible to open the bullet–proof windows, but I could see that the heat outside was intense, shimmering. It seemed too hot for even the olive trees to survive. I tried to imagine the life of these people who had once had the freedom of the desert, now cooped up in crude settlements. Why were they treated like this, how did they survive, what crops were they tending, what facilities did they have? It was as if, in this extreme situation, this unfamiliar territory, my sensibility was somehow heightened and my mind was bristling with questions, my whole being ringing with adrenaline.

TFH was speaking again. 'You also need to know that it's only with political support at the highest level that we've achieved anything with any IDF investigations. Problem is that with media pressure alone they hunker down under the anti-Semitic charge which they level against anyone who dares to criticise.'

This last comment hit home. It touched something in me and I felt my own anger. At times like this you have a strange feeling of striving to look down at yourself, of taking an aerial view in order to get the broad picture. It's an effort, but in the end it's what you have to do.

The colonel's last words reminded me acutely of Tom's Jewish friends with whom I had hardly had time to talk before leaving, and of the many Jewish people we knew in London. The present situation was not about race, religion, or getting sucked into any propaganda or political agenda. We wanted nothing but an objective search for truth, even if it meant believing that my pacifist son, Tom, really had dressed in army fatigues and been foolish enough to shoot at a watchtower, which was what that first absurd broadcast in Israel had stated.

That was the bottom line. We were a family that tried to build on insights and understandings about the reasons why people – in this case a foreign government and its army – did what they did. But there was no question that we wanted the truth. I knew this would be Anthony's view. And Tom's.

The nearer we got to Be'ersheva, the less we spoke. The dark knot in my stomach grew tighter as I went over in my mind what Anthony had told me and tried to imagine precisely what Tom's condition was, what the future really held for him and for all of us. Soon we were driving alongside the palm trees of Be'ersheva's central boulevard. With its buildings of sand-coloured stone the fifth largest city in Israel looked to me as if it had risen straight out of the desert. It was relatively new, built in 1948, TFH told me.

'That's the hospital, there,' he said pointing to a large blue semi-crescent-shaped building on one of the slight hills in the centre of the town. Now we were approaching the hotel where Anthony and Billy were staying and I called Anthony's mobile. He must have been wide awake and waiting for the call, for he answered instantly. The hotel was an ugly skyscraper block and as we entered the drive I was once more aware of security, of the spikes in the tarmac that slashed your tyres if you drove over them the wrong way, of the uniformed guard waiting at the front entrance to search us as we went in. I would soon become accustomed to all this, to the fact that it mattered not who you were – a habitual visitor, a bereaved parent, a near-death stretcher case, the most trustworthy looking person on the planet – there was no differentiation. The routine at every building was the same: you were always searched. Now, though, I was mildly surprised, since we were in a diplomatic vehicle with distinctive white number plates, and our unusual circumstances would have been known.

A sullen girl whose eyes never met mine telephoned Anthony's room, and we took the lift to the seventh floor. As he opened the door to his room Anthony's face told me everything. I had never seen him look so pale and drawn. TFH hung back tactfully as we talked and Anthony assembled a few things. Billy was still asleep and we decided to leave him and drive to the hospital on our own. It was still not yet 8 a.m.

I have no recollection of walking up the stairs of the hospital to the second floor, and along the passages and long corridors. I have a dim memory of benches along a wall on which Arab men in white robes were sitting, smoking, and of stepping over sleeping bodies in what seemed like a waiting room. I did not know then, Tom, that these were people who had come from all over Israel to be with you. The antiseptic smell struck me first as I was shown where to wash, and put on rubber gloves and a green gown. The crucial health and safety ritual added to my sense of the fragility of the lives of those in the Intensive Care Unit.

I don't think I breathed as I walked down the ward, past the semi-enclosed beds of the very sick. There were sounds but no sounds, smells but no smells. I approached your bed and recognised your face in spite of the bandages round your dreadfully swollen head, covering your eyes. Lights, moving wavy or straight lines on a screen with tubes, plugs everywhere, and a wide orange neck brace that came up over your chin. You were still bleeding from your left ear. There were cuts on your nose and hands where you must have fallen. Your hands and feet terribly swollen. I looked down at you surrounded by dials with changing numbers, luminous lines measuring blood pressure and heartbeats with the blip of a machine, searching for meaning for the state you were in.

I seemed to be looking at you from very far away, down a long tunnel. I do not know what the meaning of that tunnel was. Perhaps the shock of seeing you caused me to distance myself for that moment. I was there, gazing down at you, and yet I was not there. This was you, and yet it was not you. Too frightened to touch you for fear of hurting you. Unable to whisper for the choking in my throat. An echo, in the centre of my being, reverberated round my head, banging the drums of my ears. A voice spoke through me. It was you, Tom. Yet I knew I could not reach you, however

*many times I called your name. The moment I saw you reality had begun
to creep slowly towards me, invading me like a dark shadow.*

*Dearest Tom, at that moment, life stopped for a part of me, as it had for
you. My heart reached out to you, and I broke down. I was filled with
terror at your absolute fragility and your uncertain future. I could not even
pray.*

I don't know how long I stood gazing down at my son in total
disbelief. It was as if time had stopped, and the past, Tom's past,
our past, had disappeared, to be replaced by a colourless space. A
veil seemed to stretch round him on this bed, blocking out
everything else. This was the centre of our existence now,
nothing else mattered. I felt like two people, one looking at
the other. But as I gradually became aware of my surroundings I
realised that there was someone else standing beside the bed. As I
slowly raised my head I saw a lovely young woman with dark, sad
eyes overflowing with tears. She took me in her arms and, with
both of us in a state of complete distress, she repeated over and
over, 'I am so sorry for my country. I am so sorry.'

Those real, human words coming from an Israeli were like a
kind of explosion in my head. What must it have taken for her to
voice them? What must she have experienced in life to be in a
position to say them? What pain had she been through that she
could relate so intimately to other people's suffering? Two parallel
paths opened up. Her words came from another pain, another
story, which now seemed to be part of my own.

'I am Michal,' she said simply.

We stood there together beside Tom's bed, our arms around
each other, and this moment of sharing, of human compassion,
seemed to me at that moment to represent the epitome of
civilisation, of humanity, of what we are put on earth for.
And I wept even more because it contrasted so starkly with
the extreme inhumanity, the brutality, of what had happened to
Tom.

After a while she gently disengaged herself, laid her hand on my arm, and when I looked round she had slipped away. I had no idea then how close we would become to Michal and her family, or what a significant part they would play in Tom's story. At this moment I was too shocked and bewildered even to ask who she was.

After a while Anthony joined me. He stood looking down at Tom with an expression of infinite pity and sadness, and I could see the strain of the past forty-eight hours on his face. We left the ward and stood talking quietly about the meeting he had had the day before with the medical staff.

'We must be prepared for him to go at any time,' he said. 'It's unbelievable that he's lasted this long.'

We agreed that we must arrange for Sophie and Fred to fly out as soon as possible. I knew how painful it was going to be for both of them to see Tom in this condition. But I knew that it would be even worse if they were unable to say goodbye to him before he died. Even then some part of my brain remembered that Fred's passport was out of date, and that we would somehow have to arrange for him to renew it.

Some of what Anthony was telling me was hard to absorb. At the previous day's meeting, it seemed, one senior doctor had suggested that Tom's wound was 'commensurate with a blow from a baseball bat'. I looked across at the body of my son, swathed in bandages, connected to a battery of machines. I could see now that there was something terrible at the back of his head, where blood was still seeping through the bandage. Blood was seeping from his left ear. His long hands and feet were grotesquely swollen. Could any sane person, possibly – *possibly* – connect these terrible injuries with a blow from a baseball bat? When we looked at the notes at the foot of Tom's bed, the summary of his injury, which appeared at the top of each page, quite clearly stated that Tom had suffered a 'gunshot wound'. A senior hospital official had described the entry and exit wounds to Anthony, but he had seemed to backtrack when Anthony expressed surprise at the 'baseball bat' suggestion. Anthony had somehow gathered, too, that the consultant in charge of Tom's case had asked for a member of the IDF medical team to visit him.

What could all this mean? Uneasy as we already were about the possibility of a cover-up, and remembering the extraordinary reports which had appeared in the Israeli press, soon after Tom was shot, of a gunman in fatigues targeting an Israeli Defence Force watchtower, I began to feel the ground shifting under me – especially when I thought of TFH's uncompromising remarks about the IDF. From what little I had been able to take in, it seemed that Tom was receiving the best and most up-to-date medical care, but when it came to the medical evidence, to the politics of this situation, we both, I know, began to wonder whom could we trust. Yet at that moment I was too exhausted to pursue this train of thought. All I wanted to know was what had really happened to my son, how he had come to be where he was at the time he was shot, and what I, or anyone, could do now to help him.

Eventually we went out through the double doors with their porthole windows into the waiting room. It was still relatively early in the morning, and the scene there was like a campsite, with sleeping bags, rugs, pillows and rucksacks taking up most of the floor. Water bottles, soft drink cans and packets of half-eaten food lay here and there. A group of young people were standing by the window smoking the first cigarette of the day. It was impossible to imagine any of this happening in a London hospital. As we stepped carefully between recumbent bodies, several of the group by the window saw us and came towards us, and Anthony began to introduce me.

'This is Alison,' I remember him saying as a tall, slim, dark-haired girl in slacks held out her hand. 'Joe, Laura, Raph, Michelle, Nathan. Nathan and Michelle were with Tom in Baghdad . . .' A young woman with olive skin and dark eyes came forward and took my hands in both of hers, looking at me sadly and intently.

Apart from those two I had only the vaguest impression of a crowd of serious faces, of tousled heads and T-shirts and baggy trousers, as the group clustered round. Someone put a hand on my shoulder, someone hugged me, someone else took my hand. It was impossible to register names and information, though it did occur to me to wonder who on earth these young people were and why they were there. I think I remember hearing someone talking about the 'ISM', but it meant nothing to me. What I felt strongly was their affection and the warmth of their concern. Like an automaton, I heard myself asking them about themselves – how long they had been at the hospital, where they had come from – but was unable to take in a single answer. It felt important to respond but it took every ounce of energy I had. The tension in my head was so great that I was simply staring without seeing, hearing without registering. Yet at a deeper level I was already aware that these, too, were people who were in shock.

As I heard my voice asking these normal questions I wondered how I could be operating at these two levels. Shouldn't I be showing grief, weeping, collapsing even? Yet I already knew the answer. I was in a place beyond tears.

By this time Billy had arrived. Everyone greeted him by name when he came in and it was obvious that he had already become part of the group. But as I reached out to touch him, I was alarmed by the change I saw. Billy looked tense and drawn, and I could see immediately how much my sensitive, thoughtful second son was suffering – and suffering in silence. Billy is an unselfish person and his main concern, I knew, would be not to make things more difficult for anyone else. He'd always been like that. Almost as soon as he was born he lay on his side in the transparent-sided hospital cot with his eyes wide open, looking out at the world in the most peaceful and trusting way.

Yet I soon became aware that in this new situation something had shaken his trust. I tried to ask him how he was, but, as always, he found it difficult to talk about himself. But when we began

talking about Tom I was taken aback to discover how extremely
suspicious Billy seemed to be. Though normally so equable, he
has a passionate, outspoken streak when roused, and at these times
nothing one can say can change his mind. The comment about
the baseball bat had poisoned the atmosphere and he had con-
cluded that he must keep a very close watch on his brother and
anyone who treated him. Tom and Billy were different personalities, but their unspoken love for one another was absolute.
Though it was hard for us to say very much at this point, Billy's
few caustic remarks only added to my own uneasiness. What was
really going on here, I wondered again. How impartial were the
hospital staff, how much pressure were they under from forces as
yet unknown to us?

When TFH finally appeared in the waiting room at about
11 a.m. and announced that it was time for us to start for Rafah –
an expedition I knew he and Anthony had planned the day before
– Billy decided he wouldn't be going with us. I sensed that he
wanted to stay near to Tom. Billy was Tom's self-appointed
guardian, and he rarely left his brother's bedside during the month
he spent in Israel.

THREE

We left Billy sitting, immovable, beside Tom's bed and once again joined TFH for the journey to Rafah. Leading the way was another Range Rover containing Andy Whittaker, the second secretary from the British Consulate in East Jerusalem who covered issues in Gaza. TFH explained that the Embassy and the Consulate worked closely together. The Ambassador in Tel Aviv was accredited to the Israeli government and dealt with all issues in Israel itself. The Consul General in Jerusalem was accredited to the Palestinian Authority and covered everything that happened in the Occupied Territories – that is, East Jerusalem, the West Bank and Gaza. The Embassy was in Tel Aviv because the city was recognised by Britain as the capital of the State of Israel, while Palestine wasn't yet recognised as a state.

'But the fact that we and a lot of other countries have Consulates in East Jerusalem gives an important message to the Israelis,' he said

We were told it was Embassy policy always to go into the Occupied Territories in pairs. It was a safety measure. 'You never quite know what you'll come up against,' TFH said with a laugh. 'And by that I don't mean any threat from the Palestinians. I'm much more worried by the IDF. I'm not saying it's anything deliberate. More to do with lack of accountability and loose rules of engagement. It's easy to be mistaken for someone else – even in an Embassy Range Rover.' As Defence Attaché, he told us, he was the point of contact for all matters involving the IDF, both for the Embassy and the Consulate General.

With his wry humour, his military bearing and authoritative manner, I found TFH deeply reassuring. Later I was to learn how his thinking on the conflict had changed when he first visited the Occupied Territories and what deep anger at injustice was hidden behind his calm rather aristocratic exterior. But now I was too emotionally drained and physically exhausted for discussion of any kind.

We drove southwards along tarmac roads, through lush farmlands and well-tended fields of lemons and maize. I was astonished by the abundance of this prosperous landscape. We were in the waterless area of the Negev, yet huge shining sprays of water played continuously on the fields. From a distance they looked like hazy fluctuating mirages that glistened occasionally, but as we drew closer I realised the sheer extent of the irrigation. I'd never seen water used so freely.

Half an hour later we were approaching the Erez Crossing, the checkpoint which marks the Israeli-imposed 'border' between Israel and the Gaza Strip and is the only entry into Gaza from the north. We joined a queue of vehicles drawn up outside a low concrete building, with a guard box on either side of the gated checkpoint. TFH explained that over the past days he had been in contact with the Consulate in East Jerusalem about whether it was safe to go into the Occupied Territories – in other words, to discover whether the Israelis were planning another incursion – and had been given the all-clear. The Israeli authorities had been given notice of our impending visit, and had been provided with all our details – our names, our passport numbers, the 'purpose of our visit'. As I would learn, going into Gaza is not something anyone does lightly.

'But don't imagine all that's going to speed things up much,' he said as he got out of the car and disappeared into the office building with our passports and documents.

The minutes ticked heavily by. I think I dozed a little, my half-dreams full of Tom, of Billy, Sophie and Fred, while Anthony sat preoccupied, gazing out of the window. When I opened my eyes

I could glimpse, beyond the checkpoint, concrete stretching into the distance, and I could see people moving about behind the glass and steel windows of the checkpoint building. Eventually TFH came out.

'I'm sorry about this,' he said, 'we're just going to have to wait. This is what they do. They make you wait. It's even worse for the Palestinians. They can be here for days or even weeks. Sometimes they wait and wait and after all that they're still not let through.' Sitting in the luxury of the air-conditioned Range Rover, I tried to imagine what it would be like to be on foot, waiting and waiting in the horrendous heat. There was no comparison.

Some huge grey armoured Chevys with American flags flying drew up beside us. Some uniformed personnel went into the checkpoint building, the rest lounged around the vehicles. TFH explained to us that US Embassy cars always travelled in convoy. 'As you can see,' he said, 'they're not taking any chances. They roar in and roar out. They're not very popular in these parts. They try not to get up too close to the ordinary, local people. They have an overwhelming fear of casualties so they just don't travel in the Occupied Territories.' Ten minutes later the Americans were hopping into their vehicles and the whole ungainly procession lumbered through the checkpoint. It looked menacing, over-bearing, all shiny chrome and darkened windows. I couldn't help comparing the impression the Americans made with that of the English contingent, which was unobtrusive and low-key. TFH, I would discover, carried nothing more menacing than a bag of sweets in the Range Rover's glove compartment.

Thirty minutes . . . forty minutes passed as we waited in the car park. Finally TFH was back, this time with a young man who introduced himself as Inigo Gilmour, a correspondent for the *Daily Telegraph*, who would be coming with us to Rafah. Suddenly I registered who he was. His mother was a friend of Julia, a close friend of mine. In the confusion of arrangements before I left London, I dimly remembered Julia telling me that Inigo would be getting in touch. It felt comforting to have someone along with such close links to the family, who spoke the same language in every sense, and who could easily have been a friend. After a moment or two's conversation the barrier gate was lifted, and we were through into no-man's-land. Inigo followed in a taxi.

My first impression was of a sterile greyness, like an airport, a huge tarmac area with high concrete walls topped with barbed wire rising on either side. TFH pointed out some metal cages, approached by covered alleyways and turnstiles. 'That's where they search the Palestinian workers as they come through,' he said. 'X-rays and everything. They call it "processing". Makes me think of a concentration camp.'

We drove slowly, zigzagging between giant clumps of concrete. It was rather like being in a maze, except that there were no choices. On either side of us, about every fifty yards, were machine-gun posts guarded by tanks and at intervals tall posts with what looked like cameras on them. It was truly no-man's-land, a place with no sign of human occupation. The Israeli military were hidden, watching us through slits in their guard posts, which bristled with masts and antennae for electronic monitoring. It seemed a place devoid of humanity, empty and menacing. It sucked your hope away.

It came to me forcibly that this checkpoint was not just a formality. We were in the midst of a fearful conflict, where life and death hung in the balance. There was threat in the air, a feeling of oppression that weighed me down. It was a feeling I recognised, though at first I couldn't place it. Travelling back to England on leave from Mauritius where we had lived when I was five, we had stopped off briefly in South Africa. I was shocked and bewildered when I understood the meaning of the notice on the park bench that said 'Europeans Only'. It meant that if my much-loved Indian nanny Hannah had been with us, we wouldn't have been allowed to sit together. I can still remember my anger, even then, at the injustice of apartheid, though I did not know its name. The oppression of apartheid was what I felt I was witnessing now. Nobody had told me to look for it, but from the minute I entered the Occupied Territories I was piercingly aware of it. The stench of it hung in the air and went straight to my stomach.

But nothing had prepared me for what was to come next. As we were let through the Palestinian side of the checkpoint – an exchange which seemed to consist simply of a smile and a wave from the border guard – and out the other side, all I could see at first was mud, a brown quagmire stretching into the distance as far as the eye could see. Where the car had sped along tarmac roads on the Israeli side, now it sank into ruts and jolted over potholes, bumped and swerved, its speed slowed almost to walking pace. I'd travelled across the world that day, but one mile on Palestinian roads shook me up more than any other part of the journey. Everything in this desolate landscape seemed to have been dug up, bulldozed or flattened, the land pulped into muddy chaos. Great clumps of upended tree roots lay exposed. It was like some battlefield of the First World War. The terrible inequality bled through the crushed earth.

As we drove TFH pointed out to us the places where there had once been orchards, which had been ripped out of the ground and cleared by the bulldozers of the Israeli Defence Force. He described the countryside as it had once been, a land covered by acres of orange trees and olive groves hundreds of years old, passed from father to son by generations of Palestinian farmers. Yet however bruised and abused this landscape, I felt that a soul lingered in the churned-up earth that had once provided people with a living.

The journey took us through Gaza City, one of the most densely populated cities in the world, where we stopped to pick up an interpreter. The car crept at snail's pace through narrow streets so thick with people that there seemed to be no distinction between the pavement and the road, a heaving, shifting mass of women carrying bags of fruit, men on bicycles, wooden carts pulled by donkeys. Yet though the crowds moved they seemed to

be going nowhere. There was a sense of aimlessness and disor-
ientation, though here and there we saw groups of cleanly dressed
children on their way home from school. The feeling was even
more powerful in the Khan Younis refugee camp. TFH told us
that in this destroyed economy there was huge unemployment,
and everywhere the poverty was evident. Coming from the steely
efficiency of Israel into Gaza, we had moved from the Developed
World into the Third.

As we drove towards Rafah, TFH pointed out Israeli settlements off in the distance, clusters of attractive looking, low
bungalow-style buildings, some with beautiful views out over
the Mediterranean. What on earth were these settlements doing
in Palestinian territory, I wondered. It astonishes me now to think
how little I knew then about the situation in Gaza. Like so many
people in the West, I'd had no need to. TFH explained that these
settlements had been part of the stealthy land grab encouraged by
Ariel Sharon twenty or thirty years earlier. From time to time he
would point to a road saying, 'That's a road Palestinians don't
use.' It was all extraordinary and bewildering.

All the settlements were surrounded by dark, ominous-looking
watchtowers built of concrete or scaffolding with grey steel cabins
perched on top. Bizarrely the cabins were crowned by great lumps
of thick camouflage netting made from rope, like giant hair nets,
which made them look doubly menacing. What, I wondered,
could be the purpose of these? The Palestinians certainly had no
possibility of bombing from the air – their only airport had been
closed. It seemed simply another detail in the process of intimidation.

As we approached Rafah we passed through the infamous Abu
Houli Crossing, one of the many that the Israelis use to control
the movements of the Palestinian population in the Gaza Strip
and elsewhere in the Occupied Territories, and here we sat again,
patiently waiting to be allowed through. A tower on either side
controlled the traffic coming in both directions, with only a single
line allowed through at any one time. I was surprised to hear the

clunk of the vehicle's central locking system and wondered what the danger was.

The dust and the brilliant sunshine drained colour out of everything so that it was almost impossible to read the warning traffic light. Little boys ran along beside the line of waiting cars, peering in through the windows, gesturing to the drivers. Occasionally a door would open and a child would get in. TFH explained that cars with a single person in them weren't allowed through, because the Israelis feared they might be suicide bombers. The children made a little money by hopping into the passenger seat to get the car through the checkpoint. Other small boys moved up and down the line of cars selling chewing gum and sweets.

'Not so bad today,' TFH said as we finally drove through. 'Sometimes you get here to find it's closed for no apparent reason. You could be waiting hours or days, so you have to decide whether to sit it out or turn round – and that includes ambulances and UN vehicles. I try to get down into Gaza once or twice a month, and into the West Bank twice a week, just to check up on what's happening, use my eyes and ears, ask a few difficult questions. It's remarkable what an effect just parking near a checkpoint can sometimes have. When the soldiers on duty realise there's a diplomat watching, the traffic queue often starts flowing again quite quickly. Very satisfying!'

So this was what it meant to be a Palestinian in Gaza – constant humiliation and frustration, your every movement checked and controlled.

The first indication that we had arrived in Rafah was the sight of dense clusters of watchtowers on the skyline. Soon we found ourselves directly beneath their terrifying Big Brother gaze as we drove into the desolation that is Rafah. It must, I suppose, once have been an ordinary town, where people went about their ordinary lives, but it was hard to imagine that now. For every crumbling house left standing, its stucco pockmarked with black bullet holes, there were whole streets that had been demolished.

Here and there a single wall stood up like a broken tooth. In some places only the upper floors of houses had survived, balanced precariously on concrete piers, and in the rubble beneath them children were playing. Balconies hung crazily, windows gaped, mangled steel girders hung silhouetted against the sky like left-over strands of blackened spaghetti.

Sometimes a family had erected a tent beside their demolished house, and these small shelters looked tragic and vulnerable, clinging to the place that had once been home. Rafah seemed to me a ghost town, filled with dispossessed souls who had nowhere else to go. TFH told us that many of the population lived in the open, on the streets, on football pitches, forced from their homes by bulldozers and tanks. In the previous thirty-one months the Israeli Defence Force had demolished 788 homes in Rafah, according to Palestinian sources. 'Why?' I kept thinking. 'How can all this be happening?'

We were heading slowly into the Yibnah district, to the headquarters of an organisation TFH kept referring to as the ISM, where, we were told, we would meet people who would be able to tell us about Tom's last days there; some of them had been with him when he was shot. Anthony was determined to speak to as many witnesses as possible. My overwhelming need was to know, to understand, why Tom had been in this desolate place and what he had been doing here.

Our vehicle wove a tortuous path through the streets, man-oeuvring to left and right as we encountered roadblocks, made from the rubble of bulldozed houses. Here, it seemed, even the fabric of people's own homes was used against them. Whole streets were sealed off. Nothing could enter them, not even ambulances.

We turned the final corner into a central square and there was a large crowd. We could see that we were expected.

The two Range Rovers pulled up on a potholed piece of waste ground between two buildings which, when it rained, must have been a sea of mud. Everything in sight here had a temporary look

– corrugated-iron sheets nailed over damaged doorways, patches of unpainted plaster slapped on to hold disintegrating brickwork together. At the back of the waste ground was a crumbling wall, and across it was written in black and red letters:

> Rachel, Who Came To Rafah
> To Stop The Tanks, We
> Remember her with Love
> And honour as an Inspiration.

I turned towards TFH. I knew that Rachel Corrie was the American girl who had been crushed by an Israeli bulldozer only weeks before, and although I had no inkling then of her significance in Tom's story, I wanted to know more. But TFH was busy directing the driver.

'Park round so we're facing outwards,' I heard him say, waving at the other Range Rover to do the same. As the vehicles reversed, I wondered why this was necessary, though I would soon become familiar with these basic safety precautions.

Our driver, whom TFH now introduced as Sgt Hogan, released the central locking system and we climbed out, picking our way across the potholed patch to the square. My impression was of damaged or half-finished buildings, of breeze-block and cracked stucco, of flat roofs covered in a sharp forest of TV aerials, washing lines and huge water tanks. What seemed like hundreds of people, including a group carrying microphones and hand-held television cameras who were clearly from the press, were waiting patiently, almost blocking the entrance to one of the houses. There was no hint of aggression – in fact the crowd seemed strangely subdued – but I could tell that both TFH and Andy Whittaker were uneasy as they shepherded us quickly through the crowd, past some fruit and vegetable stalls filled with luscious tomatoes and oranges, into an open doorway and up a flight of stone stairs. Inigo Gilmour followed quietly behind.

To describe the room we entered as sparse would be an

understatement. There were a couple of mattresses on the bare floor against the far wall, and a few battered plastic chairs dotted randomly about. The most striking feature was a tattered banner draped against the right-hand wall. For a moment it reminded me strangely of the ancient banners I'd seen in English country churches, transparent with age. There was very little left of this one; it seemed to have been almost torn apart, but it was just possible to read the words: 'We are Internationals – don't shoot'.

There were a number of people in the room and they immediately came towards us, holding out their hands and introducing themselves. Anthony was ashen-faced, but he was immediately focused, asking questions and collecting facts. By this time my terror for Tom, my lack of sleep and the sense of being outside my body had induced a kind of mental paralysis, and I found it impossible to take in people's names, or indeed, initially, very much of what they were saying. After shaking hands I sat down on one of the plastic chairs, and a tall olive-skinned young man with thick curly dark hair and deep-set, intelligent eyes came and sat next to me.

'I am Mohammed. I was with Tom when he was shot,' he said in excellent English. 'I knew him for only a few days, but he had become my friend. He cared about us and about what is going on here. He is a special person. I am very, very sorry for what has happened and I miss him very much.' He put his hand over his eyes and turned away.

I realised with a lurch of my heart that, for the first time, I was with someone who had witnessed what had happened to Tom, who knew, perhaps, his reasons for coming here and what he had been doing in those last hours before the bullet struck.

I put my hand on Mohammed's arm, and we sat in silence for a moment.

'Please,' I said, 'do you know what Tom was doing in Rafah? We had no idea he was here. How did you meet him? Why was he shot? What was he doing to be targeted? I still don't understand.'

'I met him first when he came here to the ISM headquarters,' said Mohammed. 'He stayed the first night with the family of Dr Samir, right on the border there, where they are shooting at the houses day and night.'

The depth of my ignorance seemed like a chasm. 'I'm sorry,' I said. 'I know nothing about the ISM. What do the letters stand for? And what did Tom have to do with the ISM?'

'This here,' said Mohammed, sweeping his hand round to take in the rest of the room, 'is the headquarters of the ISM, the International Solidarity Movement. This is a peaceful movement, though the Israeli army and the Israeli press will tell you many lies about us. We try to stop the destruction of Palestinian homes, to monitor and bring attention to what is happening here, the shootings of civilians, the abuses of human rights.' Here Mohammed struck his forehead with his fist and sat for a moment as if in deep gloom. He himself, I felt sure now, was a Palestinian, though there seemed to be young people of many different nationalities in the room.

I had brought a notebook with me and I forced myself to concentrate, writing down Mohammed's replies to my rather incoherent questions, knowing that all this would be of importance later on. When I look at my notes now they seem scrappy and unconnected, but I no longer need them, for I know the story of Tom's last days so well that it has become a part of me, like a continuously running film.

Mohammed told me he had first met Tom a few days before the shooting. Mohammed, Alison and Raph had gone to meet him at the bus stop when he arrived. He had come from a refugee camp in Jordan, where he had been helping to put up tents with the Red Crescent. He had travelled to Gaza from Jerusalem, where he had spent some days in a student hostel on the Nablus Road.

'He had been travelling all day,' said Mohammed, 'and he was thirsty, yes, very thirsty. Tom, he sat on one of those mattresses over there and drank a couple of cans of Coke.'

Yes, that would be Tom, I thought. He drank gallons of Coke, despite my occasional protests. I could just picture him sitting in the corner with his long legs against the wall, tired and dusty, good-humouredly observing the scene around him. Though Tom appeared laid-back, his eyes missed nothing.

Mohammed told me that Tom had come through the Erez Crossing to Rafah under the auspices of the ISM. 'He had heard what happened to Rachel – you know about Rachel Corrie? – she was making peaceful protest here with the ISM, defending Palestinian homes, when the Israeli army ran over her with a bulldozer,' said Mohammed, and there was simmering anger in his voice. 'Tom told me that when he heard about Rachel he wanted to see what was going on here in Gaza, to make a record. He had with him his camera, always his camera, and his little book and pen.' He made the motions of someone writing.

So that was why Tom had come to Rafah. After leaving Iraq, he must have moved on to Jordan, and then come on down here.

For the first two nights in Rafah, Mohammed told me, Tom had stayed with the family of a Dr Samir, whose house was in an area the army were in the process of clearing – that is to say, demolishing – which they called the 'security zone', right on the Egyptian border. The army's way of doing this began, apparently, with intimidation. Each night a tank stationed permanently nearby would position itself at the end of the street and fire warning shots at the houses, terrifying the inhabitants, especially the children, and often injuring and killing civilians. During the day it lurked outside a mosque, making it impossible for local people to go in.

On the day of Tom's shooting, the ISM had decided to stage a peaceful protest by pitching a tent outside the mosque. Tom and Mohammed had met in the morning and gone to a café, where they talked about the proposed demonstration. Mohammed had been feeling very down, very depressed about the whole situation. Tom had asked him what the matter was. 'How are you feeling?' he'd said.

'I told him,' said Mohammed, 'that to me everything was

hopeless. Nothing is ever going to change here for my people. There is no future. But Tom, he put his arm round me and told me I must have hope. That he and the others of the ISM are here to give support, to try to change things for us. He really tried to give me hope.'

When they left the café to go down to the ISM headquarters, Mohammed had felt irritated because, as usual, they were followed by a crowd of inquisitive children and Tom seemed to be encouraging them. 'Already that morning he had been out playing football with some of them,' he said, with some exasperation.

I could easily picture the scene. Tom was at ease with children and was always ready to engage with them, whether it was by showing them his camera or kicking a football around. I could see that particular expression of his which carried a challenge, an invitation to stretch the boundaries, a mischievous look that said, 'Come on then. Have a try!' Whereas Mohammed, depressed as he was, would have seen these youngsters as a nuisance, Tom would have seen them simply as children who needed to have a bit of fun. And my throat suddenly constricted when I thought of Fred.

Now other people began to join us. Anthony, his pen poised over his notebook and now in deep conversation with an older woman I would later discover was called Alison, came over to where we were sitting. A pale, strained-looking young woman with very short hair, whom Mohammed introduced as Alice, appeared with a tray of tea in glass cups. Alice told me that she had been with Tom and Mohammed that day when they had set out from the ISM headquarters, carrying tent poles for the proposed demonstration.

By this time I had given up trying to record what people were saying but Anthony was still asking questions and making detailed notes. Looking at his drawn face I could see how much the experience was costing him. But this, I knew, was his way of dealing with our new and tragic reality. I didn't realise at the time that without it we would have got nowhere. It was the first step of our intense investigation.

It seemed that a couple of other young ISM members, Laura and Amjad, had been sent on ahead to see the lie of the land and had quickly returned to report to the others that there was shooting in the area of the mosque, probably from one of the Israeli Defence Force watchtowers which overlooked the square. By this time the remainder of the party had reached a mound of rubble blocking the street which led to the mosque. They could hear shooting, though they could not see where it was coming from, the tank or the watchtower. A quick discussion ensued, and it was decided to cancel the demonstration – it simply wasn't safe, they decided, and it was the policy of the ISM never to demonstrate in an area where there was shooting.

Meantime the shots continued, and they could see bullets ricocheting off the building beside the mound, on which a group of about twenty or thirty children were playing, apparently accustomed to the danger. But gradually the shots hit lower and lower, flying close over the children's heads, and when they began scuffing up the sand, most of them jumped off the mound and ran away down an alleyway between the houses. Only a boy and two little girls, about six years old, stayed rooted to the spot, terrified and crying for help, not knowing which way to turn.

Apparently Tom had seen a little boy shot in the shoulder after throwing stones at a tank only five days before. Now he saw what was happening, handed back his camera to one of the group and went towards the children. He beckoned to the boy, holding out his arms, lifted him off the mound and carried him down the street out of range of the shooting. Then he went back for the two little girls, bent down and put his arm round one of them.

'They shot him,' said Alice. 'Right there. When he was rescuing those two children. The IDF shot him.'

It was a stark and brutal statement. 'But why?' I said. 'Why would they do that? Surely they could see what he was doing. Couldn't they see he wasn't armed?'

'Oh, sure,' said Alice bitterly. 'He was wearing an orange jacket – we were all wearing orange jackets. Everyone recognises that means you're a non-combatant. Do you think that makes any difference to them? They don't like the ISM. They know we see what they're doing here, and they want us out. Just the way they want the Palestinians out.'

'Do you think it could have been a mistake?' I said. 'The shooting?'

'A mistake?' said Alice. 'You don't make mistakes with telescopic sights like the IDF have got. You could shoot the buttons off someone's coat with those.'

I remembered the reports of the Palestinian gunman targeting an Israeli watchtower.

'But was there any other shooting going on? Was there crossfire?' I said.

'None,' said Alice emphatically. 'Absolutely none. There were no Palestinian gunmen in the area that day.'

There seemed so much more to say, and everyone in the room had something they wanted to tell us, but I could see that Andy and TFH were becoming restless. Andy seemed impatient and tetchy and kept looking at his watch. Finally he stepped out on to the balcony, looked down into the square and came back. 'Right,' he said briskly. 'Come on. It's time to go.'

Alison had disappeared for a moment, but now she was back, and as we began to move towards the door she came over to me. She was holding something wrapped in a plastic bag. 'We've been keeping these to give you,' she said.

'Thank you,' I said automatically, taking the bag and opening it. Inside there was a camera, a notebook and a small green canvas shoulder bag. I recognised the bag. It was Tom's.

FOUR

It was time now to see the place. Numbness enveloped me as though protecting me from napalm. It was my body's anaesthetic, and, strangely, I understood this at the time. What was I about to witness? I knew only that it was another step in confronting the reality of what had happened to Tom. So with Anthony, Andy, TFH and Inigo leading the way and Mohammed and the other ISMers following behind, I descended the stone staircase to where the crowd was still silently waiting. Our visit was clearly a significant event. We were the parents of a non-Palestinian, a Western European, who had reached out to save some Palestinian children. Members of the press surged forward to meet us and Anthony made a short statement.

'We have come here in search of the truth,' he said. 'We want to know who fired this bullet. We have asked the Israeli Defence Force for an open and honest dialogue and an exchange of information. We only want to discover the facts and we are determined to be fair and open-minded. It is, I know, what Tom himself would have wanted.'

Of course, I thought, it *was* what Tom would have wanted. Despite what we had just heard in that upper room, until we had firm evidence it was vital we keep an open mind.

We and the young ISMers climbed into the two vehicles for the journey to Kir Street, near the Egyptian border, where Tom had been shot. Mohammed leaned over to introduce me to another young Palestinian. 'This is Amjad,' he said. 'Whenever anyone is shot by the IDF you will find Amjad there. He has made it his job to rescue the wounded. Often he risks his own life. He also was with Tom on the day he was shot.'

'*Whenever* anyone is shot?' I thought to myself. It sounded almost matter of fact, a normal occurrence. What kind of existence was it, I wondered, that had produced the mixture of compassion and vulnerability that showed in this young man's eyes. Amjad, I later learned, was only seventeen, but he looked far older. In the coming weeks I was to discover more about his almost obsessional mission. He had developed a name for himself in Rafah, and when a slight figure in pyjamas appeared on television at the scene of a shooting, people immediately recognised Amjad.

As we drove towards Kir Street I realised we had an escort. The Palestinian Authority's military police had been waiting for us. They drove in front of us, jolting along, tightly packed into a rickety looking jeep or hanging perilously off the sides and back. Dressed in black and heavily armed, they looked ominous. As they bounced along at considerable speed, the guns hanging from their shoulders swung violently with every bump in the road. I wondered why they were coming with us – to control the crowds? Did we need protecting and if so what were they protecting us from? Looking at Mohammed I could tell he was angry. 'They shouldn't have come,' he said quietly. 'They are only attracting attention. They make the Israelis jittery.' The media followed us in a procession of cars and trucks.

Hundreds of people, including crowds of children, were running with us, moving along the pavements and from time to time blocking the road so that we had to stop. As we approached the street, Mohammed began pointing things out: over there the street called Salah El Din Street which runs parallel to the Egyptian border marked by Israel's huge new steel 'security wall'; over there the Israeli Defence Force watchtowers.

We parked and got out. The street itself, Kir Street, was wide, its barren but still inhabited buildings studded with holes, like colanders. It ran at right angles to the Egyptian border. At the border end was a square containing a crumbling mosque, into which Salah El Din Street also ran. Beyond that was wasteland – part of the so-called 'security zone' Israel was creating along the border by demolishing Palestinian homes. Overlooking the square – now also part of the security zone and in line for demolition – we could see, very clearly, the IDF watchtowers.

Mohammed pointed out to us the tank, motionless and menacing in some long grass, heavily camouflaged so that it was hard to see it at first. This was the tank that positioned itself in front of the mosque, and every night after curfew peppered the houses in the street with intimidating shots – shots, we were told, that had recently wounded two boys from a house nearby known as the Abu Jabr house. It was this routine violence and intimidation, we now knew, and the fact that the tank had been preventing people going into the mosque, that had caused the ISM to plan a peaceful demonstration, a plan which had brought Tom to this street on the day he was shot.

In the middle of the street was a mound of sand-covered rubble and tangled iron girders, the customary IDF barrier made from the ruins of demolished houses. This was where the children had been playing. 'They're like playgrounds for the children,' said Mohammed. 'They run up and down them. The IDF shoot from the watchtowers all the time for no reason, just to frighten, and if the shots are at high level the children go on playing. They are used to it. It's when they start shooting low that it gets scary.'

I tried to imagine the scene on that day. The group of children playing on the mound. A low bullet suddenly scuffing up the sand, and then another. The children scattering, a boy and two little girls hesitating, rigid with fear, not knowing where to turn. Tom, in his orange jacket, gesticulating to the boy, lifting him to safety, holding out his hands again as he came back for the girls. And then . . .

Slowly Anthony and I approached the mound. I felt frozen with terror at what I was about to see. The crowd moved and swayed with us, involved yet silent and respectful. Beautiful children with lovely spirited, open smiles, ran in and out of the crowd and jumped on and off the mound – among them the same children perhaps who had been playing on it that day. Amjad indicated a large lump of concrete near the foot of the mound. There was still blood on ground: Tom's blood. This was where he had fallen. Beside the mound was a building with a pitted garage door . . . bullet holes at eye level . . . its wall was spattered with blood. I felt a physical pain, as if my heart was breaking. At the end of a long tunnel in my mind, I could see Tom lying on the ground, hurt, bleeding. Anthony and I stood silently, looking, utterly bereft.

Tom, dearest Tom, I pray that you suffered no pain, that the shot which entered your head and shattered your quick brain did so too swiftly for you to feel anything. That simple human gesture of reaching out to those children, which made you vulnerable, was so typical of you.

The ominous top of the IDF watchtower rose menacingly at the end of the street, to the side of some derelict buildings and behind a massive wall, with the tank squatting further over to the right. Although you could discern no movement we were aware that the military could see us, that we were being observed through those darkened windows encircling the watchtower, though the spot where Tom was shot was not in the 'security zone'. I could feel the eyes of the crowd on us too, sympathetic yet also wary. We were people from another world, another place. We know suffering, their looks said. We've seen it all before. I was painfully aware of the number of disabled people among the crowd, people with thin faces and unseeing eyes, people who limped or moved on crutches, or nursed misshapen hands.

After a few minutes we moved cautiously out beyond the mound of rubble into the 'security zone' so that we could see the watch-tower and the surrounding area more clearly. I couldn't understand why TFH and Andy were suddenly bristling with vigilance until they told us that many Palestinian civilians stepping into the zone had been shot. It made me wonder what policy allowed such casual shooting so near to a civilian area. But today the IDF had clearly been forewarned, and hundreds of Palestinians moved with us.

Anthony, with his lawyer's ability to apply himself to the task in hand, to concentrate on detail, began observing the scene from different angles and heights, trying to gauge what would have been in the sightlines of both the watchtower and the tank. Tom's height, both standing and crouching, the height of the mound of rubble, the block of concrete – he was taking them all into consideration, I knew, as he continued to measure and make notes. People crowded round, which made the task difficult. Others motioned them to stand away, but as soon as the crowd had parted it flowed back again, like sand.

A man came up to us and started pointing to the bloodstained wall. At first I couldn't understand what he was trying to tell me, then I realised he was pointing at the bullet holes, starting high and going lower, lower, lower. 'He's telling you they shoot low, they shoot children,' said Alice. Amjad stood on the mound, gesticulating: 'This is where Tom stood. This is where he reached out his arms.' Mohammed began telling Anthony and me again how Tom had fallen and how Sahir and Amjad had managed to lift him and carry him down the street away from the mound, while Alice screamed at them to try to staunch the blood. How they had laid Tom down and pressed a wad of cotton to the wound, how Alice tried mouth-to-mouth resuscitation, while Raph got out his mobile and his notebook and phoned the British Embassy, giving them Tom's name and passport number, shouting into the phone that a British civilian had been shot. 'Please will you tell the Israelis to stop shooting, please tell them to stop shooting,' he had pleaded over and over again. A young man called Nicola had made signals with his hand for the shooting to stop, and the tower had stopped shooting. Clearly whoever had fired the shot was aware of what had happened.

I looked at Alice. She was silent and very pale. I knew from Mohammed that only three weeks before she had been with Rachel Corrie when she died.

I turned to our interpreter and asked him about the little boy Tom had rescued. His name, he told me after some enquiries among the crowd, was Salem Baroum. Someone went off to find him, and minutes later he appeared, led by a woman I took to be his mother. Clearly she knew who I was, and the interpreter told me she wished to thank me. 'She weeps with you,' he said, 'that you have lost your brave son who saved her son. She prays with you. She knows that it is only because of your son that her son is alive.'

Little Salem hung back, withdrawn, behind his mother. He was a handsome, serious-looking child of about five. He was completely silent, utterly traumatised, I was told, by the shooting. He had not spoken a word since the previous Friday. I smiled at him and knelt down, taking his hand, speaking quietly to him, hoping the sound of my voice might reassure him, though I knew he could not understand me. He stood mute and rigid, gazing at me. On an impulse I put my arms round him and lifted him up. When there was a flash of cameras, it alarmed us both, and I could feel his body tauten. Perhaps it wasn't the right thing to do, but I was overcome by the thought that this was the last human being who had touched Tom before he was shot.

The women came closer but the men stayed on the edge of the group eyeing me warily, even with a kind of cynicism. Whatever they were feeling, I didn't blame them. These incidents, I now realised, were a daily occurrence for them. How different was our life experience, how different the backdrop to our own personal loss. But from the women I sensed empathy, solidarity. It made me feel guilty – it seemed the wrong way round. They wanted to talk, to tell me their stories through the interpreter. I learned of a son killed on the way to the supermarket. Another shot through a misted window as he took a drink of water. A mother shot as she hung out the washing to dry on the roof. An engineer picked off as he tried to mend a rooftop water tank riddled with bullet holes, which was the family's only source of water. These were some of the multitude of stories held within these shattered streets, within their homes, their families, only reaching the world occasionally through the reports of courageous foreign correspondents: days and nights of loss, intimidation, humiliation and destruction.

As they talked they seemed painfully resigned, without energy. 'This is the way we live', they seemed to be saying. 'This is how it is.' Yet underneath it all I felt the tremendous strength of spirit that I came so to admire among the Palestinians. I was struck by the contrast between the adults and the children, who hadn't yet lost their energy and their ability to smile. The older they got, the fewer smiles there seemed to be. Feelings seemed deadened and you could see it in their eyes.

I wanted to tell these women that I shared their loss, their exclusion, their humiliation. I wanted them to know that though Rafah was a place of tragedy for me, it was now inscribed on my heart, a never-to-be-forgotten part of my daily life and thought, linked by an unbreakable thread to my home and family far away in London. Were they wondering whether it had been worth-while telling me their stories? Would it matter to me? Could it make any difference?

We were being called back to the Embassy cars, and reluctantly I turned and walked away to join the others. TFH had arranged for us to call on our way back at the European Hospital in Gaza City, where Tom had first been treated, and he was insistent that we must be back at the Erez Crossing before dark. As we climbed in an old man with pleading eyes and reaching hands tried to prevent me from closing the door. I leaned towards him. What was he trying to tell me?

'Close the door,' commanded Andy.

I heard the clunk of the central locking system. I couldn't even wind down the window to wave goodbye. I could only stare in shocked silence at the old man through the bullet-proof glass. As our vehicles pulled away from the crowd I caught glimpses of faces. They looked fragile and vulnerable, accustomed somehow to being forgotten. During the years of conflict the world had repeatedly turned its back on them and you could tell that they were used to it.

I knew that I would never forget them. The image of the old

man, the whites of his eyes browned from the sheer hardship of life, is with me to this day. I had been in Rafah less than twenty-four hours, but what I had seen had shaken me to my foundations. Before I had only seen television's censored images. It was the first time I had truly come face to face with the obscenity of what oppression had done to this community. I felt a huge responsibility. I made an inner vow to return to Rafah, this town that had previously been wholly unknown to me, but next time with something to give.

The European Hospital was a modest, low-rise building in a relatively green and quiet area of Gaza City. Anthony, TFH and I were met in the entrance hall by a small group of doctors, one of whom introduced himself as Dr Jihad Abu Daya. We followed him into a meeting room where we all sat round a table and Dr Abu Daya, after expressing his sympathy in a most touching and sincere way, described to us the afternoon Tom had been brought in.

Directly after the shooting Tom had been taken by taxi to a small local hospital in Rafah, where they had been unequipped to treat him, and he had been sent on to the European Hospital by ambulance. 'When he arrived your son was bleeding very, very heavily from the wound in his head,' said Dr Abu Daya. 'We stopped the bleeding by compression and gave him fluid and many pints of blood. He had multiple fractures in his skull – the bullet entered the side of his head and exited at the back. His life was clearly in danger and he needed surgical intervention. Unfortunately we were not equipped to make such an operation here. We took a number of CAT scans, however.'

We asked if the fractures could have been made another way, perhaps by something like a baseball bat. The doctor smiled. 'Let me show you,' he said.

Dr Abu Daya rose and we followed him once again to a small office further up the corridor. The blinds in the windows were lowered, and suddenly on a screen I saw the ghostly outline of

Tom's skull. As one scan followed another Dr Abu Daya described the damage and pointed to the concentrations of irregular
sized dark marks that appeared on each. So transfixed was I by the
sight of Tom's skull that it was hard for me to take in the detail of
what he was saying, but I understood that these countless marks
were fragments of metal, shards of the bullet with which Tom had
been shot. The bullet had exploded on impact and these hundreds
of tiny pieces of metal had lodged in his brain and caused terrible
damage. My mind seemed to have travelled outside my body and
I couldn't breathe. Voices, words, registered in a far-off space.

'We have never seen this kind of bullet before, and we think it
may be a dumdum,' said one of the doctors.

'A dumdum bullet?'

'A bullet that explodes on impact. It does much more damage
than an ordinary bullet would.'

Later we would learn from a ballistics expert that any bullet
fired at such close range as this one explodes on impact – it need
not be a dumdum. But these were doctors, not ballistics experts.
One thing I knew – that the damage to Tom's brain was more
extensive even than I had imagined. Here for the first time, even
though imperfectly understood, was the medical evidence. For a
while I sat silent with distress, dimly aware of the empathy of the
doctors and of TFH. But gradually questions began to surface and
I was struck by the calm and open way in which the doctors
answered both Anthony and me. While Anthony continued to
write in his notebook I asked for copies of all the CAT scans and
medical notes. The doctors could not have been more human and
helpful – I knew that they probably witnessed such cases every
day. It was clear that they had put themselves at our disposal, and
were prepared to spend as much time with us as we needed. The
atmosphere felt very different from that in the Soroka Hospital –
closer and more encircling. There, though I was aware of the
technical sophistication, the efficiency of the care, I had somehow
felt shut out, but here I immediately felt included by the doctors'
warm humanity.

As we left we were handed copies of the CAT scans and Tom's medical notes. I noticed on the way back to the car park that TFH was carrying a black plastic bin liner, but I didn't ask what was in it.

The journey back through the desolate countryside and the grim wastes of the Erez Crossing was silent and subdued. Darkness was falling as we drew up outside the hotel, and suddenly I felt depression, like a stifling grey blanket, enveloping me as we got out of the Range Rover and TFH followed us into the lobby. So this was our reality now – a bleak hotel where no one met our eye in a country where no one in an official position had yet seen fit to acknowledge our existence, our family separated, and our son lying at death's door less than a mile away. I felt disorientated and at a loss. The day had shown us all too clearly that nothing in this chaotic situation was simple. But where were we to begin?

Now TFH handed me the black plastic bin liner. 'Tom's clothes,' he said. 'You'll need to keep them as evidence. I should ask the hotel to put them in the deep freeze.'

Upstairs in Anthony's room we sat on the bed. On the floor in front of us were the black plastic bin liner and the carrier bag Alison had given me containing Tom's spiral-bound notebook, his camera and his small green canvas bag.

Silently I opened the bin liner and began to remove its contents: first Tom's cotton trousers, slashed up the sides where they must have been cut off him; his T-shirt, similarly cut; his orange fluorescent non-combatant's jacket; his black photographer's waistcoat with its many pockets. Everything stiff with blood.

I felt in the waistcoat pockets and pulled out the familiar cigarette lighter and a packet of Camels. There was something so strangely ordinary about what I was doing. How many hundreds of times in the past had I pulled mud-caked clothing out of plastic bags, felt in the pockets before putting them in the washing machine? It's what mothers do, I thought. Yet now it was not mud, but the evidence of our son's shooting. Here was his blood.

In another pocket I found the Swiss Army knife, Anthony's last present to him. When he saw this Anthony turned and moved towards the window where he remained for some minutes, hunched over the sill. I felt desperately concerned for him, knowing how hard it was for him to talk about his feelings. It was all too much to bear.

We opened the small green canvas bag. This was the only luggage Tom had brought with him from Jerusalem, so he couldn't have imagined staying more than a couple of weeks. Silently we unpacked it and I was struck by the neatness and economy of the packing. Everything was absolutely organised – boxer shorts, T-shirts and socks tightly rolled, plasters and nail scissors packed away in one of the inside pockets. His foreign currency was in another, the money for different countries separately wrapped. There was a small pencil case with numerous pens – I remembered Tom had told us in one of his e-mails that they dried up in no time in this kind of climate.

I upended the black bin liner to make sure there was nothing left in it, and a small package fell out. It was Tom's watch, and, seeing it, a pang of the sharpest grief shot through me. I could see it on his wrist. He was never without it, and somehow it conjured him up as nothing else had.

Our brains and bodies were too blasted for us to do much else that night, though the phone kept ringing with calls from journalists of every nationality. There was a sense of urgency which was to become part of our daily life. Anthony answered the calls patiently, courteously and concisely. The message was always the same. We were seeking the truth, not revenge, and we were keeping an open mind.

After frustrating and ineffective telephone calls early in the day between Anthony and the British Passport Office over the renewal of Fred's passport, Ann, the mother of Fred's close friend Joe, had taken charge, and arrangements had now been made for Sophie and Fred to fly out the following night. We called Sophie. Her voice, when she answered, sounded faint and very far away.

'Hello, darling,' I said. 'Are you all right?'

'Yes. How's Tom?' I could hear the quaver in her voice.

How could I possibly describe at this distance what I had seen and experienced that day?

'It's a very modern, efficient hospital,' I said. 'Everything's being done that can possibly be done. Billy's at the hospital now. It's all quite complicated. I think you'll understand more when you see Tom.'

There was a pause. Then, 'Mum, I'm not sure I really do want to,' Sophie said. 'Not now anyway. Maybe I should come later. It sort of feels right being at home. I've got Catherine staying here with me and everyone's helping . . .' Her voice tailed off.

I understood. In a matter of a few days everything in Sophie's life had been turned upside down. We were all in deep distress and she was terrified, particularly at the thought that Tom might be in pain. No wonder she was clinging to the secure, the familiar. The thought of seeing Tom was just too much to bear. But if she didn't come now, she might never see him again.

'Darling,' I said, 'you must do what feels right. But I think you and Fred need to come. Everything's so uncertain.'

'You're right,' she said, after a while, with typical directness.

We talked a little more about Fred, who was staying with friends, and about the arrangements for the following day. TFH would meet them both at Tel Aviv on Wednesday morning and drive them down to Be'ersheva.

' 'Night, Mum. Give my love to Dad and Bill,' she said finally in a small voice that stabbed at my heart.

' 'Night, darling,' I said, relieved that in forty-eight hours we would all be together, but devastated by the thought of what she and Fred had to face.

I went to bed deeply disturbed, going over and over the events of the day, my thoughts always returning to Tom, like a compass returning to the north. The noise in the corridor outside made sleep impossible. I knew it was Passover, and the seventh floor, on which we were sleeping, was full. In fact, it seemed to be the only floor of this big hotel that was being used. Children were running up and down, shouting and laughing. Groups of adults went backwards and forwards to the lift talking in loud voices. At one point there was a thump on my door, as if it had been hit by a football. I looked at the clock. It was well past midnight.

Suddenly outraged, I got out of bed, put on my dressing-gown and opened the door. As I stepped out into the corridor, a body cannoned into me, almost knocking me over, and a young boy of about ten took one look at me, turned, and skidded away across the polished floor. His father, dressed in Orthodox black coat and homburg was a few steps behind him, and I fully expected some kind of apology, some reproof to the child for running and for bumping into another guest so carelessly. But the man gave me not a single glance, carrying on up the corridor as if he simply hadn't noticed me. I stood there, astonished by the bad manners, the lack of acknowledgement that this was an inconsiderate way to behave when there were people staying in the hotel who might wish to sleep.

I closed my door, sat on the bed and turned on the bedside light. On a table by the telephone was the carrier bag that Alison had given me, containing Tom's camera and his notebook. I took out the little spiral-bound book and held it. It felt so precious I was almost unwilling to open it. Eventually I turned back the cover and there, on the first page, was Tom's careful, even handwriting. I had an image of him in his room at home, writing, always writing and recording, with his feet up on the window ledge. But these were words written in very different circum-stances. The first pages described his days in Jerusalem, waiting to go into Gaza with the ISM. I would come back to those. Now I turned quickly to his arrival in Rafah. The place so haunted me, I seemed unable to leave it.

'Since I arrived I have been shot at, gassed, chased by soldiers, had "sound" grenades thrown within metres of me, been hit by falling debris and been in the way of a ten-ton D-9 bulldozer that didn't stop', I read.

'As we approached, I kept expecting a part of my body to be hit by an "invisible" force and shot of pain. It took a huge amount of will to continue. I wondered what it would be like to be shot, and strangely I wasn't too scared.'

It was so personal, so immediate, seeing Tom's handwriting, hearing his voice. This was Tom speaking, in the last days before speech was lost to him. I read on, traumatised by the sight of the words, unable to put the notebook down. In it Tom described his activities with the ISM during the previous week. On the first night he had slept in the home of a Dr Samir and his family, whose house was the only one left standing in an area bulldozed by the IDF, and who had refused to move. The family was subject to constant intimidation, and it was policy for ISM members to sleep in such houses as a gesture of solidarity. It was the house in which Rachel Corrie had stayed before she died.

'There is an Israeli tank less than 20 metres from my bed that was posted there two weeks ago,' Tom wrote. *'The room next to mine has several large-calibre bullet-holes in each wall, many of them having travelled through the brick . . . I asked Dr Samir if his children slept OK with the tank so close. He said, "For the first few nights they cried. Now it is OK. They are more used to it."'*

The journal conjured up pictures of Tom and other ISM members, highly visible in their orange peaceworkers' jackets, sitting guard while Palestinian plumbers fixed the sewage system which had been dug up by the Israelis.

'Gaza is the most densely populated place on earth', I read. *'1.2 million people in an area 10 km by 40 km, with 40 per cent of the "Palestinian Land" owned by settlers.'* This was followed by a page of mathematical calculations, and the conclusion: *'The average settler in the Gaza Strip owns 115 times as much land as the average Palestinian. The plan is to make life so bad that they all just get up and leave and the Israelis are using every trick in the book . . . They are creating their own holocaust, but using bureaucracy to cover it . . . What is going on is far beyond what is necessary, or even relative, to national security and it is all underhand.'*

As I read on I could feel Tom's passionate anger at what he was seeing, yet I could also hear him arguing with himself, playing devil's advocate, determined not to be carried away by propaganda from either side. He wrote of '*the frustration of being in the middle of various factions and their hype and being unable to ascertain what the truth is . . . in situations like this half-truths can build on each other exponentially to create a massive wrong conclusion*'. Though he liked Dr Samir enormously, did he really know the full story? he asked himself: '*The thousands of bullet-holes in south frontier houses may have been in response to direct fire. I know nothing about Dr Samir's history.*' I could feel the tension between what human decency and his own instincts were telling him, and his determination to be fair.

Anthony had mentioned to me that, in the car on the way to Heathrow before Tom had left for Iraq, they had been discussing the situation in Palestine, and Tom had actually been putting the Israeli point of view. It was part of Tom's nature to try to see both sides. As I finally turned out the light and lay down to attempt to sleep, along with the ever-present grief, I felt the most immense respect for his thinking and for what he'd done.

FIVE

I woke early and, as on every morning since the previous Friday, it took only a split second before reality closed in. After breakfast in the impersonal hotel dining room, Anthony and I prepared to go to the hospital. I felt disorientated – even the process of finding a taxi in this unfamiliar and unfriendly place was a mystery, and it was clearly no good appealing for help with anything to the staff on the reception desk, whose reactions seemed to range from unco-operative to rude. When I'd spoken to the girl on the desk about storing Tom's clothes in a freezer she had broken off, without apology, in mid-conversation to take a phone call. I stood waiting with the bloodied clothes in a bag. With media interviews being held in the foyer, the hotel staff must have known why we were in Israel; it was hard to understand this unfeeling blankness.

In the taxi Anthony and I worried again over the doctor's bizarre suggestion that Tom's injury was 'commensurate with a blow from a baseball bat'. Having seen the scans at the European Hospital it now seemed doubly incomprehensible. What on earth could it mean? Was the implication that Tom's wound had been caused by someone at close range – a Palestinian?

Yet there it was – 'gunshot wound' – written clearly on Tom's notes. And this was at an Israeli hospital experienced in dealing with gunshot wounds.

We felt deeply uneasy, and angry too, at what seemed like an attempt to mislead us. We were due to meet the medical staff that morning, and now we felt unsure about how to approach it.

I fully understood that we were feeling our way into another culture, and that this was likely to be uncomfortable. The 'benchmarks' were bound to be different and I had to keep a check on my own personal responses. But my sense of alienation, indeed irritation, was sharpened by the jarring sight of the blue guard posts at the entrance to the hospital. They were manned by the usual young armed soldiers – or were they military police? – clearly bored and uncomfortable in the already intense heat. Every visiting vehicle was stopped at the barrier and searched. The soldiers spoke peremptorily to our driver in Hebrew, checked his identification, opened the boot, peered inside the car. Before we were permitted to enter the hospital itself, we stood in a queue while my bag and Anthony's briefcase were opened and searched. I didn't question the need for security, but the sheer level of it everywhere we went had begun to seem almost provocative. Whose interests were being served, I wondered, by this state of advanced paranoia?

Again we mounted the stone stairs to the second floor, passed the rows of white-robed Arab men sitting smoking under the 'No Smoking' sign. Yesterday, on that terrible first visit, I had been almost too numb to feel fearful. I knew at some level that we had already lost Tom, and it was as if a part of myself was dying. Now I was filled with dread, partly at the thought of what we might learn from the medical staff about Tom's condition, partly because I knew I was in uncharted territory where I could not, at the moment, distinguish who was for us and who against – or, indeed, whether such divisions existed at all.

We found Billy in the waiting-room, drinking a cup of coffee with the same group of young people we had met there yesterday, amid the same confusion of sleeping bags and cast-off clothing. He was very quiet, even for Billy. Deep shock was still written on his face. He looked drawn and strained round the eyes, and I guessed he was not sleeping much. I also wondered whether he was drinking enough water in this hot climate. Though I had accepted that the hospital was where Billy was living for the present, and that this was where he wanted to be, the situation worried me. Yet I pushed these anxieties to the back of my mind. At present what energy I had was concentrated on Tom and I couldn't help it.

Anthony went to speak to the medical staff and returned to say that the consultant in charge of Tom's case, Professor Gurman, and his team, would meet us in half an hour. Tom's dressings were being changed; in the meantime we went in search of a quiet place where Anthony could settle with his laptop and his mobile phone. We found a secluded corner in the large hospital cafeteria, which looked out on to a pleasant garden in the centre of the building, aflame with red camellias and orange canna lilies. It was a place which would become a focal point for us during the coming weeks.

As I sat gazing out of the window, I realised that I was looking directly across at a grassy fenced-in compound – the helicopter pad where Tom had first arrived. Terrible pictures of him arriving in the dark, being rushed on a stretcher to the Accident and Emergency entrance with medical staff running alongside flashed into my mind. During our time at the hospital I could never pass the helicopter pad without feeling inwardly clamped by fear, and I found myself conflicted, alternately drawn to stare at it and then immediately blotting it out.

Anthony was single-minded about collecting witness statements from ISM members and others who had been in Rafah on the day of the shooting. One or two of them had by now left Israel and would have to be tracked down. He was keen to make contact with a young South African photographer, Garth Stead, who, we were told, had been present and had started filming seconds after Tom was shot. We had also received a call from a journalist called Sandra Jordan who had been filming in Rafah on that day for the Channel 4 series *Dispatches*. She had been in Kir Street within minutes of Tom's being shot and had filmed the subsequent terrifying scenes when he was transferred from Palestinian ambulance to Israeli helicopter. She was anxious to interview us and to provide any help she could.

Anthony's mobile rang constantly with calls from the international media asking for interviews, updates and our views on the situation. All we could say at present was that we had requested a meeting with the Israeli Defence Force through our Embassy in Tel Aviv, and had so far received no response. As I sat looking out on to the garden while Anthony took one call after another, it seemed to me that everyone was concerned to speak to us about Tom's shooting except those most closely involved – the Israeli government and the Israeli army. We had received no word of sympathy or sorrow for Tom; no official had come to meet us at the airport, the hotel or the hospital. Despite our requests for a meeting, so far there had been no reciprocity, no reaching out. It felt as if we were in a vacuum, with nothing to respond to or relate to. Was this a society so cocooned in a kind of membrane of unawareness, a society so insular and self-absorbed that it had no concept of how others see it, of why it was necessary to behave humanely? I was not looking for acknowledgement because our son was special in any way, but because he was a human being who had been seriously wounded, in all probability by the Israeli army. Why was it so difficult for the authorities to make a private statement, let alone a public one? Was so little value put on an individual life? It would have been a human response due to anyone in those circumstances, whether from Britain, Palestine or anywhere else. Yet such empathy was entirely lacking.

It was time for our meeting with the medical staff. Anthony, Billy and I were shown into a room inside the intensive care area where Professor Gurman, three other doctors and a nurse were waiting. Professor Gurman was tall and greying, with a slight beard, professional but kindly. We all sat at a table and Professor Gurman, with the help of the other doctors, described very clearly the operation they had carried out to remove some of the detritus from around the wound in Tom's head. Further operations would be needed, they told us, because, though they had managed to stop most of the bleeding, there was still bleeding from Tom's left ear.

All three of us had been deeply shocked and upset by the sight of Tom's terribly swollen head. We asked whether anything could be done to reduce the swelling.

'Unfortunately there is nothing we can do,' said Professor Gurman. 'The bullet entered above the left eyebrow and exited at the back of the skull. There is very severe damage to the left side of the brain and because of this there is enormous pressure. Now I am afraid this has also begun to affect the right side of the brain.'

At this point Billy rose quickly and left the room. I could see that he was in acute distress. My instinct was to follow him and hold him tight, but I was uncertain whether to go or stay.

Professor Gurman paused sympathetically for a moment. Then he said, 'I am not sure whether you quite understand that there is very little hope at all of any recovery. From the severity of your son's wound, we are surprised that he has lasted these few days. I am sorry to have to say this, but it is best to tell you the truth.'

We sat in silence. Then Anthony said, 'This wound was clearly caused by a bullet, was it not, as stated on the medical notes?' Professor Gurman inclined his head. 'So you will understand,' Anthony continued, 'if we ask you to retain any detritus, any shards of metal or relevant tissue that you remove during the operations. It will be important as evidence.'

I sensed a certain tension in the room, but Professor Gurman said, 'We will, of course, do what we can.' I could only guess what he and the other medical staff were feeling. I had no doubt, now, that they were highly professional, and that they would do their best to save the life of any patient, whether British, Palestinian or Israeli. Yet here they were faced with a highly contentious situation – a foreign national, a civilian, who had entered what they would term a war zone and had been shot by their own army. I felt they were choosing their words carefully, conscious that this was a high-profile case and that they must not put a foot wrong. They were all no doubt aware of the international media interest in Tom's shooting, of the political and diplomatic implications of the case. For some of them it must have raised personal conflicts – and how were we to know that there were not other pressures too?

We sought answers to many questions. Was there any possibility of improvement for Tom, however slight? Would he ever be in a condition to be moved? Had he any awareness at all of his surroundings? Did he feel pain? One of the young doctors explained that they had carried out a Glasgow Coma Scale Assessment. This test is used in traumatic brain injury to monitor the patient's level of consciousness. Eye, verbal and motor responses are tested on a scale from three to fifteen, anything below eight indicating a severe brain injury, and three being the worst, denoting that nothing more than the main organs were working. Tom was on three.

I was fighting back tears as we eventually left the room, and Anthony looked straight ahead of him. What we had heard seemed so final. Tom was never going to regain consciousness. His body was barely functioning. Yet a part of me still could not accept it, could not entirely give up hope.

We stood helplessly in the ante-room for a moment. Then Anthony said he must get back to the cafeteria and his computer – there was so much to do, so many calls to make and answer, so many witnesses to trace. This, I knew now, was his mission – to gather every shred of evidence he could. It was his way of coping with the situation, of doing his very best for Tom. Though shaped by his lawyer's training to question and assess, I knew it was not this that was driving him. For Anthony, as for both of us, uncovering the truth was a moral question. It was what he expected of himself, and was part of the person he was. And we both knew that Tom would have done the same.

I went in search of Billy and was told that he was in the Intensive Care Unit. A kind nurse called Netta, who spoke some English, helped me with the ritual that was to become so familiar: the washing of hands, the putting on of gloves and gown, then the slow, painful walk down the disinfectant-smelling ward, past all the anonymous beds with their tragic occupants to where, at the end, I could see Tom lying, still and pale, with Billy stationed beside him.

I stood gazing silently down at him – so near and yet so far. I was still too frightened to touch him in case I should dislodge some vital wire. I wanted to take his hand, but there was a clip on it and I had no idea what it was for. His face was covered by an oxygen mask.

Tom, how can I reach you now that you have no words – you to whom words have been so important, who used them so thoughtfully? What is left for someone who has no language? How can I reach you in your blank and solitary world? How can I comfort you?

I began trying to recall my research into particular neurological impairments and the highly complex functions of the different parts of the brain. Without the left side of his brain, he had lost the use of language, the ability to think mathematically, at which he had been so brilliant. But perhaps with the right side some awareness remained. Perhaps he might recognise the perfume I usually wore, and feel that I was near him. I must always remember to wear it. I must find some hand cream with a familiar scent – lavender perhaps – and massage his hands and feet when I dared. Yet if the parts of his brain associated with emotions were damaged, would he be able to feel comfort?

Billy and I sat silently on either side of Tom's bed. From time to time a nurse came to check the various dials and graphs. I had no way of understanding what was happening, what the nurse was seeing. All I could see was my son, lying utterly vulnerable. I knew that we could lose him at any moment. How had he clung on to life until now? Was he in pain? Could he feel pleasure?

Occasionally I looked across at Billy. He was quite still, his eyes always on Tom, though when a nurse arrived he became suddenly alert, with the kind of streetwise awareness I knew so well. I don't know how long we sat there together, but by the time I rose my whole body ached with concentration, with the weight of anguish and responsibility I felt. Billy looked far away, but I wondered if he felt this too.

I found Anthony still in the canteen. He had been joined by two of the human shields who introduced themselves as Michelle and Nathan. Michelle had a fine-boned face and olive skin, and looked Latin. Nathan was fair-haired and softly spoken. I quickly formed the impression of two sincere and thoughtful people. Anthony explained to me that they had been with Tom in Baghdad. They had left with him for Amman, and the three had spent a fortnight in Jordan in the Al Rweished refugee camp as volunteers, putting up tents and looking after Iraqi refugees. They had finally parted company in Jerusalem some days later, Tom to go to Rafah, Michelle and Nathan intending to go to the West Bank.

'We were walking along a road near Nablus when someone told us that a British national called Tom had been shot in the head in Rafah and was in hospital in Be'ersheva,' Michelle said. 'We knew it must be him and of course we came straight here.' There was an intensity about the way she spoke and her eyes filled with tears. I could tell that Nathan, too, was deeply shaken. They had all been through so much, and I was deeply moved at the affection and care this group felt for Tom and for one another. I was beginning to gain a very different impression of them from that put about by the Israeli media. These were no foolish, impulsive troublemakers, I could tell, but serious people with a social conscience and an awareness of human rights, and the integrity to take a stand.

So many things seemed to be happening simultaneously. Sophie told us of a letter from the Features Department of the *Guardian*, explaining that for a long time the paper had been campaigning for peace and equality in the Middle East, and that every time they heard of the death of an innocent person it

stiffened their resolve to bring it to the world's attention in order
to prevent it happening again. Recently they had published some
e-mails Rachel Corrie had sent to her parents and it had provoked
a huge response from around the world.

'I know Tom was doing photographic work in the region', the
letter went on. 'And I wondered if, when you felt it was appropriate, you might consider running his work in the *Guardian*. I
know he was there documenting the daily life of Rafah and we
would really like to reprint his work in a similar way to our
reproduction of Rachel's e-mails.'

I thought of Tom's camera, back at the hotel. There had barely
been time even to look at it and I had put it and his journal aside.

'I have a huge amount of video footage of Tom to show you,
taken during the seven weeks when we were together,' said
Michelle. I believe you have Tom's camera, and I can help you
select and e-mail photographs to the newspaper if you wish.'

So it was with Michelle, later that day, that we began to look at
Tom's own photos taken in Rafah – and not only in Rafah.
Anthony had now, finally, accessed e-mails and photographs in
which Tom recorded a day he had spent in Gaza City on 9 April –
two days before he was shot. The previous day two F16 rockets
had been fired into the city in an attempt by Israeli Intelligence to
target a group of Hamas and Fatah members who were travelling
together in a car. The first rocket missed, but the second hit,
killing everyone in the car and wounding three dozen civilians in
the area, four of whom had later died.

Tom had got caught up that day in what was called the 'march
for the martyrs'. There were pictures of the assassinated men's
families and friends carrying the bodies wrapped in green Hamas
flags through the streets, of running, shouting crowds and masked
gunmen, '*It's kind of intimidating when you're the only non-Palestinian
out of 850 and they're chanting: "Kill the Americans and Jews, drive
them out of Palestine"*,' Tom wrote. I admired his boldness. He
could have been mistaken for an American. Yet somehow I knew
that in such a situation he would probably have been safe. Tom

had such an unjudgemental way of looking directly at you with those friendly, intelligent, slightly challenging eyes. He had the true writer's desire to move through situations unseen, to observe and experience without disrupting the flow of events in his presence. Everything about him told you that that he was unthreatening and open-minded.

There were many more photos too, dozens of them, for, as Michelle showed us, Tom had concealed one photo beneath another as a security precaution. They showed Rafah's tragic, crumbling buildings with their gaping windows, tottering upper floors, shattered beams and trailing wires; ISM members standing in the path of a gigantic advancing bulldozer as it attempted to demolish a Palestinian house; and the smiling children of Dr Samir's extended family. *'Yesterday morning, two of the brothers were shot by snipers in the tower within two hours of each other,'* Tom wrote in one of his e-mails. *'Mustafa, 19, was hit in the leg outside the front of the house, but should be all right. Rushdie, 15, was shot in the throat while in the bathroom (through a misted glass window) and has been taken to a hospital in Gaza City. Ironically, his best hope for survival is if his family pays $4,000 (£2,500) and applies to take him to Israel for treatment. They don't have the money and Rushdie is still in critical condition.'*

And there was a photo of Tom that I loved. Someone else must have taken him, looking quizzically at the camera and wearing a cameraman's helmet with 'TV' on it. I cherished this image of him, so teasing and alive.

Sophie and Fred arrived early next morning, 16 April, delivered to the hotel by the unfailingly supportive TFH. As soon as the phone rang Anthony and I took the lift down to the lobby and found them standing by the reception desk with their rucksacks. They looked exhausted by the journey and clearly both terribly apprehensive. We hugged and hugged. I felt huge relief that the family was at least now in one place.

TFH had matters to attend to back in Tel Aviv, but we spoke

briefly. He told us that the Ambassador, Sherard Cowper-Coles, was pressing for a meeting with the IDF, so far without success. It seemed incredible to us that the army's only response to such a serious incident was total silence. We asked him to ask again. And again if need be.

'I don't think Sherard is hopeful of getting anywhere with them,' said TFH, 'but he'll go on trying. I'm in routine contact with the IDF but obviously this has to be dealt with at the highest level. I know the ISM aren't popular with them. The IDF people simply can't understand why someone like me doesn't support what the army's doing in the Occupied Territories. They've often said to me: "You're a soldier like us. You understand the problems an individual soldier has to go through" – things of that kind. They're impervious. For them there is no other point of view. There's nothing to discuss.'

'And what about No. 10?' Anthony asked. 'Will they be putting any kind of pressure on at governmental level?'

'Unlikely,' said TFH crisply. 'I don't think I'd better give you my views on that.'

So now we knew. Essentially we were on our own.

Fred and Sophie were both too tired and strung out to rest. We all tried to eat some breakfast and we heard how things had been in London since we had left. Media interest in Tom's case had been intense. Sophie had had to cope with the continual stream of calls from all the major television channels and had been interviewed by the national and local press. She had brought press cuttings for us to see, and the truthful and dignified way in which she had stood up to the ordeal didn't surprise me.

Fred, white as a sheet, sat very close and didn't say much. Hanging over us all was the knowledge that soon they must see Tom. I wanted to prepare them, yet I didn't want to frighten them. Knowing Tom was in a coma was one thing; seeing the reality was quite another. We described the Intensive Care Unit and the procedures for entering, told them that Tom was wired up to life-support machines, that Billy was staying at the hospital with a group of young people who had been in Rafah with Tom.

Billy wanted to be the one to take Fred in. He led him down the ward, past all the other patients. 'I didn't know which one was Tom,' Fred said later. 'I was only able to tell by recognising his arms.' Later, as we all stood round Tom's bed, I knew they had understood the worst. Fred, ashen-faced, looked silently down at his brother with an expression of such anguish and disbelief that it broke my heart. He was so shocked his body was rigid, he couldn't even shake. Sophie turned away in tears, utterly vulnerable, and buried her face on Billy's shoulder. There was nothing any of us could say.

Now we had somehow to find a way of existing in this new situation, this hostile terrain. The centre of our life was the hospital and at the centre of that was Tom. Each day we would set out, ferried by Ya'alon, a friendly Israeli taxi driver we'd got to know and who always seemed to be available to take us wherever we chose. He knew why we were in Israel and it was a relief not to have to answer questions or explain ourselves afresh every day. Ya'alon was an important peg in our daily organisation, and after the hotel, which was so devoid of any human warmth or connection, we appreciated his friendly willingness.

Once at the hospital we tended to separate, Anthony to the canteen to continue with his phone calls and investigations and to rendezvous with Michelle and Nathan who were helping him sort photographs and trace witnesses, Fred, Sophie and I to the Intensive Care Unit and its chaotic waiting room, where we would find Billy and the other ISM members, all of them taking turns to spend time with Tom. Very gradually, as the days passed, I began to know them a little. They were from various countries and all walks of life, and they all had their different reasons for being there. There were Joe and Laura, a couple of Americans who had been out in Israel with the ISM for several months; Phil, a lovely young Irishman who got on well with Billy and

immediately seemed to understand what it must be like for Fred
and took him under his wing; slim, dark-haired Alison, who had
left a responsible job back in the UK; and Raph, an intense young
Jewish man in his thirties, an Oxford graduate fluent in Hebrew
and Arabic, who had been with Tom when he was shot. It was
Raph who had phoned the Embassy on his mobile to tell them
that a British national had been shot by the Israelis.

During those first long days, we would all take it in turns to
spend the mornings around Tom's bed, leaving for a break at
midday and returning in the late afternoon. We were all expecting
he might stop breathing at any minute. There was a constant sense
of yearning, searching for something to do that would help him.
My body ached with the strain of watching – aware of all the
worrying dials, of the lines and tubes that might become disconnected. Sometimes the regular bleep from one of the machines
would change to a continuous sound. Usually it would bring a
nurse quickly to Tom's bedside, a button would be pressed or a
switch flicked, but if not I would rush, petrified, to find someone.

Tom's eyes were open. Occasionally he would blink, but he
was unable to close one eye, and eventually they were both gently
taped closed to try to prevent recurring infections. He would
need another operation, we were told, to drain some of the fluid
from the region of his ear. The hospital staff were at pains to
explain to us, as gently as possible, that he could see and hear
nothing. Yet despite what anyone told us I know we were all
desperate for some sign that he was aware we were there. Fred
remembers how Tom shook when Anthony's phone went off. 'I
didn't believe it was coincidence,' he said. And when he squeezed
Tom's hand, 'I felt sure he squeezed it back. I told Michelle and
Sophie – Michelle believed me.'

Gradually I reached the point where I knew that it was safe to
touch Tom, provided I didn't dislodge any of the equipment. We
would take turns to massage his swollen hands and feet, and I was
always on the alert for anything that might indicate he was in pain.
He was subject to constant infections, and I could read the level of

infection from the feel of his skin. I knew I must find a way of interpreting for him now he could not speak for himself.

Sophie had brought out a tape of songs and messages that Tom's friends had made for him, and she laid it close to his ear and played it to him one afternoon. I wasn't allowed to hear it. I could imagine the kind of messages that might be on it. I could see 'the boys', as we always called them, Tom's close inner circle, getting together on Primrose Hill to make the tape. They'd probably sworn at him and told him to get his act together, joking about it to push away the unbearable knowledge of how serious things were. A handful of our very close friends were keeping in touch by phone and thoughtfully took on the responsibility of keeping a wider circle of friends informed. But apart from that we were out of contact with England, living in limbo with no idea of when we might return.

SIX

Gradually evidence about Tom's shooting was accumulating. Anthony was obtaining witness statements from a number of the ISMers, as well as from the South African photographer Garth Stead, who had been filming ISM activities on that day. Any variations were minor and on the key facts they all told the same story. That the shot that had felled Tom could only have come from one of two IDF watchtowers on the Egyptian border, that it had not been a single shot, but one of a number, and that there had been no other gunfire in the area at that time. The 'gunman in fatigues' shooting a pistol at a watchtower, described by the IDF in their various statements, was clearly a fabrication. In his statement Garth Stead wrote:

> I am clear in my recollection of the gunfire that took place. I have some experience of firearms from family activities in South Africa (my father was in the defence force and an active member of the practical shooting club) and from various combat and similar activities I have covered as a journalist. While no expert, I can recognise different types of gunfire. I am confident that all the shots I heard while at the end of the street were rifle shots coming from the same direction into the street and that there was no other gunfire. I am certain that there was no pistol fire. At that distance I would have heard it and clearly distinguished it from the sniper rifle fire from the border tower.

Raph, in his statement, said:

I have been made aware of a suggestion that there was a gunman who was in the building on the other side of the square . . . and that he came out of this house and fired three pistol shots in the air and then two in the direction of the tower, immediately before Tom was shot and that it was him they intended to shoot. There was no gunfire audible from such a point being fired into the air or towards the tower. The shots which could be heard were easy to correlate with the concrete flying off the buildings and the dust flying off the earth mound. Other shots would have been recognisably anomalous.

Now Anthony was keen to visit Rafah again, to test these statements on the ground and to take photographs. Our first visit had been so bewildering, so traumatic, and the crowds had been so pressing that it had been difficult to photograph or get a proper view of the scene. So via TFH we got the all-clear to go into Gaza again. We talked it over with Sophie, Billy and Fred and there was no question: all three said they wanted to go. Any thought of protecting them would, I knew, have been unthinkable. They needed to see with their own eyes where their brother had been shot, to understand why he had been in Rafah and what he had been trying to do there. It was part of the coming to terms.

Michelle agreed to come with us this time. As a skilled photographer she would be indispensable, and she and Nathan were spending most of their time now assisting with Anthony's investigation. A shared love for Tom made everyone want to do whatever they could to help, and we worked alongside one another, using our different skills. Anthony and I valued this greatly.

We were all very quiet on that second journey. TFH and Andy escorted us as before, but even TFH's robust presence did nothing to dispel the dread we all clearly felt as we drove through the grey no-man's-land of the Erez Crossing and along the potholed roads towards Rafah. As the landscape unfolded and we passed through the Abu Houli checkpoint and beneath the looming IDF watchtowers on the Rafah road, I could see shock and disbelief on Sophie's and Billy's faces. As we approached the Yibnah district the desolation increased.

By now we were well aware of the IDF's rationalisation for all this destruction – to expose tunnels built by the Palestinians for smuggling weapons in from Egypt, and to deter suicide bombers. I felt deep sympathy for the Israelis living under this threat. Yet it wasn't the whole story. This level of destruction, however close to the border, simply could not be morally justified. What these bulldozers were aiming at was clearly total wipe-out. The army was behaving as if it had *carte blanche* to do as it chose.

Everywhere there was rubble and more rubble. The ground-floor walls of many of the houses had been pulled apart or pushed inwards, leaving a mound of debris mixed with personal posses-sions – a shoe, a saucepan, a piece of plastic tablecloth. Steel girders wrenched upwards out of the mess. And everywhere there were people, hordes of people, climbing round and over the rubble in a matter-of-fact way, as if this was what they did every day – which of course they did, in order to get on with their lives. Though Anthony and I had seen all this before, I know we were as shocked by it on this second visit as the rest of the family were. Yet we were all too preoccupied with thoughts of what we were about to see to say very much to one another. Under the layers of my own disbelief was the feeling that people, friends back in Britain, just wouldn't believe what we were witnessing. It might be a cliché, but I found myself saying inwardly, 'This needs to be seen to be believed.' But how could it all be conveyed? What could make people *feel* this situation, rather than complacently observe it on their TV screens? I had been guilty of that myself.

Again we parked at the end of Kir Street. If we had thought we would be able to make a quiet, private visit to the scene of the shooting, we were soon disabused. Drawn by the sight of the Embassy cars, a small crowd had appeared seemingly from nowhere and stood, watching quietly. Old men squatted in doorways surveying the scene. Children with mischievous smiles ran round us calling 'How are *you*?', 'What is your name?', 'How old are you?'. Yet, oddly, all this did not feel intrusive. It was not idle curiosity I felt from these Palestinian people who were virtual prisoners within their own territory, but a desperate need for connection. I felt a human warmth here, in such contrast to our experience in Israel, where no one met our eyes.

We walked slowly towards the spot, holding hands tightly. There was no need to point it out – there was still blood on the ground, dark bloodstains on the wall. When she saw them Sophie began to sob. I shall never forget the hopelessness and helplessness I felt at the sight of our three children holding one another, devastated by the loss of their brother, lost for words. Were they afraid to come to me because of my distress? This barrier of rubble seemed a thing of such significance, a border between life and death. One moment Tom had been standing here, whole and young and full of life, a thinking, feeling human being; the next he was lying on the ground, bleeding and unconscious, with no hope, no future. I think we were all seeing him as he had been and as he was now. It was not just our loss that we were weeping for, but all that he had lost – life, love, friendship, language, joy and imagination, the beauty of the world. And this was where it had happened.

Eventually we walked sombrely back to where the others were waiting. They had been joined now by Mohammed and Amjad, and by Alison, an older, Scottish ISM member we had met briefly on our first visit. While Michelle and Anthony set about photographing and taking measurements – again with some difficulty because of the crowd of people, which was increasing all the time – we stood in the shade of a crumbling balcony and talked. Mohammed told us again about Tom's arrival in Rafah.

'He didn't really talk very much, maybe because it was too hot,' he said. 'He was always drinking Coca-Cola. He got criticised by the others for it. They thought these companies were an emblem of capitalism. But Tom grinned. He didn't mind the teasing much.'

No one could have been less of a materialist than Tom, I thought, but he was not a hugely thoughtful consumer, and his unfortunate passion for Coke was irresistible.

Almost as soon as Tom arrived a call had come through about a house demolition, and they had all rushed to respond, snatching up orange jackets, loudhailers, torches and cameras.

'I never wear an orange jacket now,' said Mohammed. 'Since Rachel was killed I've begun to think it doesn't have any effect. You never know what the Israelis are thinking.'

'You mean people wearing orange jackets might actually be targeted?' I said, and Mohammed nodded.

'So is this what the ISM is doing?' said Sophie. 'Trying to save people's homes.'

'That's right,' said Mohammed. 'We can't stop the bullets and missiles and rockets; we can only place ourselves between these targeted homes and the Israeli army with their bulldozers and APCs.'

'APCs?'

'Armoured personnel carriers, a bit like a tank. An APC always comes along with a bulldozer. It waits in the background or suddenly it appears, driving in a threatening way towards you, very fast. It gives protection, kind of observing the area while the bulldozer is demolishing. These bulldozers weigh sixty tons, and I've seen them driving over people's homes.'

'What must you feel when you see this happening to the homes of people you know?' I asked.

'It's so painful,' said Mohammed. 'Good homes, crumbling like biscuits. Everything you worked for gone, not even photos left. Nothing can stop these bulldozers. They're just massive. Very cruel. Very powerful.'

Amjad told us, in his broken English, more about the two young brothers from what he called the Abu Jabr house, who had been shot two days before Tom. 'They live on the same street as my family – over there,' he said, pointing towards the border. 'That watchtower is right behind their house.'

On the evening of 9 April, Amjad told us, Rushdie, aged fifteen, had gone to get a drink of water and while he was drinking was shot through the neck, in front of his two young sisters. His mother presumed the soldier in the watchtower had seen her son through the window as he lifted the water to drink.

'He was bleeding real heavy. Everyone start to scream and call for help from the neighbours,' said Amjad. 'It was horrible. They take him first to the Rafah Hospital, and then to the Al Shifa Hospital in Gaza City. It's a half-hour drive, but the ambulance was held up at the Abu Houli checkpoint and it took very long. They kept giving him blood, and the ambulance got through in the end. He didn't die but he is in intensive care. The family is very sad, very worried.'

Later Mustafa, Rushdie's nineteen-year-old brother, went out to the shop and was shot in the leg. 'I think he got shot from the tank,' said Amjad. 'They took him to the hospital too.'

Alison told us that she and Tom had both stayed at the house of Dr Samir, whose name I recalled from Tom's journal, and at the house of Abu Jamil, both on the Egyptian border.

'Dr Samir's house was riddled with bullet holes, like all the buildings along the border,' she said, 'and one shell hole had gone right through two walls, so the family lived mostly in the back rooms for safety. Tom was very gentle and concerned, especially for the children. Dr Samir's kids loved him. He'd take their photos and show them the pictures on his digital camera, and lie on the floor playing noughts and crosses with them.'

When Tom learned that Abu Jamil's house was more directly under threat than Dr Samir's he asked to move there. 'I'm not sure whether it was testing himself against a challenge,' said Alison, 'or the feeling that he needed to be there with the people who were suffering the most.'

The two of them had provided cover, with other ISM members, while engineers mended water tanks that had been holed by Israeli fire. They had helped erect a banner on a threatened house saying that internationals were sleeping there.

'The Israelis shot it to ribbons. They used it for target practice,' said Alison, and I had a sudden picture of the ghostly banner at the ISM headquarters with its almost unreadable writing.

Alison had been near Tom when he was shot. 'The first call I got afterwards was from a man with a heavy Israeli accent who kept asking over and over if Tom was dead,' she said. 'I explained that he was on life support in Be'ersheva, so was still technically alive, though we had been told he was brain dead. I asked, "Who am I speaking to?" and he said "Err . . . Ron Brown". Then he said "So he is not dead? – then we will have to postpone our celebration." After that I cut him off. They hated people like Tom, because he was taking photographs of what they were doing.'

I turned away, feeling sick. It was one of the most chilling things I had yet heard.

TFH joined us and pointed out the extent of the so-called security zone at the end of Salah El Din Street, a barren no-man's-land extending one hundred metres to the border. 'It's hard to believe, but this was a thriving residential area,' he said. 'The Israelis claim they need to clear it for security reasons. I understand they've totally demolished nearly eight hundred homes in Rafah in the past thirty-one months.'

'Sometimes they have another strange kind of vehicle which digs vertically into the ground, looking for tunnels,' said Mohammed.

I looked up at the two armoured watchtowers, the tops of them clearly visible above the intervening buildings. There was absolutely no sign of movement, but we knew that the IDF was watching us through the horizontal slits near the top. What horrendous power and danger those watchtowers held. It would take only one false move, I realised – raising a hand, looking through binoculars, drinking a glass of water even – to call forth a shot from an IDF sniper.

About two hundred yards from the end of Salah El Din Street we could see the tank – the same tank that Tom had described, whose indiscriminate firing down the street and shooting of the two Palestinian boys the previous day had prompted the plan for a demonstration. How was it possible for people to live their lives with this daily level of threat, I asked myself. Yet people carried on because they had to. When you are living in such devastation, with the world looking the other way, at what point, I wondered, do you simply give up? At what point do you run out of hope, the essence of life?

Alison described the evenings she and Tom had spent with Dr Samir's family in the small backyard where Dr Samir tended a vine and some fruit trees: 'We would sit on the terrace drinking tea or coffee and talking a bit while Dr Samir's wife prepared the evening meal. You could almost believe in normal life then, because the wall screened off the border and the tank, which was usually parked nearby. Sparrows had nested in the bullet holes up above and you could hear them chirruping.' And this in the only house left standing for hundreds of yards around.

While we were talking, Anthony, Billy and Michelle had been at work. They crouched at different heights on the precise spot where Tom had been shot, working out the exact level at which his head would have been, then photographing the two watch-towers from various angles to gauge the line of vision from each. Anthony, surrounded by onlookers eager to help, was taking meticulous measurements and recording them in his notebook.

It was at this point that a British journalist, who must have got word that we had returned, appeared on the scene. Fred was standing a little away from the rest of us, watching Anthony, Billy and Michelle at work. The journalist went up to him and said something to him I couldn't hear. But I heard Fred's reply: 'My brother was doing something good, he was rescuing little children, and they shot him,' he said, looking far into the distance. 'They shot him, they shot my brother.' His face was white and swept of all expression. The memory of it comes back to me so often.

By now the heat of the day was intense in the barren, sun-baked street. We were all emotionally and physically exhausted, and Andy and TFH were clearly anxious to be on the move. So, saying goodbye to Mohammed, Amjad and Alison, we climbed into the Range Rovers for the long drive back to Be'ersheva. It was impossible to imagine that we wouldn't see them again, but we left feeling we'd had too little time with them. Yet again this had been a fact-finding mission. I wanted to return to talk with them at an ordinary human level.

That night my head was full of disturbing images: Dr Samir's family in their small garden, drinking coffee only yards from where a tank lay in waiting; a young boy raising a glass to his lips as an IDF sniper took aim; IDF bulldozers crushing Palestinian homes . . . I opened Tom's journal, which lay on my bedside table, and there in front of me was a passage about the death of Rachel Corrie. *'Being crushed by a bulldozer is not just losing your life. It is your body being pulled apart as people stand and watch. Your arm may be dislocated by the tons of metal grinding it against some piece of rusted metal wire, while one side of your face is crushed in and the skin and flesh torn away on the edge of the metal sheet designed to clear boulders and huge amounts of rubble quickly. You don't die immediately . . .'* But I couldn't read on.

Our days began to fall into some sort of pattern. My heart was wrung to see how the children gave themselves up to caring for Tom, each in their own way. One or other of us was constantly watching over him, sitting by his bed, hands near his on the coverlet. We would gently massage his hands and feet, searching for the smallest signs of consciousness or improvement. There were lighter moments too. Sophie remembers chatting to Tom, even teasing him, pretending there was booze in his drip, or that they'd brought him a pizza, threatening to take it away if he didn't wake up. This was the kind of playful relationship they'd had with Tom. It reminded them of what he would have laughed at, and by doing this they helped each other through. Yet though we were there together, surrounding Tom with all the love we had, we still felt isolated, cut off from one another by a private grief too deep to express; aware of my incapacity, I feared for all my children.

Our isolation was greatly eased by the presence of the ISMers – Raph, Phil, Alison (who I came to think of as Young Alison, to distinguish her from the older Alison we'd met in Rafah), Laura, Joe, and of Nathan and Michelle – who were still camping out at the hospital, anxious to stay near Tom. I often came across them in the waiting room or the canteen, talking on their mobiles to family and friends. They took turns to sit with us at Tom's bedside, and we would talk quietly – about Tom, about the shooting, about their own lives and plans. One day, when we were there alone, American Joe told me again of the horror of the day when Tom was shot.

'I heard a woman scream, turned to look thinking a child had been shot, and then saw the orange jacket on the ground,' he said. 'I rushed over as Amjad picked him up. I screamed for them to put him down and covered his head with cotton pads. A taxi appeared and they pulled him in, though we pleaded for them to wait for an ambulance. We caught a taxi and went straight to the hospital, me still clutching a bloody pad. He was stabilised and shipped off to Gaza City before I even knew what was happening, and I just sat outside the hospital clutching that pad, looking at all the blood on my hands for over half an hour.'

I still had a sense that information was coming at me so fast that it was passing over my head. But I needed to hear the ISMers' accounts, to share what they'd been through. They were conscientious, thinking people, many of them working out what they wanted to do with their lives, and I respected their seriousness and sincerity. The more I got to know them, the less they seemed like the group of 'terrorists' portrayed by the Israeli press.

I also became aware of another figure, a quiet, dark man who seemed to be camped out in the waiting room. He was there when we arrived in the mornings and we would smile and nod. He seemed to know his way around and I sensed that he had been in the hospital some time. The ISMers told me he was a

Palestinian gynaecologist whose brother was dying in the Intensive Care Unit. He had been there for six weeks without leaving the hospital. He dared not go out because he had come with his brother from Gaza and didn't have a permit to be in Israel. Leaving the hospital was too risky because he could be arrested.

I was concerned by his isolation, this obviously intelligent young man, alone here with his dying brother, cut off from the outside world by these inhuman regulations, and I tried to find some Arabic newspapers for him. But I was too late. As I waited on the bench outside the Intensive Care Unit a few days later, the doors opened and a trolley was wheeled out with a body on it, covered with a sheet. Behind it walked the young gynaecologist. Our eyes met and he acknowledged me with a smile and a movement of his head. Then the trolley was whisked into the lift and he followed it. I heard later that he had been prevented from returning to Gaza with his brother's body. I felt both sorrow and outrage.

I began to understand that the row of white-robed men who sat smoking on benches outside the Intensive Care Unit were Palestinians from the Occupied Territories. Those who could pay brought their relations to be treated in Israel, for although the Palestinian health service did its best in their destroyed economy, the quality of care it could offer was inevitably greatly diminished. But what of those who could not pay, I thought. Especially those civilians wounded by the bullets of the IDF?

Sometimes, to my relief, some of the group would tempt Fred away to the canteen, or for a walk to the local shopping mall, and he would trot off, released for an hour or so. They all knew how close he was to Tom, and they did their best to amuse him and take his mind off things, especially Phil, the warm, sensitive young Irishman, and the ever thoughtful Michelle and Nathan. Already so used to his brothers' and sister's friends, Fred slotted easily into being with an older group.

It was during a conversation with Raph, the young Hebrew-speaker, that I learned more about Michal, the mysterious Israeli girl who had been at Tom's bedside when we first arrived. Her parents, Danny and Erella, lived on a kibbutz a bus ride from Be'ersheva, and they had come to the hospital on the night Tom was shot, having heard the news from Michal. Raph told me that Erella was a bereavement counsellor, and that she had offered her home on the kibbutz as a refuge to the traumatised group of young people who had gathered around Tom, some of whom had witnessed the murder of Rachel Corrie only days before. I had heard mention of 'the kibbutz' and had been aware that people sometimes disappeared for a day or two. Now I knew where they had gone.

'They're wonderful people, Danny and Erella, so generous and hospitable,' said Raph. 'Erella is there for anyone who needs her – it doesn't matter what nationality you are. You might like to come out there with us some time. It's a beautiful place. They don't mind how many people arrive – there's always food and talk and a floor to sleep on. It's like a bit of normal life after this place.'

Billy was the first to visit the kibbutz, but soon Sophie and Fred made the journey too. They came back with vivid descriptions of the peaceful surroundings and lush vegetation, of Erella's warmth and kindness, and of the evenings they all spent on the vine-covered balcony talking to Danny, an engineer on the kibbutz, about the situation in Gaza and on the West Bank. I could see getting out of the hospital had helped them to unwind. In fact over those early weeks Sophie visited several times and I saw that she and Erella hit it off wonderfully. I was grateful. I knew how much she missed the support of her London friends, how threatening, confusing and difficult she found the present situation.

I think that at this time I was still so shocked, so distanced from myself, that I was functioning almost automatically, and this must have been very difficult for Sophie, Bill and Fred. While Anthony spent his days dealing with the outside world and pursuing his investigations, I spent them in the Intensive Care Unit where Tom still lay, pale and unmoving. The orange brace remained around his neck, but the bandage round his head had been replaced by a smaller dressing, so that I could see more of his face. His head was still swollen, and it was impossible to bear the thought of the intense and painful pressure this must be causing. We were told that a section of his skull might have to be removed to relieve it, leaving his brain even more unprotected, and this seemed a terrible option. He would probably also need a tracheostomy.

Day after day I sat watching him, wondering how well I had really known him in the twenty-one years we had spent together. Only the past now seemed to have any meaning, and those twenty-one years were all concertinaed together, everything leading up to this point, nothing beyond it having any reality. Scenes and conversations flashed through my unfocused mind: the Saturday Tom had come home with 'Defy the Stars' tattooed on his arm – Romeo's challenge to fate from Tom's favourite Shakespeare play; the evening I had gone up to his room and found every piece of furniture covered with my best white linen, and every surface flickering with candles, awaiting the arrival of his girlfriend Libby. Tom, so romantic, so idealistic, and yet so grimly realistic too, vividly aware, as I knew now, of what he was letting himself in for when he arrived in Gaza. *'It is on the decision of any one Israeli soldier or settler that my life depends. I know that I'd probably never know what hit me. . . .'*

At night my mind could not shut down. The tension of watching with Tom, interpreting for Tom, my anxieties about the rest of the family and the strain of this alien environment registered in every fibre of my being. I felt it physically, emotionally, neurologically, chemically. Every part of me ached and I faced the mornings empty. One morning Sophie found me in the bathroom beside myself with grief, and was so upset that she phoned a friend of mine in London, who immediately phoned a friend in Jerusalem. Within hours a sympathetic doctor who lived in Be'ersheva was knocking at my bedroom door. We talked for a while and he gave me a prescription. I didn't take the pills, but I hung on to them, tremendously strengthened by this wonderful, direct support. At the same time I was distressed that for the moment Sophie and I seemed to have exchanged roles, and I knew it left her feeling terribly exposed. Before I had always coped, never given way. Now, seeing my vulnerability, feeling she had to care for me on top of everything else, it was too much.

At about this time we were disturbed to hear of a story that was going round the hospital. Anthony and I were approached rather hesitantly in the corridor by two young women who introduced themselves as Palestinian medical students. They expressed their sympathy, then told us that the other students in their classes were saying that Tom had been shot by a Palestinian. It had created bad feeling. Was it true?

We invited them to join us and we sat together on some shady benches beside the medical library. Anthony told them that this was not the case, that his researches indicated Tom had been shot by a member of the Israeli Defence Force while rescuing a small child from sniper fire. They asked us a number of questions and were obviously relieved by our answers. They told us they would pass the information on to their fellow students and Anthony volunteered to come and explain the situation to them if this would help. Where had this story come from, we wondered – from the misleading early press reports, or from somewhere else entirely?

During our second week in Israel TFH phoned to say that the British Ambassador, Sherard Cowper-Coles, and his wife Bridget would like to visit Tom and meet us. It was becoming increasingly obvious that we were getting nowhere through diplomatic channels in our attempts to meet the IDF, and we welcomed the chance to speak to the Ambassador face to face. The IDF had simply announced that it was conducting its own internal enquiry, a similar enquiry, we presumed, to the one that had completely exonerated the army over the death of Rachel Corrie.

In the late afternoon of 28 April the Ambassador and his wife arrived to meet us at the hospital, and we went immediately up to

see Tom. We had been through so much in the preceding weeks
that we were beyond formalities, and Sherard and Bridget greeted
us not as diplomats but as one human being to another. They had
five teenage children of their own, all away at boarding school in
England, and I could see that they were both deeply affected by
the sight of Tom. Much moved, Bridget turned to me while
Sherard stood at the foot of the bed with Anthony, silent and
appalled.

Afterwards they invited us all to dinner at a Chinese restaurant; in
this informal family atmosphere we relaxed a little. It was comforting to be able to talk openly about what had happened to someone
who was officially there to give us support. Sherard was an
intelligent and experienced diplomat, approachable and very much
his own man I felt, while Bridget was warm and empathetic.

But though Sherard's manner was more measured and less
forthright than TFH's, what he had to say about the IDF, clearly
based on experience, was hardly more encouraging.

'I'm afraid I really hold out very little hope of ever extracting a
fully satisfactory account of what happened from them,' he said.
'We may end up with some mild general admission of a mistake
having been made. But that would be set in the context of the
ISM being hostile to Israel and having no right to be there in the
first place, plus the threat to the IDF in Rafah.'

'But how *can* they justify these shootings of unarmed civilians?'
I said, feeling anger rising. 'It's not just Tom and Rachel Corrie, is
it? There was Brian Avery, that young American working with
the ISM who was shot in the face in Jenin three weeks ago. Not to
mention all the shootings of innocent Palestinians we've been
hearing about.'

'The IDF have much looser rules of engagement than would be
acceptable in, say, the British army,' said Sherard. 'They're
permitted to fire on anyone they believe poses a threat. And
there's no real culture of public accountability for soldiers.'

I remembered my conversation with TFH on the drive to
Be'ersheva. I'd heard this before.

'However,' Sherard went on, 'it doesn't follow that we shouldn't keep up the pressure for an account of what happened. We owe this to ourselves and to Tom.' He spoke with obvious sincerity, yet I had an uncomfortable feeling that, as far as the Foreign Office was concerned, the pass had already been sold. It seemed to be accepted that the Israeli army was a law unto itself.

We went on to discuss Tom's condition and the possibility of bringing him back to England when he was sufficiently stable. British Embassy officials had already explored the cost of an air ambulance, which would be anything from £17,000 to £20,000. And then, of course, there was the matter of Tom's medical expenses. Although the Foreign Office would be happy to help with practicalities, he said, unfortunately it was unable to contribute financially in any way.

'What about the Israelis?' Anthony asked.

'Well,' said Sherard. 'Not surprisingly their style is to give as little as possible as late as possible. I suspect they may end up meeting the medical bills, if only because they can't stop treating Tom, and recovering the money from you could be difficult. But there could be a very nasty legal dispute – they might even prevent you from leaving the country.'

It felt extraordinary to be talking about Tom's life in this detached way, yet these were the practicalities. We had no idea when we would be able to return to the UK, and neither Anthony nor I could imagine going back to work in the present circumstances. There were the expenses of family travel and of staying in a hotel to meet, and meantime the everyday bills piled up in England. There were so many aspects to this situation – emotional, medical, financial, legal, diplomatic – and we had to consider all of them. I felt wrung out with trying to operate at so many different levels.

Sherard urged us to consider ways of raising money in the UK to bring Tom home, and we talked about how we could bring some good out of this evil thing that had happened – perhaps by establishing a trust in Tom's memory and setting up a website for information about the case which would be a point of contact for people who wanted to help.

We parted warmly, with Bridget suggesting I might come and spend a day or two at the Residence in Tel Aviv. 'It's quiet,' she said. 'We have a lovely garden, and you can just sit and relax.' I couldn't imagine being able to relax, but I was grateful for her kindness.

Next day Anthony received an e-mail from Sherard, setting out the points we had discussed. 'I see virtually no chance of anyone being able to conduct a meaningful independent enquiry,' he wrote. 'My advice would be to concentrate on getting answers out of the Israelis, and putting those alongside the statements you have, or are collecting, from ISM and Palestinian witnesses.'

Getting answers out of the Israelis? How on earth were we to do that? But at least Sherard had confirmed what we already knew: that although Her Majesty's Government might be willing to smooth our path in practical ways and in opening up important channels of communication with the Israelis, when it came to bringing the IDF to book it was going to be up to us. I would come to respect Sherard's judgement and perseverance with the Israelis. But I realised he was a diplomat and his hands were tied by No. 10.

SEVEN

We had very soon begun to appreciate the importance of the media in keeping Tom's story alive and – we hoped – exerting pressure on the IDF. There was no shortage of interest. On 17 April Tom's dramatic photographs appeared in the *Guardian*, and other cuttings, critical of Israeli action, filtered through to us, not just from the British press but from newspapers all over the world. Pictures of Tom were appearing everywhere, his bright orange vest vivid against the drab background of Rafah, indisputable evidence that IDF claims that they had mistaken him for a gunman in army fatigues were a lie.

The feeling of outrage at the shooting of Tom and Brian Avery and the killing of Rachel Corrie seemed to be worldwide. On 22 April the *Chicago Tribune* commented: 'Repeatedly the international community has caved in when faced with Israeli defiance. The difference between the docile international community, on the one hand, and individuals like Corrie, Hurndall and Avery, on the other, is that these individuals refused to be turned back. They left the safety of their lives to go unarmed, except with their principles, into harm's way, because they believed someone had to act where governments refused to do so.'

Joseph Algazy of the Israeli English-language newspaper *Ha'aretz* came to see us and published a long piece under the headline 'Dear IDF, Please Meet Us, Allow an Open Dialogue'. 'If I could write a letter to the IDF,' I told him, 'my letter would say: "Dear IDF, Please move on and let go of this negativity . . .

hear ordinary human anger, take responsibility where it is right that you do so . . . Allow this useless and perpetual dynamic of victimisation to shrivel to nothing, where it belongs . . . Please just put your head out of your faceless watchtowers and dark tanks and hear, feel, smell, breathe and taste the benefits of a more inclusive way of being."'

'Tom wanted to help the people here and we also want to contribute in some way to finding a solution that will put an end to this conflict,' Anthony told Algazy. 'From now on this is also our responsibility, just as it is the responsibility of the Israelis and the Palestinians.'

Among the many people who came to interview us were two dynamic French journalists in their early thirties who were making a television documentary about Tom's shooting. They could have been slightly older versions of Tom, fearless and energetic. On several occasions they had been locked up and detained by the Israelis while travelling out to film in the Occupied Territories. They told us numerous stories of these exploits, and of how they had managed to hide a mobile phone in order to keep in touch with the French Embassy. They were streetwise and full of nous, and had had enough experience of the IDF, they told us, to know what we were up against.

At the end of the day they suggested we all have dinner in Jerusalem and we called on the faithful Ya'alon to take us. It was thirty years since I had been in Jerusalem, and my heart leapt at the first glimpse of the Old City, standing on its hill, its pale walls glowing in the evening sunlight. Did we know the American Colony Hotel one of them asked, as we drew up outside a familiar leafy doorway.

How could he have known that the American Colony Hotel was part of my history? As soon as we walked into the cool reception area with its arched ceiling, mellow stone floor and antique blue wall tiles I was twenty-one again, dressed in a crushed red dress that I'd brought along for 'best' but which had languished for weeks at the bottom of my rucksack. 'You must visit the American Colony Hotel and meet Mrs Vester,' my father had said to me before I left England. So off we had gone, my friend and I, and ordered a cream tea with strawberries, which we ate in a courtyard which I thought then – and still do – must be the most beautiful courtyard in the world.

'Do you by any chance have a guest book for 1964–5?' I said now to the girl at the reception desk. I was overcome by a kaleidoscopic sense of different parts of my life coming together in a new pattern, of standing with my family in a place my father had known so well, a few days after my son had been shot. I longed to have something of my father, to see his familiar writing, to feel his steadfast, reassuring presence. 'My father used to stay here, and he knew Mrs Vester well, you see,' I said by way of explanation.

'Of course, we will look for you,' said the receptionist with a dazzling smile. It felt that nothing was too much trouble. Now we were in East Jerusalem, a predominantly Palestinian area, and we were being welcomed with Palestinian warmth.

'Would you like me to see if Mrs Vester is still up?' asked one of the waiters who was standing by the desk.

I couldn't believe it. I'd imagined that Mrs Vester had died long ago. She was related to the members of the old American colony who had settled in East Jerusalem in the nineteenth century and her name was synonymous with the hotel, which was still owned by the Vester family, though they no longer ran it. She and my father had become good friends during his visits to Jordan, and I'm sure they would have discussed the two main interests in his life – aspects of theology and saving the world's resources. Soon the waiter returned to tell me that Mrs Vester had gone to bed. But she would be at breakfast as usual, he said.

We talked late over dinner, and at some point one of the journalists left the table to make a phone call, returning to say that he had permission from his company to invite us to spend the night at the hotel. Billy declined, saying he would prefer to stay at the hospital. This was now the centre of Billy's life and he had made friends with several of the ISMers. I could tell that these friendships, and his grief over what had happened to Tom, had opened Billy's eyes and sharpened his awareness.

Next morning I saw Mrs Vester, seated at her own table, patrician, upright and immaculately dressed. Although she was in her nineties she was entirely on the ball and aware of the news, and had heard all about Tom. She and her son, who lived in London, had spoken about it, she said. She shook her head sadly. I knew from my father that she came from a colonial tradition based in care for the local community. The family into which she had married, the original American colony who came to Jerusalem from Chicago, was known for its charitable works, and the hotel they founded was always a place where Jews and Arabs could meet on neutral ground. Mrs Vester had retained that tradition, and in the middle of troubled East Jerusalem it still felt like an oasis of tranquillity. Talking to Mrs Vester I felt I had touched another world.

We sat in the lovely courtyard after breakfast, drinking our coffee, listening to the soothing sound of water splashing into a basin where goldfish swam hypnotically, catching the sunlight in flashes of red and gold. Above our heads were baskets of sharply scented geraniums, and around us carefully tended formal beds filled with pansies and tulips. Over in one corner of the courtyard was a piece of old stone pipe which had been made into a kind of sculpture. I remembered it from my last visit. I even had a photograph of my father, sitting beside it at one of the wrought-iron tables topped with hand-painted blue and green tiles. He was drawn to Palestinian art and craftsmanship, and would return home from Jordanian Jerusalem, as it was then, with glowing Palestinian pottery, butter dishes, ashtrays, mugs and glass from Hebron. I had inherited some of them, but there were only two pieces left now.

Doves cooed. Being here felt surreal. Everything was peace and warmth and colour, yet only miles away was the sterile grey ward of a hospital where Tom was lying, the violent mud-caked desolation of Gaza. I closed my eyes and held my face up to the morning sun slanting through the leaves of a jacaranda tree. Yet I dared not give myself up to the moment. *Dear Tom, it is not possible to believe you will never know this beauty, the sound of the fountain, the light on the stone, the shadows in the colonnade.*

This part of East Jerusalem was the last place where he had walked before he travelled down to Rafah. When I looked back on his life now, everything seemed to have been leading up to that point. It was almost as if I could have predicted it. Tom had always wanted to challenge, wanted to look – not look away as some of us do. I could see him in my mind's eye, loose-limbed and at ease, striding observantly through the narrow streets with his camera. Not far from here he had sat in a little rooftop café overlooking the Dome of the Rock, and wondered that there could be such peace in the middle of such turmoil.

'I saw children of ages between 5 and 15 fighting viciously, with sticks and shards of broken mirrors, throwing the sharpest rocks they could find at each other. This place is saturated with anger, resentment and frustration. You can feel it in the air. And it occurred to me; what would it do to the mind of a child growing up under these conditions? I can't imagine the number of tears they have cried and what they have thought they had to turn into just to survive.

'And then I came across a church and in it was the most serene atmosphere. In the centre of the Venetian-set slums and maze of alleys there was silence. The church of the Holy Sepulchre; the tomb of Jesus where he was crucified, etc. It drew me in, an agnostic verging on atheism, and it touched me. I'm not saying I came out a believer, but something really moved me, me, who am never moved.'

The maze of alleys drew me like a magnet. I wanted to be near to Tom, to hear what he had heard, see through his eyes, feel with his heart. It seemed important, too, that we should make the most of this visit; who knew when we would have a chance to see this historic place again? Fred was keen to look for a football and that seemed important, too, something ordinary for him to hold on to.

Sophie wanted to see the market, Anthony wanted to post a letter. So we set off.

Before long we were accosted by a guide. We tried to put him off. No, we didn't want a tour, we just wanted to post a letter, we told him.

'No, no – come. I will show you where postbox is,' he said. He was very insistent, in the way of all guides. We just wanted to be on our own, but none of us had the strength to resist. I was annoyed with myself for failing to stand up to him.

He led us towards the majestic Damascus Gate. Crowds were thronging in and out of the great dark archway leading through the massive grey stone wall into the Old City. This was the gate my father used, his door into old Jerusalem, and I wanted to stand there in the shadows and savour the place, but the man was hurrying us on. Down, down, down the wide stone steps we went into a cool well where the air was full of the sound of human voices, pungent with the smell of herbs and spices. Women crouched on the ground beside boxes of almonds and spring onions and vine leaves and dill, stalls overflowed with oranges and lemons, cauliflowers and cucumbers, all fresh and beautifully set out. From time to time narrow, high-sided barrows laden with fruit would come trundling towards us at an alarming pace, accompanied by warning shouts. On the back of each was a hook with an old tyre attached by a stubby chain. This was the braking system. When the stallholder needed to slow down he unhooked the tyre and stood on it – often only just in time.

Everywhere there was vibrant colour – trays of nougat and Turkish delight, displays of pottery, racks of Bedouin clothing. I noticed two young Israeli soldiers lounging against a stall selling cheap baby clothes, tensely observed by the stall's owners. And from time to time, through all this pulsating life, this connected-ness, this humanity, would walk a pair of men in the long black overcoats of the Jewish Orthodox, looking neither to right nor left, apparently entirely unconnected to their surroundings. They were just getting from A to B, but they seemed not so much single-minded as insulated. The sight of them made me ponder the apparent depth of separation between these two cultures. To me their demeanour was thought-provoking, incomprehensible.

Down and still down our guide led us, until we came upon a falafel shop which I seemed to recognise from thirty-odd years ago. Limited as his tastes were, Tom was notoriously difficult to feed, but I was sure he would have stopped there to buy falafels. Now we were being shepherded along narrow streets that led upwards towards small patches of sky, past moneylenders and moneychangers and shops full of lamps, musical instruments, tourist paraphernalia. We bought some Jerusalem plates – 'and this is for you, a gift,' said the shopkeeper, slipping in an extra plate with a picture of Yasser Arafat's face on it – and looked for a football for Fred. Our guide talked on. We were having the full tourist treatment and everyone was quietly grumbling. Sophie, I know, found it unbearable to see the groups of IDF soldiers crowding the holy shrines. Every bone in my body ached, my shoes were uncomfortable and my feet were hurting. It all felt unreal, inappropriate. Yet here we were, following this man as he whisked us round the sights, too dulled to bring this intrusive guided tour to an end.

Finally we were once more back at the Damascus Gate, and we said goodbye to our guide with some relief. It had been an uncomfortable experience, the very antithesis of what we had wanted. I had gone in search of Tom but I had not found him. To do so I knew I would sometime have to return, alone.

EIGHT

Sophie had decided to go home. I knew she was finding the situation in Israel isolating and stressful, but I felt sad that she was going, and concerned. We were all so preoccupied that it was hard for us to get together as a family and talk openly about the things that were on our minds, but I realised that Sophie felt she had already lost Tom. Yet Tom had not died, and she could not mourn. It was the tragic dilemma that faced all of us, and we all tried to deal with it as best we could. I sensed that Billy too, in his quiet, realistic way, had accepted the loss of his brother, but despite the doctors' insistent message that Tom would never recover, the rest of us clung to some sort of hope – for what? We didn't know.

So at the beginning of May Sophie left for London. She wanted to get on with raising funds to bring Tom home, so he could have his friends and family around him. She also badly needed the support of her own friends.

By this time we had managed to escape the hotel and move into a flat near the hospital generously lent to us by a lively, bright, human rights lawyer with whom we had been in contact. A group of human rights workers, lecturers at Be'ersheva University, had simply arrived one day and moved us in, even providing us with furniture, and we were touched and grateful. It was a slick, brand-new, purpose-built flat, furnished simply, with mattresses on the floor, and it was a great relief to be there after the noise, expense and chilling atmosphere of the hotel.

Sherard and Bridget kept in regular contact. Sherard was still negotiating behind the scenes with a General Eiland, the officer in charge of the army's enquiry into Tom's shooting, for a meeting between us and the IDF. So far he'd made no progress. The only glimmer we had had was through *Ha'aretz*, which reported an IDF spokesperson as saying the military authorities would 'meet with the Hurndall family, and on conclusion of investigations and the formulation of conclusions would present them to the relevant people'. We wondered what kind of investigation this could be – so far they had contacted none of the witnesses.

Now Bridget invited Fred and me to spend a few days at the Ambassador's Residence in Tel Aviv. So on the first Saturday in May an Embassy driver collected us from the flat, dropped us both at the Residence and took Sophie on to catch her plane. I felt that I should go to the airport with her, but my head was throbbing and my temples seemed gripped in an iron vice. All I wanted to do was lie down, and Sophie insisted that she would be fine. I stood on the steps watching the car with her gallant, determined figure waving in the back until it was out of sight. I hadn't the time or the emotional resources to respond to her needs. It was as if the carpet had been pulled from under my feet and I hardly recognised myself.

The Residence was a secluded single-storey building set among lush terraced gardens in a residential area of Tel Aviv. On the topmost terrace was a swimming pool, on the lowest level a basketball court and in the middle a lovely garden designed for diplomatic entertaining. Fred, a natural athlete, was able to have a break from the intensity and sadness of the hospital, racing between the pool and the court. Although he seemed carefree, he told me later he couldn't wait to get back to Be'ersheva and Tom. 'I needed to be with my big brother.'

Bridget and Sherard welcomed us, tactfully leaving me alone for most of the time to lie in the shade on the terrace outside my room. I longed for the warmth and kindness and peaceful surroundings to work some kind of magic, to disperse the tension in my back and shoulders, release the iron band around my head, but I had long passed the stage when I could let go. So I lay in a basket chair, trying to read or gazing through half-closed eyes at the bougainvillea that covered the wall, the vibrant purples and blues of the lilac and the jacaranda. But I wasn't seeing the flowers. My inner world was full of shifting monochrome images – Tom, lying deathly still on his hospital bed, the bloodstained ground in Rafah, my last glimpse of Sophie as she waved good-bye, concerned friends back home in London – round and round they went in my troubled brain, like an old film on a loop. When would we ever see home again? What would happen if no one in authority would meet us? Did we even exist in their eyes?

In the evenings we gathered for drinks and dinner on the marble-pillared verandah. It was here, I think, that Sherard and I discussed again the possibility of setting up a foundation in Tom's name. And it was here that I learned of the death of a young British cameraman called James Miller, shot in the neck by the IDF as he filmed for a television documentary on the children of Rafah.

According to *Ha'aretz*, as James and his team were preparing to leave a Palestinian home after curfew on the evening of 2 May, they realised they were trapped and could not leave without putting themselves in danger, though the soldiers were fully aware of their presence since they had been shouting over to them, even singing at them, during the day. So they had come out with the translator carrying a white flag and James walking close beside him, shining a flashlight at the flag, waving his arms and shouting to make sure the soldiers saw it. It was inconceivable that they had not seen it, but James was shot, nonetheless. The IDF were now claiming he had been caught in crossfire, yet several witnesses claimed there had been no other shooting at the time.

'The IDF is sorry at a civilian death, but stresses that a camera-man who knowingly enters a combat zone, especially at night, endangers himself,' said the predictable IDF spokesman. It was all painfully familiar. The young man with a concern for children, the tragedy, the excuse – no, my scepticism told me, the *lie*. It was no good beating about the bush. It had become impossible to believe these murders of peaceful civilians were accidental. This growing certainty was unbelievably shocking.

One evening Bridget and Sherard suggested I join them in a local bar to hear a well-known Israeli singer. I very much wanted to go, but at the last minute I knew I couldn't do it. It was just as well. At around midnight, a young British Muslim walked into Mike's Place, a bar only a few doors away from the one we had planned to visit, and blew himself up, killing three people. It was my first experience of suicide bombers. Israeli TV and Al Jazeera showed graphic footage of the resulting terrible human injury.

Reaction from the British government was swift and crystal-clear in its public condemnation. Jack Straw, the Foreign Secretary, announced in the Commons that he would give Israel every support in relation to the bombing and offered his condolences on behalf of the British public. The Chancellor, Gordon Brown, ordered the Bank of England to freeze all bank accounts belonging to the bomber's two suspected accomplices. Premises in England were raided and arrests swiftly made.

The Times reported that the raids 'followed a warning from Israel that the British Government must deal severely with Islamic extremists'. Yet the British government had not so far seen fit to make a public statement or put pressure of any kind on the Israeli government over its shooting of young British citizens. We were outraged, and we made our feelings clear to Sherard.

'I have expressed to the Embassy strongly my unease at the fact that immediately following the bombing at the bar in Tel Aviv and the killing of three Israelis, the British government jumped to give a statement of support for Israelis and to freeze funds and make arrests,' Anthony told the *Guardian*. 'There's an enormous difference between how the British reacted to British citizens' involvement in killing Israelis and the complete lack of cooperation and a complete silence over what happened to British nationals here.'

Only after this statement did we receive a communication from

Jack Straw, offering us a meeting when we returned to England. The Foreign Office belatedly stated, almost a month after the incident, that it was 'shocked and saddened by the shooting of Tom Hurndall' and was 'pressing the Israeli army for an investigation'.

Our hopes of a proper investigation were utterly dashed when we met Sandra Jordan, the young journalist working on the film about events in Rafah for *Dispatches*. Not long after my return from Tel Aviv she came to the flat in Be'ersheva and showed us the transcript of a conversation she had had with an IDF representative, Major Sharon Feingold. Much of the interview would have been laughable if its subject had not been so tragic. Under the pressure of Sandra Jordan's quiet but persistent questioning, it became clear that the major had not even troubled to identify the correct site of Tom's shooting. Her arrogance was breathtaking. Asked what evidence she had for the claim that the IDF had been fired at, Major Feingold replied: 'I don't think the onus is on us. I think the onus is on the Palestinian side – as I say we do not fire unless we are fired at. We have one of the highest standards of morals in the Israeli Defence Force.'

'But what independent evidence – witnesses – do you have that you were fired at that day?' Sandra persisted.

'We don't need witnesses,' replied Feingold, 'we, again as I say, have very strict instructions . . . The first responsibility that we have is to provide security for Israelis, secondly is to ensure that our soldiers are not targeted and if they are, they are there to protect themselves and this day, and every other day along the Israeli–Egyptian border, Palestinian gunmen are shooting.' And of the soldier who shot Tom: 'I am very proud that he followed the procedures and did exactly what he needed to do.'

Challenged to make public the army's internal recordings of conversations between the soldier and his commander and CCTV footage of the incident, Major Feingold clearly became rattled.

'I don't appreciate the fact that the IDF is being put on a stand or a pedestal on trial and has to prove that we are innocent,' she replied. 'I don't believe that the Israeli army has to be holier than the Pope in trying to prove that what we are doing is just. You will have to take my word when I say we are fired at and we return fire.'

So, case dismissed. In other words, the IDF saw itself as accountable to no one, a law unto itself.

Sandra Jordan was impressive. Slight, dark-haired and intelligent, with a deceptively low-key manner and a lilting Irish voice, she missed nothing and was clearly affected by what she had seen. She sat with us on the balcony of the flat and told us what had happened in the hours after Tom's shooting. Filming in Rafah that day, she had been on the scene within minutes, and had filmed Tom's transfers from hospital to hospital until he was finally airlifted out of Gaza to Be'ersheva. I still haven't watched the footage which finally appeared on *Dispatches*, and I don't think I ever will. Sandra's description of the horrors of that journey was enough, and I wept as she told us.

'After Tom was taken off in a taxi, I went with Joe and Alice and Amjad and some of the other ISM people to the hospital in Rafah and we all just waited around,' she said. 'We were stunned – completely silent. Amjad's clothes were covered in Tom's blood and Joe was still holding the cotton pads he'd used to try to staunch the bleeding.'

Sandra and her cameraman had followed the ambulance which took Tom on to the European Hospital in Gaza City where they waited until word came that he was to be transferred by helicopter to a hospital in Israel. I knew from talking to TFH that Andy Whittaker had phoned him that day while he was at a meeting of international defence attachés to say that a British national had been shot in Rafah. The US Defence Attaché Roger Bass, who was present at the meeting, had urged TFH to ask the IDF to evacuate the wounded man out of Gaza to a hospital in Israel.

Protracted negotiations had then taken place as Tom lay in a critical condition at the European Hospital. 'I was arguing and cajoling the IDF to agree and get moving and thought we had done a pretty swift job, but when I looked at the time it took it was about three to four hours – far too long for someone in his condition,' TFH had told me.

At the European Hospital Sandra learned that the transfer was to be made at Karem Shalom, one of the Israeli settlements near the border with Israel, and she made her way there. 'When the ambulance arrived it was horrific,' she said. 'There were all sorts of delays and difficulties because it was a Palestinian ambulance, but finally it arrived at the place where the helicopter was waiting. Someone signalled the driver to go ahead, but for some reason he went into reverse – I suppose he was thinking about how best to transfer the stretcher into the helicopter. People had gathered to watch, and suddenly there was complete hysteria – they thought it was some sort of terrorist ploy. Everyone was screaming and shouting, and Tom was just left unattended, I should say for the best part of an hour. It was so shocking – the degree of fear and mistrust. He was at death's door, but there was such confusion and paranoia he was completely forgotten. He could easily have died while all this was going on.'

Sandra had also interviewed a number of the ISMers who were there on that day, and was well aware of the picture of them put out by the Israeli media and the IDF ('I wouldn't say they were peace activists and I wouldn't call them non-violent,' Major Feingold had declared).

'You can see why the army don't like them,' Sandra said. 'They're in the front line in a way that even the UN isn't, and they see everything. They're the only people who will go and stand right in front of the bulldozers to prevent houses being demolished. The fact that they're peaceful and unarmed just adds to the aggravation.'

Ironically, it was not long after this meeting that we learned the International Solidarity Movement had been nominated for a Nobel Peace Prize.

'Although this nomination is for the ISM as a whole', read the citation, 'three young individuals merit particular recognition for the courage and resolve they displayed in their acts of non-violent civil disobedience in defence of peace and human rights in the Palestinian Occupied Territories.

'These individuals are Brian Avery and Tom Hurndall, who miraculously survived sniper shots to the head by Israeli forces while they were defending Palestinian civilians from Israeli troops, and Rachel Corrie, who was crushed to death by an Israeli Defence Force bulldozer while attempting to prevent the demolition of the home of an innocent Palestinian family.

'A Nobel Peace Price for the ISM would be a fitting testament to the fortitude and principle exemplified by the members of this organisation and these three individuals in particular.'

I felt immensely proud, but it was a deeply painful pride. Yes, Tom had 'miraculously survived', but he would never hear this praise.

Back in London Sophie had thrown herself into raising money for the 'Bring Tom Home' appeal. Before she left, the five of us had also discussed establishing another longer-term charitable fund with which we might do something positive for the people of Gaza. We decided to call one the Thomas Hurndall Fund and the other the Tom Hurndall Trust Fund, and there was a lot of work to do in setting them up.

Friends rallied round, offering their support, both practical and financial, as did the press – in particular the *Evening Standard* and our local paper, the *Camden New Journal*, which had followed Tom's story closely from the beginning. 'Help Bring Tom Home to Die' said the stark black headline. Contributions came from all over the UK. It was deeply affecting to know how many people had been touched by the story of Tom and what he had done.

On familiar ground again, Sophie dealt competently with the administration and talked confidently to the media, but I knew how fragile that carapace was. In mid-May she was asked to speak at a Free Palestine Rally in Trafalgar Square to mark the fifty-fifth anniversary of the creation of the State of Israel, and courageously she accepted, standing beside the actress Juliet Stevenson and Tony Benn to address a crowd of twenty thousand. She spoke passionately, from the heart, and friends told us later what a striking and emotional impact she had made standing there in her jeans and T-shirt, with her strong features and alive, expressive face framed by her glossy dark hair. She described vividly what had happened to Tom, and the situation in Gaza.

'If we don't take a stand to make the Israeli government accountable for its actions, then there will be no end to this terrible loss of life in Palestine. Help us exert pressure for proper accountability and an end to this indiscriminate loss of life,' she appealed to the crowd. 'Please contact the Foreign Secretary, Jack Straw, to reinforce our demand for an independent public enquiry. Help us to make a difference.'

Now Billy was talking of going home. We had been in Israel for over a month and during that time my second son had largely kept his own counsel, as was his habit, watching, hawk-like, at his brother's bedside, or sitting smoking and drinking coffee in the waiting room, listening to the conversations of the ISMers and sometimes joining in. Now, accepting that Tom was not going to recover, he felt it was time to go.

So a week after Sophie's departure Billy also left to join her at home. I knew I was going to miss his solid presence, his trenchant remarks and wry sense of humour. There is something utterly grounded and reassuring about Billy, though intensely vulnerable too. Yet I was almost relieved to see him go. All his concern was focused on Tom, and I wasn't even sure if he was eating and drinking. Under the unforgiving lights of the ward he looked strained, and I sensed an underlying panic, which the rest of us shared. In this limbo we were all beginning to feel disconnected.

We had been in Be'ersheva a month. Friends were starting to ask about our plans. One evening the phone rang and it was Tom's godfather, Max. 'Isn't it time you thought about coming home?' he said directly, after we had filled him in on what was happening. 'Tom could be in that state for a very long time.'

No doubt the authorities were hoping we would leave – our presence in Israel and all the media attention it attracted must have been a constant embarrassment to them. But we knew, and Sherard had also made the point, that we were in a much better position to force a meeting and to negotiate with the Israelis over the expenses of Tom's repatriation if we stayed. And leaving without Tom was unthinkable, absolutely out of the question.

But with Sophie and Billy back in London, we began to think more about how to bring Tom home. Touching messages reached us, reminding us of the life we had left behind. Ann Manly, wife of Guy Protheroe, the director of the English Chamber Choir, with which I had sung for many years, phoned to ask how we were and to say they were all thinking of us. 'Jocey,' she said, 'the choir would like to do a concert for Tom when you get back. Please think about it, and about the music. What would you like and what did Tom like?' Hearing this was truly heartwarming. But Ann's call put me in touch with another sense of loss. Music had always been central to my life. One of my greatest sources of comfort and inspiration, it affected the deepest part of me, but now I could not listen to it – could not hear it even. It had been entirely blotted out. There was no way of playing music in the flat, and I would not have done so even if it was possible. I once heard Daniel Barenboim comment that music brings peace because it 'enables you to have a dialogue with yourself'. It was a dialogue I could not bear to have.

Another friend told us that soon after Tom was shot there had been an announcement before a home match at Arsenal, and people had stood in silence, in tribute to Tom. Arsenal was our local team and all the boys were keen supporters. Anthony had taken Tom as soon as he was old enough and those had been some of their best times together. The two of them would set off on cold winter Saturdays or weekday evenings, Tom in his heavy biker's jacket with the red stripes on the shoulders, and bulky leather gloves.

I thought of Tom's friends – the two Adams, Daniel, Sam, Angie, Caelia, Antonia, Ollie, Cassie, Alex – his close-knit circle, some of whom had gone up on to Primrose Hill together to make that tape I hadn't been allowed to hear. They all loved Tom. We knew how hard it must be for them and trusted our messages were getting through.

We were very worried, too, about Tom's girlfriend, Kay. When Tom was shot she had been on her way back home from India and at the airport had accessed scores of e-mails from Sophie asking that she get in touch. It wasn't until she'd spoken on the phone to Sophie that she'd found out what had happened. Distraught and on her own, she had tried to change her flight to Tel Aviv without success, and had then returned to London.

These thoughts of home, the loving, empathetic messages we were receiving, threw into stark contrast the situation we were in. We were struggling so hard to remain impartial, not to lay blame or condemn anyone before all the evidence was in, even though it all seemed to be leading in one direction. Yet from time to time people would ask me, 'Do you hate us, do you hate the Israelis?' It seemed a bizarre question, and it made me recoil inwardly. How could anyone think that, just because the soldier who had shot our son belonged to an army whose policies we found shocking, we would therefore hate an entire people? Another question was: 'Are you a friend of Israel?' How could I reply? The question seemed to indicate a political immaturity, a black and white view that allowed for no subtler shades of opinion: 'You are either for us, or against us.' How could I explain that we didn't hate anyone, were nobody's special friends? We simply wanted to know the truth.

Sophie rang us one day to say that a Jewish friend in London had generously contributed to the 'Bring Tom Home' fund, but only on condition that the money 'wasn't put to any political use'. Sophie was shocked and hurt by this proviso from someone who should have known us better. It seemed to be part of the same siege mentality.

We were now well into May. A number of the ISMers were still camping out at the hospital, unwilling to leave, perhaps not quite knowing what to do next, paralysed by what had happened but comforted to be involved. Apart from their sincerity and concern for Tom, I was glad for Fred's sake that they were still there. I felt he was spending too much time in the Intensive Care Unit. It was such an unnatural situation for a twelve-year-old, but I knew he was always watching for signs, that in his heart he couldn't give up the idea that one day Tom might recover. Any other possibility would have been too terrible to bear. Other people tried to provide diversions for him. The human rights lawyer who had lent us our flat and his Russian wife often invited him to their home. They were exceedingly kind, and Fred liked their children, but he was always slightly reluctant to go.

So I would always feel relieved when I heard the words, 'Mum, we're going down to the Mall', or, 'Mum, we're getting the bus out to the kibbutz', and I'd see him trotting off between a couple of the group, arms linked on either side. I knew he was in safe hands. We and the ISMers were like an extended family. Anyone who went out of the unit to buy a cold drink would buy a drink for everyone. Talk in the waiting room was quiet and serious. They were all doing their best to support us and to help one another.

Anthony was still deeply preoccupied with gathering witness statements, sifting evidence, talking to the press, working at his laptop in the canteen or back at the flat. Some of the witnesses had now scattered and it was laborious work making contact since e-mail connections were often difficult. By now his immediate impulse to bring the facts of Tom's case to light had hardened into a strategy – and a crusade. He wanted to follow through what Tom had started, to make his sacrifice meaningful, and hoped by establishing the facts of what had happened to Tom and the Abu

Jabr family, he could bring some openness and honesty to the Middle East situation. Tom's shooting and that of Mustafa and Rushdie two days before were part of a pattern, and Anthony was determined to engage with the media, government and law at every level to highlight this and so turn around the juggernaut of IDF policy. For him it was not an exercise in finger-pointing but his chance to contribute to peace in the area. He was utterly driven.

With Michelle's help we had now been able to uncover all the pictures in Tom's cameras. They were powerful and intensely personal, like his journal. I felt I was seeing through his eyes. This was what Tom had witnessed, these were the people he had stopped to talk to in the weeks before he was shot. Among the photos was one of a young smiling man taken on the bus from Amman to Baghdad. He was looking directly at Tom, and somehow you could see them relating. From press reports I recognised him as the cameraman James Miller. It seemed poignant that they had met and talked on this coach journey, perhaps shared the fear and adrenaline of possible death, discussed the effects of war on children. There were fearsome pictures of the ISMers confronting the bulldozers and APCs of the IDF ('*I'd heard that D-9 bulldozers were big, but this was fucking huge*', Tom wrote in his journal. '*It towered up like a lookout tower or airport control tower*'). Looking at these gigantic machines rearing up in front of the unarmed peaceworkers, it was impossible to believe that Rachel Corrie's death could have been accidental, that neither the driver of the bulldozer nor the nearby APC had seen her. This, despite all the evidence, was what Major Feingold had brazenly claimed in her interview with Sandra Jordan.

Michelle and Nathan had met Tom in Amman and they had stuck together until they arrived in Israel. Among Michelle's many images of Tom, most of them taken in the Jordanian refugee camp they had travelled on to, there were two pictures that moved me particularly. One was of Tom playing football with a young Iraqi boy. He was about to kick the ball, swinging his long leg and twisting his body, with that particular set of the head that was so familiar. You could see from his expression and from the angle of his body that he was giving way to the little kid – it was so absolutely Tom. In the other he was showing his camera to another small boy, encouraging him to look, letting him hold it. It was a moment of real communication, a gesture of absolute trust.

By now Tom had had a tracheostomy; some of the time the oxygen mask was removed and he was able to breathe on his own. I sat with him every day, watching the slight rise and fall of his chest, alert for any variation in the pattern of his breathing, panic-stricken if it seemed to change. One afternoon when I was alone with him it suddenly appeared to me that he had stopped breathing. I put my face close to his, listening for the gasp that comes when someone asleep and dreaming stops breathing for a moment and then suddenly breathes in again. But it never came.

Suddenly all my control gave way and I ran down the ward, tears streaming down my face, desperate for help from someone – anyone. It felt to me at that moment as if Tom had been completely abandoned, as if no one cared any more whether he lived or died.

A young doctor was walking towards me and we almost collided. 'Are you still looking after Tom?' I asked him through my tears. 'He's stopped breathing. Are you just going to let him go?'

When we reached Tom's bed he was breathing again, but I was distraught. The young doctor seemed astonished, bewildered. 'Why are you crying?' he said.

The question astonished me. I thought I had lost my son.

Yet part of me had accepted that I had lost him already, that that fine brain of his was damaged beyond repair. It frightened me, in the heat of the night, that I could not conjure up pictures of Tom as he was growing up – Tom going to school, Tom with his friends, Tom writing, drawing, taking photographs, playing football. I knew he had done all these things, but I could no longer see them in my mind's eye. Was this normal – not being able to picture your child in this way? Was it just shock? Would these images ever be retrievable? It was as if a door had closed, a curtain had come down. I tried to speak to him, but there was silence. And I knew, in my heart, that Tom was not really alive.

At about four o'clock one morning, after a terrible, wakeful night, I got up and opened the sliding doors on to the balcony, looking across the night lights of Be'ersheva to the distinctive outline of the hospital on the horizon. The beauty of the night sky and the stars made me ache. Tom, too, had loved the Middle Eastern sky, had wondered that so much bitter conflict could co-exist with such beauty. I remembered so clearly another hospital, another early morning: Friday 27 November 1981, the day of Tom's birth. He was only a few days overdue, but Friday was the day of inductions and Anthony and I drove in early. Tom was born at five o'clock that afternoon. It had been a long day in the bustling labour ward, yet what I remembered now was the absolute stillness following Tom's birth, the joy as Anthony handed him to me. How keenly we felt our responsibility. All your instincts, as a parent, are focused on keeping your child alive. But what was the reason now for keeping Tom alive? Perhaps our responsibility as parents was to do the unimaginable, to enable our child to die.

Somehow I couldn't fit these responsibilities together in my mind. My reason fought with my emotions and I felt torn in two. I wandered aimlessly around, not knowing what to do, but aware I had to do something. Eventually I dressed, wrote a note for Anthony and set out towards the hospital. The sun was coming up and it was already warm as I walked along the main boulevard, but the heat was still bearable. I passed quickly through the security checks, went up the stairs and along the familiar wide corridors where, even at this hour, people were waiting in the treatment rooms on either side. I could hear the tap of footsteps on shiny lino floors, caught glimpses of medical staff grabbing a cup of coffee before going home after the night shift.

Professor Gurman's door was open, and he was already at his desk. I stood in the doorway, obviously distressed, and when he saw me he rose and came towards me.

'Please,' he said, indicating a chair, and pulling up another in front of me.

It was a minute or two before I was able to speak. 'When you bring a child into the world,' I said finally, 'you never expect to have to make the decision to end that child's life. Is this really what we have to do?'

Professor Gurman simply inclined his head, looking at me quietly. 'I can think of no greater sadness than the loss of a child,' he said at last. 'Does it help at all if I tell you that I too have lost a child? But in my case there was no decision to make. My son died in a motor accident.'

Suddenly we were no longer doctor and client, but simply two parents, sharing our desperate feelings of loss, and I listened with a different kind of sadness. He told me about his son and the circumstances of his death, I talked to him about Tom, and we both shed tears. It was a conversation that crossed all professional barriers, all cultural divides. I became aware that I was talking to someone who was in constant touch with the experience of death. People know about death in the Middle East, they face the reality of it every day, and it is one of the things that gives life there its vibrancy. In the West we are not forced to look death in the face in the same way. We barely acknowledge its existence. We take our lives very much for granted and because of it we lose something. It made me understand that an awareness of our own mortality is a gift, for it gives life itself, every minute of every day, such value.

I shall always be grateful to Professor Gurman for that conversation. I continue to carry it with me, though I doubt if he realised the impact it had on me at the time. Although we did not speak directly of Tom's future, I felt as if it had brought some kind of peace, some sort of resolution – an acceptance of what would be.

NINE

Someone else who helped me find some kind of peace during this time was Erella. We'd been hearing a lot about her and her husband Danny from our children and from the ISMers. Her home on the kibbutz seemed to have become a kind of family-run youth hostel and counselling centre rolled into one, an all-healing place where they could crash out and feel completely at home, and I grew curious about meeting this unusual person. Before there had been too many other priorities, but now the time felt right. So one morning, before it became too hot to breathe and the whole of Be'ersheva was covered in a pall of desert dust, we called Ya'alon who drove us out to the kibbutz.

As we drove through the Negev I remembered arriving at another kibbutz, in the Golan Heights, right on the border with Lebanon. It was 1972. I'd landed at Lod airport with a group of other volunteers and we'd been driven north for several hours through the clear starry night. At about midnight there was a feeling of getting closer to our destination – a change of speed and a sense of getting higher and higher, of having to hold on to the sides of the lorry as we revved and manoeuvred round the bumpy U-bends.

When we stopped on the border road with Lebanon I could hear voices talking in Hebrew, shouting orders. Glaring lights outlined armed soldiers milling around a parked tank and other military vehicles silhouetted against the pitch-black. 'There's a curfew,' someone explained. 'It starts at seven o'clock in the evening. So the military will have to escort us along the road to the kibbutz.' I'd never been in a society controlled by the military before; it felt strange and mildly alarming.

One day, when we were picking peaches within yards of the wire fence that marked the Lebanese border, my Scottish friend Sona let out a yell. She'd inadvertently put her hand on a poisonous snake. The kibbutzniks who were with us jumped into action, chopped its head off with a long knife and slung it over the fence. 'That's for Lebanon,' someone said. 'Lebanon can have that.' One could sense the tension.

I remember, too, being taken on a four-day trip down to the south of Israel and spending a night on the beach at Eilat. We lit a fire, heated supper and sat round on the sand singing Jewish songs of loss, hope and friendship. '*Shalom chaverim, shalom chaverim, lehidrahot, lehidrahot, shalom, shalom,*' we sang – 'Peace, my friend, we'll meet again.' Men's and women's voices mingled gently in the darkness by the fire, with the lights of Aqaba in Jordan twinkling across the Red Sea, in which we'd swum that day. Then, as now, I could feel the intense contrasts in this complicated country.

Now, more than thirty years later, I walked along the paved paths of this other kibbutz, lined with palm trees and giant succulents, past beds overflowing with roses and huge clumps of sweet-smelling herbaceous plants. It was blessedly quiet after the city, and the air seemed cooler and softer.

We went up some steps at the side of a low, cream-painted building and I saw coming down to meet us a sturdily built woman wearing a white T-shirt and baggy cotton trousers, with greying hair tied back in a ponytail and a face that was utterly alive. Erella didn't say anything. She just looked deeply at me with her extraordinary, searching eyes, put her arms round me and hugged me. Then she led me in, through a front door to which was pinned a quote by Gandhi – 'An eye for an eye leaves the whole world blind' – and asked if I would like to go and lie down.

I could feel a migraine coming on and there was nothing I

wanted to do more, but something in me held back. I had just met Erella. Little did I know how accustomed she was to seeing people walk through her door because of the death of someone close. So, unable to admit to myself how exhausted I was, I sat on the sofa, accepted a glass of water and tried to hold a conversation, while Danny took Anthony off to send some e-mails from his computer.

Erella told me that on the evening of Tom's shooting she, Danny and Michal had been coming out of the cinema in Be'ersheva when Michal received a call from a friend in Tel Aviv, concerned about a mutual friend who had been with a young English student who had been shot in Gaza. He was in a critical condition in the Soroka Hospital. It was eleven o'clock at night. Danny, Erella and Michal went straight there. Tom was in surgery and there were seven of his friends waiting in the hospital corridor, all in a terrible state.

'What made you go?' I said.

'I knew immediately I arrived that there was nothing I could do for Tom. He was in the best hands,' said Erella. 'But those other poor young people. Already they had seen that American girl killed by a bulldozer. They were in shock, far from home. I work with bereavement, and I gave them my phone number. I wanted to offer them some kind of help and support.'

Next morning as she was exercising on her walking machine she heard on Radio Kol Israel that an armed man in fatigues had been shot by the army in Rafah after he had aimed a pistol at a watchtower on the Philadelphi Road.

'I knew it was a lie,' said Erella passionately, 'a barefaced lie. My goodness, was I *angry*. But, then, we have come to expect this kind of random violence and dishonesty where the IDF are concerned. This is not a new story, believe me.'

Erella is one of those people who looks below the surface, who sees the complexities, the shades of grey. I found myself talking to her about who Tom was, about our feelings of isolation and astonishment at our treatment by the British government and the

IDF, our shock at what we had seen in Rafah, the hostility we often felt around us. It was such a relief to talk to someone for whom these issues were already familiar.

'*Oreach lerega roeh kol pega*,' said Erella at one point. 'It's a Hebrew saying and it means "A guest in a hurry sees all the worry". When you are in a place for a short time, you have to rely on your intuition. It makes you acutely aware of what's going on, what the key issues are. When you have experienced such a terrible tragedy as yours, your emotions are laid bare, and the pain of what you see is all the greater.'

Erella, in common with many Arabs and Israelis, often talks in sayings. It's a form of communication quite alien to us in the West. It gets directly to the heart of things. Whereas we are brought up to feel that analytical thinking – 'left-brain thinking' – is the best and really the only way to arrive at a judgement, the Middle Eastern way places more value on an intuitive awareness, an intense focus that goes straight to the core of a problem or a situation. It brings everything you know to bear without the intellectual filtering that often gets in the way of true understanding.

Another of Erella's favourite sayings is: 'Haste is of the devil'. It's an Arab saying, and to us Westerners, always rushing, always anxious about the fulfilment of our next goal or desire, it seems to express a general lack of efficiency. But as I came to learn from my time in the Middle East, what it really means is: 'Stop, savour the moment, feel what your senses are telling you'. It has nothing to do with efficiency or the lack of it. It is part of a deep respect for life.

As soon as I met her I felt this quality in Erella, an intense engagement with the moment, a capacity to enjoy what's around. Erella is a truly joyful person, and even in my distraught and desperate state my spirit responded and I began to relax. Later in the day it didn't feel right to be leaving. So Anthony went back to Be'ersheva and, too exhausted now to think about my inhibitions, I climbed into one side of Erella's big double bed and she climbed into the other. To her it was obviously entirely natural, and I later discovered that when any of her three grown-up daughters or her son came home, they shared her bed too; it was simply the Israeli way, the way of the Middle East. I lay awake for a while, listening to her deep steady breathing, trying to accustom myself to this unexpected situation. I hadn't yet got used to the total informality and spontaneity of life in Erella's family. But eventually, surprisingly, I slept.

Next day I felt worse. Talking to Erella had opened the door of my emotions one small crack, and the pain was terrible. It manifested itself as an appalling migraine. I could hardly see, and I sat on Erella's beautiful first-floor verandah where the breeze was soothing. Yet even in the midst of the pain I had a feeling of sanctuary, of being, for the first time since I had arrived in Israel, somewhere emotionally safe. There was nothing I needed to explain; Erella simply understood.

The apartment in Be'ersheva remained our base, but we visited the kibbutz after that on a number of occasions, sometimes singly, sometimes all together. Often Michelle was there, and she and Anthony would work side by side, Anthony on his computer and Michelle on Danny's, e-mailing questions, sending photographs, trawling the internet for information. Fred would just hang out, reading in the shade or kicking a ball, enjoying the freedom and the friendly atmosphere. Erella and Danny both loved Fred and did everything they could to amuse him and make him feel at home. When Sophie and Billy visited, Danny and Erella's warmth allowed them to thaw and gave them the space just to be.

Often I would wander alone through the lovely gardens, drinking in the warm smell of the pine trees, losing myself among the paths that wound between lilacs and palms and oleanders, and abundant bougainvillea. Sometimes I would leave the path, lured by some seductive scent, or look upwards, my attention drawn by a minute movement – the lazy stretch of a cat's paw from a branch, the silver, indigo and black flash of a woodpecker. Everything here was fragrance and colour, order and contentment

– and yet, and yet, not far away was the horror of Gaza, the wounded, orphaned children whom Tom had photographed. And at intervals, above the branches of the pine trees, I would see a sinister black gunship moving purposefully across the Negev sky.

Erella and I would talk for hours on the verandah, shaded by an overhanging jacaranda tree, or in the light, creamy upstairs sitting room where the overhead fan whirred gently, lazily moving the heavy air around. I still retreat to that verandah in my imagination. All around the edge were pots of pink, purple and peach-coloured busy Lizzies and geraniums, and a clematis wound its way up a disused drain pipe in which a small bird had nested. Erella would sit attentively, talking, listening, smoking one of her roll-ups, getting up from time to time to answer the phone. People were always phoning. This home was a refuge for anyone in need, of any religion or no religion, any nationality.

At the back of the flat was a large square window covered with a mesh panel to keep out the mosquitoes. Sometimes I would slide the panel back, scattering light on the marbled floor, and gaze out to where the yellow and green of the Negev stretched away into the distance. Again it seemed incredible that not far from this peaceful landscape, a few miles only, war was being waged. One evening we drove out into this extraordinary countryside which had been coaxed from the desert. The flat cornfields and wide skies reminded me of East Anglia – except that here and there one would see an 'illegal' Bedouin settlement, a small cluster of tents with a few tethered camels. Danny explained to me that the government had rounded up the Bedouin in the south of the country into seven Arab 'villages', of which Rahat, on a potholed road between the kibbutz and Be'ersheva, was the largest.

'It goes against their culture,' said Erella. 'They like to be free, not right on top of their neighbours.' So these were the ones for whom the call of the desert was too strong to resist. This land was what they rightly owned, what they knew, and there was great dignity in their way of life. But at any moment these tented settlements could be broken up and their inhabitants forced back into a village.

Ever since meeting Erella's daughter Michal on that terrible first day in Israel, I had been haunted by what she had said to me as we stood beside Tom's bed: 'I am so sorry for my country'.

'All I can say,' said Erella, when we discussed it, 'is that more and more many of us here in Israel are tortured with guilt when we hear of the terrible things that are being done in our name, although there are many, many, many Israelis who have no idea what is going on, in Gaza mainly, but also in the West Bank. If you don't take the trouble to know then . . . you will never know the truth and, Jozaleen, let me tell you, *it is right there in our face.*' She emphasised these last words. 'We have *Ha'aretz* where there is open reporting but it's not widely read . . . what else . . .? For myself, I have moved beyond guilt. Why? Because I no longer feel that my country, my nation, my religion, is part of my identity.'

In 1985, she told me, she initiated a project to encourage Jewish-Israeli children and Israeli-Palestinian children to work in pairs, teaching one another about each other's language. It provided a rare chance, a bridge, for two cultures to reach out to one another. As part of her preparation she attended an adult workshop – eight Israeli-Jews and eight Israeli-Palestinians – during which they were each asked to choose four ways of defining their identity. They were given various definitions and asked to put them in order of priority. People thought hard and answered very seriously. The Israeli-Jews always began their definitions with the word 'Jewish'. The closer it came to Erella's turn the more anxious she became, because she knew that the way she saw her identity was light years away from this kind of thinking.

'When the facilitator finally reached me, I didn't want to answer. I said, "I suggest you forget me because what I say is only going to cause trouble." But the facilitator insisted. So finally I said, "Identity is something very serious, very basic. For me it has nothing to do with these labels. I believe my identity is made up both of my own 'self' and the 'self' of others, and both of them are equally important. I believe that I am a channel through which something much greater than me, something infinite, can pass – a cosmic wisdom if you like. I am part of this cosmic wisdom, and this cosmic wisdom is also within me."

'There was a moment's loaded silence, then the storm broke. The seven Jews started to shout at me hysterically: "What? Aren't you a Jew? Aren't you an Israeli? Aren't you a Zionist?" It had got to them deep down. It wasn't a joke. I looked at the eight Palestinians and they were clearly bewildered by all this shouting, they couldn't understand what I had said wrong.

'So I took a deep breath and I said, "Listen, as far as I know I am a Jew, an Israeli, a Zionist and not a Zionist, a woman, a mother, a partner, a kibbutznik, and many other things. These labels are just not part of my identity. They are only the tools we use to manifest our identity. If you confuse labels and identities you are making a tragic mistake. If we could only realise this, there would be no war. We are all one, all part of a greater wisdom, but the tools we use are different. If we accept this, there is no reason to kill one another." After that there was complete silence.'

As I listened to Erella I was thinking that Tom, too, with his inclusive way of being, had known he was part of that oneness, that greater whole.

Erella, I learned, had known great sadness in her life. Her intelligent, good-looking younger brother whom she adored had been paralysed by motor neurone disease and had died at twenty-four. Erella had cared for him during his illness, and his death had affected her profoundly. Danny had been her brother's best friend. Her mother, to whom she had been very close, had developed Alzheimer's, and Erella had cared for her too for many, many years.

A close friend of whom she often spoke had also known such sadness. Like me, Daniella had lost a son. His name was Tom and he was twenty-one. Erella told me that at the time of his death he and Ayelet, one of Erella's and Danny's daughters, had been boyfriend and girlfriend, and that his death had been a tragedy for Ayelet. On 4 February 1997, as darkness fell, he and seventy-two other young conscripts had boarded two helicopters to fly to an Israeli army base in southern Lebanon. Very close to the Lebanese border the two helicopters had collided, killing everyone on board. It was the worst military air disaster in Israeli history.

Daniella lived in a community called Neve Shalom, in Arabic Wahat al-Salam – 'Oasis of Peace' – about an hour's drive away, and one evening Erella took me to meet her. This community was founded by a Dominican priest in 1972, the year I first came to Israel, and is the only place in Israel where Jewish and Arab families have actually chosen to live together. As we drove away from the Negev, into the hillier countryside around Jerusalem, I was filled with anticipation and anxiety. I wasn't sure how I would feel meeting someone whose experience was so near to my own. I had so many questions to ask. But would we be able to talk, or would it be too painful for both of us?

As soon as we met, I realised there was no need for words. Everything important was said with our eyes in those first few moments. We sat on the balcony of Daniella's airy modern home looking out over the ordered lines of green vineyards. On a hill in the distance stood a red-tiled monastery surrounded by dark cypress trees, and the old road to Jerusalem cut through the valley below. Daniella told me that this valley had been the scene of a ferocious battle between Israel and Jordan during the 1967 war, in which Ariel Sharon had been badly wounded.

The huge orange sun sank towards the hill. We talked quietly, often drifting into a silence that felt perfectly natural. The shadows lengthened, the light began to fade. The loveliness and serenity of the scene reminded me of Tuscany. But as always the beauty tore into me; I could hardly bear it. It was a searing reminder of what Tom could never see. Daniella told me that when her son was killed she, too, had turned away from beauty – from nature, art, music. We were both singers, and music had been as important to her as it had been to me. But only now, six years after her son's death, had she felt able to rejoin the choir with which she sang.

I wondered despairingly if I would ever be able to sing again. Or stand beside the sea, or watch the sun set. Or listen to a beautiful piece of music. These were the things that had always inspired me. But inspiration involved feeling, and that was a terrifying prospect. Yet talking with Daniella I began to sense, however dimly, that Tom's tragedy, Tom's sacrifice, could become a source of inspiration. First, though, I would have to face the feelings, face the anger. For the first time since it had happened I was able to imagine that there might be a future, however far away it seemed.

It was dark when we rose to go. On a chest in a corner a lighted candle stood beside a collection of photographs and small mementos – pictures of Daniella's son. He even looked a little like Tom. 'I always keep the candle alight,' she said. 'It helps me to remember.'

TEN

Ever since our first visit to Rafah I had been haunted by the memory of Salem Baroum, the silent little boy whom Tom had rescued. I knew there would be many children like him in Rafah, marked for ever by the horror of what they had seen. In some ways this was familiar territory, for I was used to working with a wide range of traumatised children in the learning support unit. Some were refugees who'd fled their country in dangerous circumstances, many had suffered the death of a parent or sibling. Bedwetting, nightmares and withdrawn behaviour were common symptoms.

So I wanted to go back and find out how Salem was, and to see other Palestinians like Amjad and Sahir and Mohammed who had been caught up in our tragedy. Our last visit to Rafah had been so packed and public that there had been no real chance to have a genuine exchange. Anthony wanted to meet Dr Samir, with whose family Tom had stayed, and the family whose two sons had been shot by the IDF. We needed to have this human contact, to share their feelings, and experience what it was like for ordinary Palestinians to survive and live their lives in what seemed a grossly inhuman situation. We had been deeply moved to hear of a demonstration in which local people, many children included, had come to the spot where Tom had been shot to lay flowers. It showed the strength of Palestinians' feeling for these people who had travelled from all over the world to stand with them and show their solidarity and support.

Entering Gaza wasn't easy, however. We knew that each time we went we were putting the people who took us, as well as ourselves, at risk. I was astounded when TFH had told us that he was one of only two defence attachés, out of the fifty or so from different countries with embassies in Israel, who ever ventured into Rafah to report back to their governments on the situation. 'The Israelis often say to me, "Why do you want to go down there? We can tell you everything you want to know",' he'd said. So we hesitated, not entirely sure how much we could ask of the Embassy. But finally we called him, and a day was fixed.

'Don't bank on it, though,' he told us. 'We'll have to keep checking with the Consulate on the situation down there in Gaza over the next few days. My sources tell me that from next week the IDF will be requiring all foreign nationals, including relief workers, to sign waivers acknowledging that they are entering a danger zone and won't hold the army responsible if it shoots them. Wonderful, isn't it? I'll keep you posted.'

Early that morning he phoned to give us the all-clear, and after breakfast he and Andy were waiting in the Embassy Range Rovers at our regular meeting point outside the hotel. Fred could have stayed behind, but he chose to come. From time to time Anthony and I discussed the extent to which we should expose Fred, but we knew that mostly he needed to see for himself. Fred has never run from death. At the age of five he visited my father when he was dying and told me afterwards, 'I know Grandad's going to die. His feet were cold.'

As usual we made good time along the smooth roads to the Erez Crossing. We were becoming familiar with this ghastly landmark – the queue of patiently waiting cars, the bored young soldiers, the cages, the turnstiles, the faceless guard posts, the insulting sign welcoming us to the Erez Crossing in Hebrew and English. TFH was right. It did look like a concentration camp. At the very least, I now saw Gaza as a massive prison. Its only airport, Yasser Arafat International, had been closed, the borders were heavily guarded, and the Palestinians' every movement through them and within them was controlled by the Israeli Defence Force.

Once we were into Gaza the pace changed. Slowly negotiating the churned-up roads, the Range Rover overtook wildly over-loaded carts pulled by meagre looking donkeys. Not long before we entered Gaza City I caught a glimpse of blue, and realised we were driving along beside the Mediterranean. I had barely noticed it on our earlier visits, but now I was struck by the beauty of the coastline. Creamy waves lapped the sandy shore, but there was no one enjoying the beaches, no one swimming. You could still see the remnants of a previous life – the demolished seaside buildings, a children's playground that had been uprooted and broken up. It seemed utterly tragic that this lovely, healthful place, which could have attracted tourists and been a source of income to the Palestinians, was now closed to them, like everything else.

I asked TFH how long the airport had been out of action.

'The Israelis closed it at the end of 2000 and the IDF tore up the runway about a year later,' he said. 'This was at the beginning of the Second Intifada, after Sharon's visit to the Temple Mount in Jerusalem, and the Al Aqsa Mosque, which is one of the Muslims' holiest shrines. That visit was calculated to provoke. Basically the Israelis sealed Gaza off then and they've been systematically destroying the Palestinian economy ever since. The human cost is indescribable, and it's all done under the guise of self-defence. They used the uprising as an excuse for loosening up the army's rules of engagement too.'

'So what precisely *are* the rules of engagement now?' Anthony asked.

'That's the million-dollar question,' said TFH. 'Since the beginning of the Second Intifada the open-fire regulations in the Occupied Territories have been classed as "confidential information". They're given to soldiers verbally, not written down, as they used to be, and I gather certain battalion com-manders pitch in and add their own. A lot of the soldiers can't actually remember what they've been told. It's a recipe for confusion and it makes them trigger-happy. Hundreds of civilians are being shot who have nothing whatever to do with the fighting. I think there's no doubt that there's a shoot-to-kill policy for anyone entering the army's prohibited areas, regardless of the reason. The IDF always denies it, of course.'

As we entered Gaza City I noticed that the Range Rovers moved closer together. Again I was struck by the seething mass of humanity crisscrossing in the streets, an air of aimlessness and desperation that was hard to pin down. Sometimes the press of people was so intense that we slowed to a halt and were overtaken by a donkey cart. People stopped to stare as we went past and I was acutely aware of the wide gap between our lives and theirs as we sat cocooned in our armour-plated, air-conditioned vehicles.

Yet I also had the sense that Gaza had somehow managed to hang on to its identity as a living city. TFH told me there was a university there. Behind the scenes there was clearly a vigorous intellectual, legal and political life going on. I later discovered that Tom had not only photographed the Hamas funerals in Gaza City two days before he was shot, but had also visited the Palestinian Centre for Human Rights and spoken to the distinguished human rights lawyer Raji Sourani.

After picking up our interpreter, we drove on to the Abu Houli Crossing at the entrance to the Khan Younis refugee camp just outside Rafah, where we joined a long line of traffic waiting to go through. As we sat in the Range Rover, with little boys tapping at the windows, trying to hitch a lift or sell us nuts and sweets, I wondered what exactly the purpose of this particular checkpoint was. 'Well, with the refugee camp here this is a flashpoint and there are settlements around – see?' said TFH, pointing to clusters of buildings on the hills. 'It's a way of keeping control of the Palestinian population. And it stops the people in Rafah getting out.'

'So Rafah is really a prison within a prison,' I said.

'That's about it,' said TFH laconically.

The queue inched forward. When we were in sight of the rickety, leaning traffic light by the checkpoint tower we could just see, through the haze of sunlight and dust, that it wasn't working.

There was no other traffic control and the way through the checkpoint was on a single raised track, so it was hard to know what to do. We simply proceeded at snail's pace, following Andy who was following the car in front.

I heard nothing strange, but suddenly TFH, who had been chatting, broke off and picked up the phone. We stopped.

'Did you hear what I heard?' he said to the car in front.

The second time I did hear it – the distinct sound of a gunshot. 'I'm going to phone Joseph Levy,' I heard TFH say. He called a number: 'Blast! Engaged . . .' After a few moments' wait he tried again, then: 'Joseph, what the hell's going on? I've got civilians in the car . . .'

There was a pause while some kind of justification was clearly being offered by TFH's IDF contact. Then: 'How the hell does anyone know when to stop? The traffic lights aren't working. They're never working. Get a grip, Joseph. This is quite unacceptable. You knew we were coming through. I'll be coming back at the end of the day and I expect to go through absolutely smoothly. OK?' And TFH, clearly furious, ended the call.

By this time Andy had decided to get out of the car. 'For goodness' sake go very very slowly,' I heard TFH say. 'No sudden movements.'

Andy, in a white shirt with the sleeves rolled up, got gingerly out of the Range Rover and stood beside it with his hands up. Then he gestured towards the tower, as if to say, 'So what do you want us to do?'

That seemed to do the trick. A few seconds later a languid white hand appeared from the tower and dismissively waved us through.

Suddenly I felt livid. I wanted to shake the arrogant twenty-one-year-old I imagined was attached to that hand. 'Just get down from there and speak to us,' I wanted to say. 'All you need to do is explain what you want of us. Where's the dialogue? We followed the protocol. You could see our white number plates perfectly well, you knew who we were.'

Soon we were beneath the watchtowers on the outskirts of Rafah, then negotiating a route round the ugly mounds of rubble, topped with huge tangles of wire and bent girders, on our way to the Egyptian border. We had phoned Mohammed and he, Amjad and Sahir were waiting for us on the corner of Kir Street, three slight, dark-haired figures looking small and vulnerable in the midst of the now familiar devastation. I thought of the picture I had seen of Amjad, his face contorted with anguish, staggering under the weight of Tom's body as he and Sahir struggled to move him further down the street after the shooting. It was a tragic, shocking picture that made me think of Michelangelo's *Pietà* with its sense of human vulnerability, of our dependency on one another. Yet I knew that carrying the dead and wounded had become part of Amjad's everyday life.

We greeted one another affectionately, and as everyone stood talking for a moment Amjad and I began wandering down Kir Street, drawn irresistibly towards the place where Tom had been shot. I asked Amjad what he had been doing since last we met, and he began to tell me about his work with the Palestinian Progressive Youth Movement, a group that had developed links with the ISM and often put themselves at risk by acting with it, as they had on the day of the demonstration.

Amjad explained to me that the PPYM supported human rights, and tried to bring education and other opportunities to young people in Gaza. This meant that they were seen as a threat by the Islamic movement. Like the ISM they were non-violent, and when they demonstrated they tried to be practical, for example by giving blood to help the victims of the Iraq war.

By this time we had reached the mound, and I was suddenly aware that Andy was beside me. 'I really wouldn't go any further,' he said, putting his hand under my elbow and guiding me back towards the cars. He seemed distinctly jumpy.

Fred and I had bought a ball and some paper and coloured crayons in the mall in Be'ersheva to give to little Salem Baroum, so it was decided that we would split up. TFH would go with

Anthony and the others to visit the Abu Jabr house where the two boys were shot, while Andy and the interpreter would come with Fred and me to find Salem's family.

By this time the usual curious crowd of children and other onlookers had gathered and it had started to rain. The interpreter made enquiries and then led us, single file, through a maze of narrow, muddy alleyways until we reached a very small house only partly covered by a roof. A woman I recognised as Salem's mother came to the door with a man and several young children clustering behind her. She beckoned us warmly into a tiny, bare room and immediately offered us a cup of tea, which we drank sitting on chairs with the rain dripping in. I noticed that she was pregnant, and tried to imagine how she would cope looking after a newborn baby in such desperate circumstances. Salem's father stood silently by, watching us very seriously, bewildered, I felt, by our visit.

Onlookers, friends and neighbours had crowded in with us, and I felt sorry that we had descended on this family in such numbers. I had wanted this to be a quiet visit. Meantime, his father lifted Salem on to my knee. I spoke to the little boy gently as I put my arms round him, and felt his small body rigid against mine. Fred leaned over and with his head close to Salem's, very sweetly and lovingly offered him the ball and the crayons, looking into his face all the while. Salem took them but he didn't smile or show any interest. His expression was blank and his eyes were dull. Six weeks after the shooting, his mother said he could still not be persuaded to speak.

She and I talked a little more through the interpreter, but after twenty minutes or so Andy rose to go. Salem's mother and I took one another's hands and stood in silence for a long moment, simply looking at each other. Then I followed Andy out of the door and we all made our way back to Kir Street through the mud and debris of the alleys.

The sky was dark, the afternoon was drawing in and it was time to go. I wished we had had more time with Mohammed and

Amjad and Sahir, but I knew, as the car drew away and they receded into the distance, standing forlornly waving on the corner of Kir Street, that they were part of our lives now. I was certain we would see them again.

What Anthony had seen that afternoon had shocked him – families so fearful of IDF marksmen that they had abandoned most rooms in their houses. 'They daren't live at the front,' he said, 'and they daren't live on the top floor either because the army targets the top floors, so they live in one room on the ground floor at the back.' One of the sons from the Abu Jabr house was still in intensive care in Gaza City and the family was distraught.

By this time we had reached the approach to the Abu Houli Crossing and we joined a long line of stationary cars snaking back from the checkpoint. We sat waiting, waiting, but after about twenty minutes there was still no movement. Cars began turning round and going back in the direction they had come.

'What's the problem, do you think?' said Anthony.

'Absolutely no idea,' said TFH briskly. 'Could be waiting for a settler coming down the road from one of the settlements. Or the chaps in the checkpoint could be bored and just feel like being obstructive.'

A ratty looking jeep full of soldiers drove up beside the queue and parked at right angles to it. They looked as if they might know something, and my instinct was to lower the window and ask reasonably what was going on. But this was not England. The quietness was deceptive, and there was certainly no question of our getting out of the car.

'Right, I'm going to phone Joseph,' said TFH finally picking up the phone. 'What's the trouble *now*, Joseph?' I heard him say. 'We're sitting here at Abu Houli . . . right, well can you get us through?'

There was more conversation, then a brief word with Andy, TFH started the engine again, and we nosed out and drove very slowly up the inside of the queue. As always I felt uncomfortable as we overtook battered Palestinian cars in these large four-wheel-drive vehicles flying the British flag, which TFH had been careful to put up before we reached Abu Houli. No IDF soldier could be in any doubt that this was a British vehicle. I think it was in all our minds that we might be shot at again. We drove up and over an alarmingly steep bank lurching diagonally down the other side, then back on to the track, and within minutes we were through the checkpoint. I looked back at the stationary line of vehicles behind us, with their patient drivers and the little boys running along the track in the humid heat and squeezing in and out of the cars, and I felt a mixture of emotions – mortification at our privileged treatment, anger and sadness on their behalf.

We reached the Erez Crossing and as we drove between the bollards and across the sterile concrete it was as if we were somehow leaving life behind. In Gaza there was desperation but there was warmth – a determination to enjoy each minute that was partly born out of that desperation. Now we were back in a colder, more hard-edged world.

TFH had to be back in Tel Aviv, so at the crossing exit we joined Andy in the other vehicle. I was just doing up my seat belt, half-looking out of the window at the empty road in front of us as we pulled slowly away when suddenly, out of nowhere, shot a smart-looking Mazda heading directly and purposefully for us at great speed. Andy's reaction was quick. He swerved up on to the pavement, there was a screech of tyres, a jarring impact and we were all thrown violently sideways as the oncoming car hit our wing with a thud.

Andy was the first to recover. He got out and calmly walked back to the other car, which had come to a halt a few yards away. The rest of us sat there, dazed. Finally Anthony walked back to join Andy, and after some conversation I saw him get out Tom's camera and photograph the scene from various angles – for insurance purposes, I presumed. Fred hopped out too and reported that, surprisingly for such a heavy vehicle, the Range Rover's wing was 'a real mess'. The impact must have been considerable.

The Range Rover, one of a convoy of two diplomatic vehicles, and essential if we, and also James Miller's family, were to travel into Gaza, was now out of action. We travelled by taxi back to Be'ersheva, considerably shaken. I sensed that beneath his calm exterior Andy was as shocked as the rest of us. He had been able to get very little out of the Israeli driver, who appeared curiously unfazed. The whole incident seemed eerie, inexplicable. Or was it? The shots at Abu Houli, this rogue vehicle – it all seemed too much of a coincidence. Was this a way of preventing us from gathering evidence?

It was early one morning towards the end of May and we were getting ready to leave for the hospital, when the phone rang. Anthony answered but I could hear what the familiar voice at the other end was saying. It was Sherard.

'I've some news for you,' he said, after the usual greetings. 'I've got the Israelis' field report into the shooting here on my desk. They presented it to us yesterday. Obviously we'd like to discuss it with you and Jocelyn. Could you make it down here on, say, Thursday if we send a car for you?'

'So what are their conclusions?' Anthony said.

'Nothing very spectacular, I'm afraid,' said Sherard. 'I think there are some major discrepancies in the report – on the location, for instance – but it's probably better if we talk when you've seen the whole thing. We put forward our key demands, i.e. that they pay Tom's medical expenses and the cost of repatriation, your expenses, and some family compensation. They very reluctantly agreed to meet the medical expenses, and they did actually say they were considering a meeting. It's a lot better than we usually manage.'

Round about eleven o'clock on Thursday we took our seats on the Residence verandah with Sherard, Neil Wigan, a clean-cut young member of the Embassy staff, and the Consul, Mike Hancock. Lovely Middle Eastern morning light shone on the garden and the overhead fan whirred gently. I saw Bridget briefly on her way out; coffee was brought. Then TFH appeared with a sheaf of papers, which he laid on the table. I could read the writing on the top page. '*Thomas Hurndall's Injury*' it said in enormous yellow italics on a bright blue background. This presumably was the army's 'field report'. It looked a bit like something designed for children.

'Well,' said Sherard. 'Just to put you in the picture, we were given the report by the IDF on Monday. It was a PowerPoint presentation in Hebrew, which wasn't immensely helpful. Here's the English version they gave us. I'll be interested to see what you think of the whole thing.'

TFH handed us each a copy. We read in silence. It didn't take long. Few of the twenty-odd pages had more than half a dozen lines on them and the type was huge. The first ten pages were taken up with pro-IDF propaganda, justifying, in simplistic terms, Israel's presence and actions in the 'Military Installations Area' near the Philadelphi Road, and slating the ISM for its 'provocative and illegal activities'.

Then came a section headed 'The Incident', set out in bullet points. This outlined a scenario in which 'an individual aged about 20 dressed in camouflage fatigues', another 'bearded man aged about 30' and two children were seen simultaneously to 'exit' from a building. The first man fired three pistol shots into the air and then fired two shots at the IDF outpost, the outpost commander fired a single shot in return, the 'gunman' fell and was pulled back into the building, and there was then 'a large gathering during which the outpost was attacked with rocks'.

This was followed by five 'Possible Scenarios Explaining How Tom Hurndall Was Wounded'. They read thus:

- Mr Hurndall was hit by Palestinian fire or by a Palestinian gunman's stray bullet (the probability of this scenario is very low).
- The soldier at the outpost accidentally mistook the second adult at the scene for the gunman.

- The soldier at the outpost aimed at the gunman but hit the second adult at the scene.
- Mr Hurndall was hit by a bullet ricocheted off the wall opposite him.
- The gunman was Mr Hurndall (the probability of this scenario is very low).

Bewilderingly, in a separate 'Timeline of the Medical Evacuation' the IDF post also identified 'three figures planting what was presumed to be an explosive device' and the wounded man was brought to 'a nearby IDF outpost' where he received initial medical treatment. None of it added up, and it certainly bore no relation whatever to the facts as we knew them.

The conclusions of the 'report' were as follows:

- It is impossible to establish with certainty the cause of the injuries sustained by Mr Hurndall.
- It is likely that Mr Hurndall was hit by IDF fire.
- The commander of the outpost acted according to the rules of engagement for the area: an armed Palestinian fired at an IDF soldier who felt an immediate danger and therefore he shot a single bullet in response.

The document was accompanied by some meaningless grainy photographs and a 'location map'.

The whole thing was ludicrous, transparent, so unprofessional it was hard to know how to respond. Did they really think we would be content with this level of investigation, this so-called enquiry, backed up by no evidence of any kind? In any case, it made no sense. According to the location map, the notional gunman appeared to have come out of two entirely different buildings. And why would a Palestinian gunman attract attention to himself by firing shots into the air like a cowboy? In the no-go area he would have been shot immediately.

I looked at Anthony, and I could see that he was incandescent with rage. But he spoke quietly, pointing out that not only were the facts unquestionably wrong on the basis of the evidence we already had, but that the aerial map was out of date and that, anyway, the Israelis had got the wrong location. The point marked with a cross was about eighty yards from where Tom was actually shot.

'Yes, we spotted that,' said TFH.

Crucially, Anthony made the point that the claim of a single shot from the tower was an out and out lie. It was well established by a large number of witnesses – not only Palestinians, but international reporters – that there had been at least five shots and possibly as many as eight. And he brought up again the shooting of other civilians, including the boys in the Abu Jabr house.

It was agreed that Sherard would take up with the Israelis the fact that they had got the location wrong, and he promised to be in touch. I think we were both too stunned by the sheer inadequacy of the report and, indeed, the lies contained in it, to say very much after that. In the car on the way back to Be'ersheva we agreed it impossible to take it seriously. It was beyond being an insult.

Next day Sherard phoned. The Israelis had apparently had very little to say in answer to our criticisms.

'I think,' I heard Anthony say finally, in an ominously controlled voice, 'that this is such an obvious cover-up that it should be exposed. I think we should go to the press.'

Sherard, on the other end of the line, was clearly objecting.

'I'm not interested that it wasn't meant for publication,' Anthony said. 'The fact remains that it's a total fabrication. They shouldn't be allowed to get away with it.' Things were clearly becoming more and more heated, and I cringed as I heard Anthony say, 'They're quite simply liars.'

Eventually, after more heated exchanges, he said, 'All right. A few days, then I shall expose it to the press', put down the phone and walked over to the window, breathing audibly.

'Sherard wants to follow the diplomatic line,' he said finally. 'Keep quiet and work behind the scenes. He says it will be more effective. I don't agree. Why should we make it easy for the IDF? They *are* just a pack of liars.'

'Absolutely. So how did you leave it?' I said.

'I said I'd wait four days. But that's it.'

'Is Sherard thinking that they might still agree to a meeting? Is that perhaps why he's being careful?' I said.

'If they can produce something like that so-called "report" I don't really see the point of a meeting,' said Anthony, bitterly.

I'd been acutely aware of the toll our situation was taking on Anthony. He looked strained, but until now he had remained, on the surface anyway, controlled. I could see how affronted he was by the tissue of lies we had just been presented with.

Clearly, if we were going to take Tom home and pursue our case from England, we needed a lawyer in Israel to represent us. Several people recommended a well-known and highly regarded human rights lawyer, Avigdor Feldman, and we made an appointment to see him in his office in Tel Aviv. The office was in a back street, a plain building with a down-to-earth, hard-working look about it. I remember being mildly surprised at the modesty of the set-up. The office of someone of comparable standing in London would, I felt sure, have looked very different. We had been told that all the key human rights cases in Israel, such as that of Mordecai Vanunu, who had revealed to the world Israel's secret nuclear capacity, ended up on Avigdor's desk.

He came across his book-lined office to meet us and introduced his partner, Michael Sfarad, a young man in his thirties with an alert, intelligent manner and a friendly, open face. Avigdor was stocky, with rough red skin and iron-grey hair. He said very little, but what he said was to the point. I had the impression of an extremely busy man who knew how to conserve his energy, who knew precisely what he was talking about.

We discussed our situation, the IDF 'report' and various legal issues including the responsibility of the chain of command. Although it was not a priority at the time, we knew that at some stage we would need to pursue our case for compensation for Tom himself and for us. Expenses of every kind were piling up. I was in close touch with the school where I worked and my salary would be paid for a short while longer, but Anthony's practice in London was being manned by someone else, and neither of us had any idea what the future would hold as far as employment was concerned. When we showed Avigdor and Michael the field report, they simply shook their heads wearily. This was familiar territory. They told us that they were, at that moment, compiling a huge report on the IDF's shoot-to-kill policy. It was clear that they understood the workings of the IDF at a very deep level and were able to explain some of the legal precedents and procedures. As a lawyer Anthony was able to grasp more than I did, but it helped me to understand the picture.

I liked them both immensely. Michael told us that he himself had been in prison as a refusenik – he had refused to serve in the Occupied Territories – and I gathered that he spent a good deal of his time fighting for Palestinian human rights. It was agreed that when the time came they would represent us, though it was not clear at present how or when. We went away tremendously reassured to be in the hands of two people of such calibre.

Meantime, Professor Reichental, the head of the Intensive Care Unit, had been conducting his own private conversations with the IDF. I knew he had been doing his best to negotiate a repatriation arrangement for Tom, and Sherard, who was also in discussions about it with the IDF, seemed happy with this two-pronged approach. Sophie reported that many generous people were donating funds for the 'Bring Tom Home' campaign into a separate bank account, but we were still struggling with all the complexities of British charity law, which was difficult from a distance. Our plan was that as soon as Tom was stable enough to travel we would take him home, come what may, and I had already spoken to my own branch of NatWest in Belsize Park about a loan. The manager there was wonderfully responsive and kind; he bent over backwards to make available the £20,000 necessary to bring Tom home, should we need it.

Various helpful people had spent hours on the phone, exploring the possibility of hiring an air ambulance, but we were now told that it wouldn't in fact be the safest way for Tom to travel. With such a badly injured patient the longer journey on a small plane and the bumpier takeoff and landing could be dangerous, so it would be safer to take a scheduled flight. There would, of course, have to be an Israeli medical team to accompany him, including an anaesthetist, and accommodation would have to be found for them in London. The complications seemed endless.

There was also the immense problem of finding a London hospital willing to take Tom. Professor Reichental gave me the name of a contact at the Royal Hospital for Neurological Diseases in Queen Square, but finally, to my immense relief, our local hospital, the Royal Free in Hampstead, agreed to accept him. The biggest complication was the unpredictability of Tom's changing state. He was subject to frequent infections, and we had to wait for a window in which he was sufficiently stable to travel.

In the second half of May he had been moved from the Intensive Care Unit into a small neurological ward, which was really another kind of intensive care. In the next bed was an Israeli man who had suffered a brain haemorrhage. His wife came frequently to visit him from the kibbutz on which they lived. My heart went out to her, for it was obviously a difficult journey, but with tremendous generosity she always came laden with chicken and rice and piles of fruit which she insisted on sharing with us. It was one of those heartwarming contacts that meant so much.

Every day I sat by Tom, holding his hands. His head was still enormously swollen, though a small section of his skull on the left side had now been removed to ease the pressure. He lay there like a shadow, Tom, and yet not Tom. Sometimes I would sit beside him writing, knowing these were moments in which to think and record and remember. I felt he was drifting further and further away from us. *Tom, wait. We're going to take you home. You're going to be among your friends, and the people who love you. They need to say goodbye to you before you go. Wait Tom, dearest Tom.*

Professor Reichental clearly understood our anxiety to take Tom home. I had come greatly to like and respect this fatherly figure. He was dignified and cultured, close to retirement, and I sensed that he understood and empathised with our position.

One Sunday he invited us to tea at his home. We had spent a good deal of time that day with an unusually unpleasant, bullying journalist. He had interviewed us at length about Tom's shooting, but at three o'clock I had excused myself and had gone off alone to Professor Reichental's, leaving Anthony to finish the interview.

Another couple had been invited. I struggled to connect, but the pleasure for me was in being shown round Professor Reichental's beautiful garden as we talked about the various flowers and shrubs. It was restful and civilised, another world from the one I had just left.

I got back at about 7.30 to find the journalist still waiting for me. For some reason he wanted a picture of Anthony and me walking through the door of the ward. I had kept them waiting. So, tired as I was, I put my overall on as requested and we entered the ward. We had made it quite clear that in no circumstances would we permit photographs to be taken of Tom. As I walked through the door, with this man behind me, I realised that the door was about to swing back and hit his camera, so I held it briefly, then walked on towards Tom.

Suddenly I realised, to my horror, that this man was beside me at the foot of the bed, filming. Devastated, I put my hands out in front of me to shield Tom. A nurse appeared and said very clearly, 'Please stop. You are not allowed to do that', but the man simply went on filming.

When he finally lowered his camera, I said with suppressed

fury, 'I had no idea you were going to follow me in. How could you *possibly* feel it was OK to do that? You know we specifically asked you not to film in here.'

'But you held the door open for me,' he said brazenly.

When he had left I simply broke down. It had been such a sly, cheap trick, and I felt devastated. Here was Tom, more vulnerable than he had ever been in his life and needing my protection, and I had let him down. The press had always been so supportive of us; I was shattered by this betrayal.

A few minutes later, a friend, Anne Perkins, who writes for the *Guardian*, phoned. 'Anne,' I said through my tears, 'something terrible has just happened . . .' She was sensible and consoling. Anthony, too, was extremely angry and we complained to the television company. Later we heard that the journalist in question had had a difficult time justifying his behaviour to his bosses, and the film was never shown. But it was an episode that left its mark on me. After that I was always on my guard.

In the third week of May Professor Reichental told us that he thought Tom was stable enough to travel, and all the complex arrangements were finally made for us to fly back to London on 26 May. At last, at last, we were going to take Tom home. But before I could fully absorb the news, two unexpected things happened. Billy phoned to tell us he was planning to return to Israel. He realised he couldn't go into Gaza, but he was planning to travel to the West Bank under the umbrella of the ISM. He wanted to see and understand for himself what the IDF were doing, and was taking his video camera.

We were both appalled. But I realised, from his tone, that Billy, though only just eighteen, was now very much his own man and there was nothing we could do to stop him. Much as I trusted Billy's common sense, it seemed like a nightmare replay of what had happened with Tom. He arrived on 24 May, looking very calm and determined, and went straight out to the kibbutz. I could tell he had done a lot of thinking while we had been in Israel. Our second son had come out of himself and had begun to look at the world through another window. All I could do was phone the understanding TFH and implore him to keep an eye on him.

And on the day Billy arrived, Sherard phoned to tell us that the IDF had agreed to a meeting. They had arranged it for 26 May, the day we were due to fly home.

ELEVEN

Our meeting with the IDF was scheduled for 2.30 p.m. Peter
Carter, the Deputy Ambassador who was accompanying us to
Jerusalem, explained that we were going to save time by cutting
through the West Bank and that we'd be driving pretty fast. 'We
don't want to hang around more than is strictly necessary. One
tends to attract attention in a vehicle like this,' he said.

There was an uneasy atmosphere in the car and no one spoke
much. Anthony and I were preoccupied with the thought of this
meeting for which we had waited so long, and Peter and Mike
Hancock, another member of the consular staff who was with us
in the car, were clearly on the alert for any sign of trouble. The
lack of road signs in the West Bank didn't help. At one point we
took a wrong turning and seemed to be climbing higher and
higher until we reached a quarry-like dead end. Peter reversed
rapidly and we found our way back on to the right road, but the
feeling of being in unmarked territory was unsettling.

Now that the time for the meeting had come, it seemed almost
an anticlimax. This should have been the day we took Tom home
and in my heart I was already on my way to London. Somehow
all the waiting had exhausted my anger. Anthony had had a
sleepless night. When we'd first received news of it from Sherard,
Anthony had felt that by this stage it was barely worth having this
meeting with the IDF. The ludicrous field report had already
shown them in their true colours, and it seemed to him pointless
to waste time and effort changing the delicate arrangements for
taking Tom home simply in order to meet them face to face.

Yet however insulting the IDF's behaviour, whatever their motive in scheduling this meeting for a time when they must have known that we were virtually on our way home, we couldn't quite bring ourselves to turn our backs. After all, apart from anything else there were still practical matters to be settled and Sherard had urged us to accept. So we were doing our best to psych ourselves up, build up the adrenaline again.

Nearer to Jerusalem we skirted the ancient city of Hebron. I remembered so well visiting it as a student with another volunteer from the kibbutz. We had taken a bus through the Jordanian countryside to visit the famous glass factory where, years before, my father had stood to watch the exquisite blue, green and brown Hebron glass being blown. It had felt good then to be following in his footsteps, seeing what he had seen – a little connection with home.

Returning to Jerusalem on the bus in the evening, to our open-air lodgings on the roof of the Armenian Monastery near the Via Dolorosa, I'd had the strange sensation that strands of my hair kept catching on something. I felt a regular, sharp little sting in my scalp and when I eventually turned round in annoyance I was just in time to catch the man behind me preparing to pluck out another strand. I was too nonplussed to say anything. I've wondered since why he was doing it. Was my fair hair unusual, or shouldn't I have had my head uncovered? Or perhaps he disapproved of my sawn-off jeans and skimpy polka-dot top. I cringe to remember how thoughtlessly we dressed in a country where women's culture was so different – despite all my father's warnings about cultural sensitivity.

Looking down at the old city, nestling in the valley, I was shocked to see what had happened since my last visit. Ugly, threatening tower blocks with darkened glass windows now covered the surrounding hills. I asked Mike what they were; he told me they were West Bank settlements. I was appalled. I had thought of settlements as groups of low-rise domestic buildings. I had never conceived of anything that looked like this. What on earth must it feel like to be the Palestinians living in the valley, with these Big Brother buildings glaring down on them? It was such a blatant and aggressive use of architecture to intimidate and oppress. I thought what a powerful positive effect beautiful architecture can have, and how it can also be used for entirely negative ends. These monstrous, swaggering buildings had clearly been designed to strike fear into a powerless minority. Their message was obvious: 'We don't want you here. We will watch your every move, control your comings and goings, and make life as difficult for you as possible.' As so often during the past few weeks, the word 'apartheid' came into my mind.

It was deeply painful to observe the erosion of this beautiful countryside. I thought how saddened my father would have been to see it and to witness such inhuman treatment handed out to a people he had come to admire and understand and who didn't deserve it. I was overcome by melancholy at the thought of this unending and apparently unresolvable conflict. It was impossible for these two peoples to shift the dark sands of history alone, yet all the words that were spoken now by the rest of the world, by the politicians and diplomats, had come to sound like empty clichés. I had come fresh and uninformed to the situation. I had no prior knowledge, no backlog of assumptions, only my pain at the loss of Tom, and I felt a sudden, urgent responsibility to use that in any way I could. At the same time I had a sick feeling in the pit of my stomach. We had waited so long for this chance to meet the IDF face to face. Would I be able to say what was really in my heart? Would we be able to do Tom justice?

As soon as we'd agreed to the meeting, Anthony and I discussed how we would approach it. To use the meeting to best effect we felt we needed to think very clearly about what we wanted to say and how to say it, and what precisely our demands were. We also wondered who we would be meeting and what level of official-dom there would be.

We'd decided that we both had different roles to play accord-ing to our individual personalities, and that it was important that we both have the space to say what we had to say. Anthony, who, when it comes to legal matters is measured and rational, would deal with the practical and investigative side of things. He would tell the IDF very clearly that we wanted to know the truth and were seeking their full cooperation in gathering and sharing evidence. He would ask for confirmation that they would cover all Tom's medical expenses, the cost of bringing him home, and our own expenses, too – in other words, take responsibility for what had happened.

My contribution would be different. I was determined that they should know something of Tom as a person, and what this tragedy had meant to our family. I wanted to look them in the eye and show them that we were human beings, with lives that had been deeply affected by what they had done. I wanted them to understand that they couldn't simply ignore us, look through us, pretend we didn't exist.

We agreed that we wouldn't be accusatory or judgemental. What we wanted was to put them in touch with the pain they had caused us and demand that they make such practical reparation as they could.

The evening before the meeting we'd gone out to the kibbutz to talk to Erella. We felt we needed someone with her knowledge and human understanding to act as a sounding board, perhaps to give us insights into the way the IDF might be thinking. We sat in the cool of the verandah and talked over the way in which the IDF had made us feel transparent, non-existent. We discussed the extraordinary depth of their denial – of us, of what had actually happened, of everything – and how we might bring this out into the open, reflect it back to them. It was something that needed to be seen. Erella's realism gave us confidence. She urged us to focus on Tom's and our absolute right to be considered as human beings.

We came away feeling we'd cleared our minds. Anthony had worked out what he wanted to say, and I felt Erella had given me strength to confront the IDF with the human aspects of the situation. But I knew that I would probably be speaking a language they were not used to hearing, and I couldn't begin to imagine what their response would be.

As we drove through the outskirts of Jerusalem I recalled something TFH had said to me when we were talking about the IDF. 'The bottom line, always remember, is that Tom is seen as a gentile, a "*goi'im*" and therefore in the eyes of God worth less than a member of the Chosen Race,' he'd said. 'It's an appalling but true fact that's rarely talked about in public. To a huge extent it explains the savage nature of their operations against the Palestinians.' A tragic mirror image, I thought, of the way society had so often treated the Jews.

Before the meeting Peter and Mike took us to lunch at an elegant restaurant overlooking Jerusalem where they entertained us in true diplomatic style. We sat looking out over the distant roofscape of the Old City, talking idly. As so often, It felt terribly unreal, as if the parts of our world didn't really join up. Suddenly Peter looked at his watch, gave a sharp exclamation and took out his phone. 'Oh, hello, Danny,' he said. 'Yes, that's right. We're just on our way. We'll be with you in twenty minutes or so.'

The Ministry of Foreign Affairs was a large modern building in the centre of Jerusalem. We left the main road and drove through the usual barriers down a sweep of concrete into a grey-lit underground car park. A clean-cut man of middle height waiting at the entrance introduced himself as Danny Carmon, Head of the Ministry's Co-ordination Bureau. His manner was smoothly charming; as he and Peter greeted one another they might almost have been exchanging golf-course pleasantries. At one level I was intensely irritated, yet I also saw that this smooth, diplomatic approach was a way of oiling the wheels, of getting us through an awkward moment. But Anthony and I both stayed silent. We couldn't have felt more grave, and we showed it.

Danny Carmon led us along corridors and through a long open-plan office. A khaki-clad figure stood framed in a doorway at the end. The very sight of the military uniform was jarring, shocking, a symbol of everything we could no longer respect. The young soldier stood aside for us to enter, and my legs kept on walking though my head felt strangely separate. I picked up bits of a conversation between Peter and Mike behind me, and the sound of their familiar voices was reassuring.

There was a row of eight or nine people seated down one side of a long table. They rose as we came in and Danny Carmon, who appeared to be chairing the meeting, introduced them. It was hard to take in names but I understood that the soldier at the door, Major Biton, was in charge of the enquiry into Tom's shooting and presumably there to defend the infamous 'field report'. He looked about Tom's age. How on earth, I wondered, could someone so young have been given such a responsible job, with all its diplomatic and political implications? Also present were a legal adviser and a desk officer from the Ministry of Foreign Affairs, and an older army captain who was Deputy Head of the IDF Liaison and Foreign Relations Department.

Danny Carmon took his place in the middle of the table and we all sat down, with Anthony directly opposite him, me on Anthony's left and Peter and Mike on his right. Danny Carmon started by offering us a formal expression of sympathy. Anthony thanked him, and said that we appreciated this meeting.

'I'm afraid, however, that it is too little contact too late,' he said. 'We have had to cancel travel arrangements in order to be here, and we shall be leaving Israel within the next few days.'

'Why *has* it taken you so long to meet us?' I said, unable to contain myself as I looked at the row of impassive faces.

Carmon hesitated for a moment, then said rather quietly, 'Perhaps we need to reconsider our policy on this . . .'

Oh yes? What are the real chances of *that*? I thought.

Anthony then said very clearly, 'We haven't come here to criticise or point the finger, but we do want to get at the truth. I'm sure it's what we all want. Our aim is to exchange as much information as possible in order to build up a picture of what really happened on the day our son was shot. Israel used to be a

country we all admired and respected. But that respect has been
eroded by the way the IDF are conducting themselves now, and
there is huge disappointment. We are saddened that our perception of Israel has had to change.'

This produced an uncomfortable silence. Everyone on the
other side of the table looked away, or fiddled with their papers. I
had the impression that they weren't used to being held to
account in this way. I knew that no family of a Palestinian victim
would ever have been given the chance to confront them, and it
clearly didn't feel good to have an English family, with all their
advantages, doing so now.

Anthony explained that we were now planning to fly home
with Tom in three days' time, on 29 May. He asked that Israel
agree to cover Tom's medical expenses, the cost of repatriating
him to the UK, and our own out-of-pocket expenses since the
shooting, including loss of earnings. To cover the immediate cost
of the flight, he told them, we planned to take out a loan.

Danny Carmon cleared his throat. 'I'm pleased to tell you that
my government has already agreed to cover, *ex gratia*, all your
son's medical expenses in Israel, and is positively contemplating a
contribution to the cost of repatriation, although I have no final
word on that yet. If we agree to contribute to repatriation, then
we would naturally wish to be involved in the arrangements.'

'What would that mean, exactly?' Anthony asked.

'Well, for example, we would prefer you to fly by our own
airline, El Al,' said Carmon, 'though I understand it may be
difficult to change your arrangements at this late stage.'

'So if we were to fly, say, by BA?' said Anthony

'Then I am not sure we would be able to meet the additional
cost,' said Carmon. 'Though naturally,' he added quickly, 'we
would still consider a contribution as a goodwill gesture.'

A frozen fury was building inside me at the use of the word
'goodwill'. *Goodwill?* We hadn't yet even received an apology.

'However,' Carmon continued, 'we are most unlikely to be
able to meet out-of-pocket expenses. Compensation of any kind

is a legal issue which of course implies liability, and I hold out very little hope that my government will agree to that.'

Peter Carter now spoke for the first time. 'I would like to remind you, at this point,' he said, 'that Mr and Mrs Hurndall and their family are also seeking an apology for this tragic incident, and a full and open enquiry into the circumstances.'

'As you know, the Israeli Defence Force field report into the incident is now complete,' said Carmon, 'and the results have been passed to the Judge Advocate General's office. I believe you already know from the British Ambassador that the Judge Advocate General would like to see any further evidence you wish to offer before he makes any decision on the possibility of a judicial investigation.'

'Yes, and I understand he wants it by tomorrow, which I'm afraid is not possible,' said Anthony. 'The witness statements are almost complete, and there's a great deal of photographic and other evidence, but that deadline is unrealistic.'

Carmon looked at the young IDF officer. 'Could you approach the Judge Advocate General's office for an extension, Major Biton?' he said.

Anthony then spoke eloquently and at length of his hopes for a proper judicial enquiry, and our wish to use what had happened to improve the army's accountability and contribute to peace in the region. 'As I said earlier, we hold no grudges against the Israeli people,' he said finally. 'We ourselves have many Jewish friends in London. I must honestly say, however, that the results of my own investigation do not tally with the findings of the army's field enquiry. They are so very far from the facts as I understand them that to me they suggest a cover-up.'

The last word went through the meeting like an electric shock. Everyone suddenly moved and shifted papers uneasily. 'On the contrary,' said Carmon smoothly, 'I think it was an impressively frank and open enquiry. I cannot imagine there are many countries which would have gone to such lengths to establish the truth in similar circumstances. I can assure you there has been no cover-up. However, if new data has become available, then clearly the Judge Advocate General should have it.'

Here was a diplomat, cool as a cucumber, praising this blatantly superficial report and complacently imagining we would accept it. It shook me to the core, undermined all my assumptions about the way the world worked. But Anthony remained calm and courteous.

'To take just one example,' he said, 'the report claims that a single shot was fired from the watchtower at the time of the incident, whereas fifteen eyewitnesses state unanimously that there were at least five shots and possibly more than eight. How do you account for this difference?'

'Not true,' said Major Biton. 'The soldier in the tower fired only once.'

'And he was using a telescopic sight?' said Anthony.

'He was using a telescopic sight,' said Major Biton, 'but there was poor visibility from where that soldier was standing.'

'Which was . . .?'

The major went over to the whiteboard in the corner and with a thick black marker drew a crude picture of the tower. On it there was a single window, halfway up, which he marked with a large cross.

'That was the soldier's position,' he said. 'Because of the intervening buildings it would have been impossible for him to have seen your son.'

'But there is surely something wrong there,' said Anthony. 'The lookout windows are round the top of the tower. There is a surveillance platform at the top missing from your drawing. I have seen and photographed them myself, as did my son two days before he was shot. I have the pictures. From these windows there would have been perfect visibility.'

Major Biton simply shook his head, saying, several times, 'No, there was no visibility.'

'Then,' said Anthony, 'the proof will surely be in the CCTV footage. May we see that?'

'We have no CCTV cameras on that watchtower,' said Major Biton.

'But in my son's photographs one can quite clearly see the CCTV cameras fixed to a mast,' said Anthony.

The major had no answer to this. He stood silent for a moment, but then inspiration struck. 'Ah, yes,' he said, 'but those cameras are pointing towards the border, into Egypt.'

It was beginning to resemble a scene from Kafka. Even a civilian like myself could see that there would be no purpose in pointing the CCTV cameras over the Egyptian border when the scene of military action was in the security zone on the Rafah side. Yet again, they seemed to imagine we would be perfectly satisfied with this answer.

'In that case,' Anthony persisted, 'I should like to hear the relevant audiotapes from the two watchtowers and from the armoured personnel carrier which was stationed nearby. I understand that it's customary for you to keep video and audio records of these operations.'

I could see the major was getting flustered, but I felt not a jot of sympathy for him. Though he had seemed very confident at first, it was difficult to hold his own in the face of such cool persistence from someone so clear and determined. But he battled on.

'There was no armoured personnel carrier in the area on April 11 as far as I know,' he said. 'And as I've already said, there were no CCTV cameras in the watchtower that could have recorded the incident.'

'What about the second watchtower?' said Anthony.

'No, that had no cameras either,' said Major Biton after a moment's hesitation. 'It was still under construction and they hadn't yet been installed.'

'You haven't yet answered my question about the audiotapes. There must surely have been some record of what orders were given,' said Anthony.

'I will check on that,' said the major, 'but I think it's unlikely', and he scribbled something on a pad.

'I have to say,' said Anthony, 'that I find all this most extra-ordinary. Is it customary for you to have no record whatever of an incident as serious as this?'

Nobody attempted to answer.

'As there seems no other way of checking, I would like to visit the watchtower to see first-hand what the visibility from it is,' said Anthony. 'I think I have a right to do that.'

The major looked down and shook his head. 'Again I will check,' he said, 'but I'm afraid there are likely to be security issues.'

'I am also troubled by the case of two Palestinian boys who were shot within the same area within forty-eight hours of my son,' said Anthony. 'Their names are Rushdie and Mustafa Jabr, and they were shot without apparent provocation. To me these shootings seem to demonstrate some kind of pattern. Too many unarmed civilians are being shot for it to be entirely a coincidence, it seems to me. I would like to see the IDF's comments on these incidents.'

It was clear that Anthony had mentioned the unmentionable. The shooting of a young Englishman was one thing, but to mention the shooting of young Palestinians was quite another. I saw Danny Carmon's eyebrows lift slightly. Everyone else either gazed silently into space, or fiddled with pens and pencils. I could sense that Peter and Mike, on Anthony's right, were sitting very still.

After an awkward pause Biton said, 'I personally know nothing about these incidents, but again, I will make enquiries.'

I had sat through these exchanges with a feeling of disorienta-tion, one that remains with me to this day. These people clearly started out from a completely different baseline from ourselves. I realised that they had genuinely imagined these monstrous eva-sions would be enough to keep us quiet. And if this was what they served up to us, what utter contempt Palestinians must be met with if they ever attempted to put their case. If this was the accountability of Israel's 'moral army', then it wasn't a morality I could relate to.

There seemed little else that anyone could say. But I was determined that I was going to try to communicate our pain to them, as I had promised myself I would. I wanted to penetrate their ivory tower, make them understand the human consequences of what they had done. It was important they knew something of our life, of who we were and what we expected of ourselves and others. In the silence I spoke quietly.

'This is a terrible, terrible thing that's happened to our family,' I said. 'It's not just a tragedy for Tom and us. It's much more than that.'

They stared at me impassively.

'I mean,' I said, 'that shootings like this, of people who can't defend themselves, have an effect on all of us. They're not just a tragedy for the people involved. We are all eroded by them. They devalue life and make us lesser human beings. Such actions go to the core of all we believe about being civilised.'

No one moved. No one spoke.

'Our lives have been completely shattered,' I said. 'Tom and his siblings were very, very close. Sophie, my daughter, has had to leave her job as a researcher, my son Billy has had to take time out to be with his brother, and my son Fred, who is only twelve, hasn't been at school for seven weeks. No homework done. As for Anthony and I, we've had to take time out from our jobs with the uncertainty that brings, and this could have serious repercussions for the whole family. Those are just some of the ways our lives have been affected. What the loss of Tom has done to us emotionally I can't begin to describe. We are distraught, devastated. I can't at the moment see how we will ever recover.'

I thought of Rushdie and Mustafa's family and all the other Palestinian families who would never have a chance to say these things. I thought that at least we had jobs to leave, and roofs over our heads, and the freedom to come and go as we chose. My voice began to break and I could feel tears pricking my eyes and beginning to run down my face.

'When my son Tom came to Rafah he was a university student,

an exceptional young man with an enquiring mind who had all his life before him. I am talking about him in the past tense, because now that life has been taken away,' I said, my voice shaking. 'A bullet fired by one of your soldiers has put an end to it. When Tom was shot he was removing frightened small children from the line of fire. However you wish to interpret what happened, that is what it comes down to. He saw small children threatened by a soldier with a telescopic sight and he did the human thing. He held out his hands to them. What happened to him was utterly without humanity.'

Looking at the row of blank faces, I wanted to go on, to speak to them about the importance of seeing rather than turning away, of entering into dialogue rather than simply looking down the barrel of a gun. But the picture in my mind of Tom holding out his hands to those children was too vivid, too painful, and I choked.

There was still no reaction from the other side of the table. No one could look at me directly. It was as if I was speaking into air. I waited, imagining, I suppose, that someone would say something, but there was silence.

'And why did you shoot at us when we were last in Gaza?' I burst out finally. 'You knew who we were. We followed protocol. We were on our way to the place where Tom was shot. Is that the way you treat a grieving family – treat anyone?'

The embarrassment in the air was tangible. Danny Carmon said, 'I know nothing about this' and the others nodded in agreement – all except the major, who, after a muttered conversation with the captain said haltingly, 'Yes . . . I am . . . aware of that incident.' No expression of apology or regret. The IDF clearly hadn't seen it as an important matter, not something they would expect us to take up with them. I was aware again of the yawning gulf between our expectations and theirs.

After a pause, the lawyer, Daniel Taub, said, 'I think we would all like to say that we respect the way in which you have approached this whole situation.'

It was a small gesture, but at least it implied some empathy. The atmosphere eased somewhat. Danny Carmon raised his head, looked round the room and after a pause said: 'Well, I think we've covered all the various aspects. If no one has anything to add, we'll finish there. I shall be in touch as promised over the matters we've discussed and may I wish you a safe journey home.'

We all stood up. I felt lost, let down, unsure what to do. As people were gathering their papers the grey-uniformed captain came over to where we were standing with Peter and Mike.

'I'm sorry about the incident at the checkpoint. It was unfortunate,' he said.

I had to speak out. 'Thank you,' I said, 'but your army needs further training, Captain. If that soldier didn't know what he was doing, then he should have. We had followed all the correct protocol.'

He seemed extremely taken aback. We stood in awkward silence, then he said goodbye and moved away again. Peter and Mike were drifting towards the door, talking to Danny Carmon, and Anthony and I followed.

So our meeting with the IDF was over. Did they feel the way they had dealt with it was perfectly satisfactory? I realised now that they had come with no expectation that we would actually talk to one another, exchange information. Was dialogue a concept they understood? I thought of the young soldier shooting at us at the Abu Houli checkpoint, the IDF bulldozers driving over Palestinian homes, the shots aimed at small children playing in Rafah. In the coming months and years I would hear it said over and over again. Force was the only way the IDF seemed to know of dealing with conflict. Weapons did their speaking for them.

II

BE'ERSHEVA – LONDON

MAY 2003–JANUARY 2004

TWELVE

Thursday 29 May

I woke before dawn, but even if I'd wanted to there was no question of going back to sleep. This was the day when we were taking Tom home, a day I had thought would never come. Our bags were packed, the flat cleared, the last piece of documentation checked, the last address exchanged. I walked round the flat, gazing out of the windows at the lightening sky, looking over towards the hospital where I knew that, soon, they would be preparing Tom for the journey.

I thought of all the people we were leaving behind – our university friends from the human rights movement who had moved us into this flat; Professor Gurman and Professor Reichental and the staff at the hospital; TFH, and Sherard and Bridget; all the extended family of ISMers; Ya'alon and his taxi: all good, kind people who, in their different ways, had done their best to make life in Israel bearable for us. I thought, with a twist of the heart, of Amjad and Mohammed and Sahir and all the other people in Rafah, trapped behind the checkpoints, threatened by IDF guns and bulldozers, just trying to survive. And of course I thought about Erella. There had been barely time to say goodbye, but somehow there was no need. She and Danny were part of our life now, and we all took it for granted that we would stay in touch.

A few evenings before, our university friends had taken us for a farewell supper in Rahat, the Arab settlement I had often seen from the kibbutz. Though we were eating in the home of a family who were quite clearly very poor, they had laid on a huge, delicious, typically Arab meal for us of rice and coriander and chicken and stuffed vine leaves. They piled our plates high and I was overwhelmed by their generosity, their kindness, their openness, their good spirits. I wished I could have responded in the same way, but I was so tired with the strain of last-minute arrangements, the heat and the language barrier, that it was hard to do justice to the occasion, though both Anthony and I were deeply touched.

And now we were leaving all this behind. We'd decided it would be unfair to put Fred through the tension of travelling with Tom and he had flown to Heathrow the previous day, where he'd been met by Tom's girlfriend Kay and by Ann, the mother of his great friend Joe. I knew he was safe and happy with Joe's family, and I shall always be grateful to them for the way they supported us and opened their house to Fred. Some day, I hope, I shall find some way to repay them.

At 6 a.m. the Embassy driver arrived to take us to the airport, where Peter Carter and Mike Hancock were to meet us. 'Phew,' he said as we drove along the main boulevard, pretending to wipe his brow. 'Your Fred nearly had us in trouble yesterday.'

It seemed that when they'd arrived at the airport, security officials had taken Fred's bags apart and had come across the beautiful blue plates we'd bought on our day out in Jerusalem. I'd wrapped and packed them carefully, and in the middle of them, without thinking about it, I'd put the 'free gift' the shopkeeper had pressed on us – the plate with a huge picture of Yasser Arafat's face on it. This caused confusion and horror at the airport. It was put through the X-ray machine three times, Fred was closely questioned about where he'd got it, and his bags were obsessively searched all over again. How far could paranoia go?

We'd reached the crossroads by the hospital now, and as we stopped at the traffic lights an ambulance swept out at terrific speed. My heart lurched. I knew Tom was inside it. We'd been

Tom, 3 years old, and me looking at photos together

Tom, 6 years old, in a fig tree in Portugal

A family cycling holiday in East Anglia

In the garden in North London; the Harwich Estuary; at Grandma's cottage gate

With Billy, Fred and Sophie

The ISM banner later used for target practice by the IDF

Schoolchildren demonstrating at a funeral in Gaza City

Minutes after this picture was taken, the little boy throwing stones was shot in the shoulder by an APC

Tom Hurndall

Rafah: ISM volunteers Alison and Nicolai sitting on a 12 foot dirt roadblock to enable workers to fix the sewerage system in 'safety'

Tom Hurndall

Rafah: ISM volunteers demonstrating peacefully in front of a bulldozer, an APC and a digger to prevent house demolitions

Tom Hurndall

Rafah: children standing in the ruins of their demolished home

Working as a Red Crescent volunteer at the Al-Rweished refugee camp, Jordan

A demonstration in Rafah: 'Palestinians and Internationals targeted by the Israeli Army'

Seconds after being shot, Tom is lifted from the ground by Amjad and Sahir; Nicolai is in the background

Garth Stead

Anthony and I visit Yibnah, Rafah to see for ourselves

The block of concrete; the mound; Amjad showing us where Tom fell; the top of the watchtower visible in the centre

Me holding Salem Baroum, the little boy rescued by Tom

Second visit to Rafah: Billy, Sophie, Fred, me and Michelle

The press conference at the Royal Free Hospital on the day
we brought Tom home to London

With the Palestinian Delegate and his wife, Afif and Christ'l Safieh, outside
the Royal Free Hospital

Erella

Sophie at the candlelit vigil outside Downing Street the day after Tom died

Billy and Sophie speaking at the 'Free Palestine' and 'Stop the Iraq war' demonstrations, Trafalgar Square

Polly Hancock

The 'Concert for Tom'

Anthony setting up Tom's exhibition, 'Peace in conflict', at the Frontline Club

Clockwise from top left: Daniel; on holiday with the two Adams;
Caelia; playing at 'Reservoir Dogs' with Ollie and Alex; Antonia; Adam

THE BOYS

Clockwise from top left: Tom and Libby; Sam; Adam and Tom; Kay and Tom; Sam; Cassie

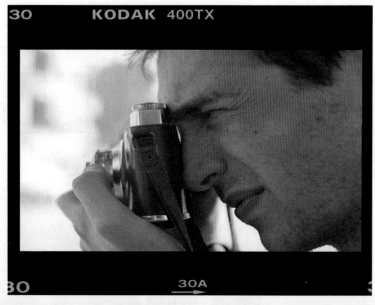

KODAK 400TX

30 30A

warned that he would be driven very fast to Tel Aviv to minimise the travelling time, which was dangerous for such a sick and vulnerable patient. I shall never forget the feeling of terrible, terrible sadness as we watched it race on into the distance and out of sight. Here we were at last, taking our son home. It was such a normal thing for parents to do, something we'd been doing all his life, but now it was all so totally, tragically different. Tom would never be part of ordinary life again, never speak to the friends who loved him, and whom he'd loved so dearly. They'd been through so much together. How would they be able to bear this new situation, I wondered, how would they react? It had been so difficult to keep in touch that many of them still had no idea of what had really happened. This was something new we would have to face. First we had had to bear the sharpness of Tom's shooting. Now we must endure the sharpness of bringing him home.

When we reached the airport the ambulance was waiting in a protected area of the car park. The anaesthetist and the nurse were standing talking in the sunshine. The side of the ambulance was open and Tom was lying on a stretcher inside. As I stood looking in at him, I could almost believe he was his old self. A piece of patterned cloth had been laid round his head, which hid the dressing on his terrible wound. I touched his hand, and his skin felt cool. Everything suddenly seemed more ordinary, more normal. Since Tom had left London in February the only place I had seen him had been in a hospital bed. Now it felt wonderful to see him lying there in the fresh air, with none of the paraphernalia of the hospital around him, just waiting for us to take him home.

As soon as we entered the airport building we were surrounded by the press. At hearings of the Israeli Parliament's law committee two days earlier Michael Eitan, the leader of Ariel Sharon's Likud party, had accused IDF soldiers of 'gross violations of human rights' in the Occupied Territories. He had demanded to know whether military leaders could tell him how many cases of human rights abuses there were a month, and, when he received evasive answers, had accused the army high command of indifference. This, from a former army officer, had caused a stir and had clearly focused new press interest on Tom's case. Anthony had just time to answer a few questions and reiterate that we would continue to press for justice, before Peter and Mike hurried us on towards the check-in.

After all our documents had been minutely inspected, a young soldier in the security section motioned us to one side and pointed to our luggage. 'We need to open your bags,' he said. I felt outraged. These soldiers knew very well our circumstances and what we'd been through, they could see that we had Embassy staff with us. How could they subject us to this? The young soldier rooted about, as if fairly uninterested, then picked up a black plastic bin liner that lay on top of my case and opened it. Inside it was another bin liner. He took that out and peered in, but quickly closed it again. Inside it were Tom's bloodstained clothes. It was vital we keep them, but once we'd moved to the flat there had been no cool place to store them, and by now the smell they gave off was horrific.

'What is that? What is in that bag?' he said.

'Those are clothes belonging to my son, who was shot by one of your soldiers,' I said, looking at him with burning eyes, my throat constricting, close to angry tears. It seemed such gross, even purposeful insensitivity. Were they trained not to show their own feelings or to respect other people's? That was our final contact with the Israeli military.

The El Al flight, a concession we were forced to make, was another ordeal. A small section at the back of the plane had been divided off with a tiny, flimsy curtain, the backs and arms of several rows of seats had been lowered and Tom's stretcher had been laid precariously across them. There was absolutely no privacy. Anybody walking down the central aisle could look over and see him. Clearly the Israeli government had wanted to keep its 'goodwill payment' for Tom's flight as low as possible.

Anthony and I sat next to Tom on one side, and the anaesthetist and the nurse sat close to him on the other, continually monitoring him and checking his pulse. I was rigid with tension as we took off, knowing that this was a dangerous moment for Tom, and even when we reached cruising altitude I couldn't relax. Anthony read quietly beside me, or looked out of the window as the map of Europe unfolded beneath us. From time to time I got up and went round to check with the medical staff that all was well, desperately needing reassurance. The plane was fairly full, with many Orthodox Jewish passengers travelling to London, and people walked up and down the aisle continually, peering over at us with undisguised curiosity. I felt we were a sort of show. It was a raw and shocking experience.

After what seemed an eternity we saw the English coastline, and the plane began its descent into Heathrow. I'd always had a feeling of warmth and security returning home from abroad, but this time I was on edge, worried about the landing and how it might affect Tom, not sure what would happen when we arrived. When the doors were finally opened and we were ushered off the plane, it was a relief to find a British ambulance team waiting. Tom's stretcher was lowered on to a trolley and we left him on the tarmac with the cheerful, competent ambulance men. Lying there in the midday sunshine, free of tubes and wires, he could almost have been asleep. I just remember seeing his long bare feet poking out from under the blanket before he was wheeled away and we followed the crowd towards the terminal.

A car was supposed to be meeting us, but somehow we were unable to make contact with it, so we took a taxi to the Royal Free, miraculously escaping the press. They were waiting inside the arrivals building, with their cameras pointing towards the tarmac where Tom was being transferred to an ambulance, and we simply walked out behind them.

It was extraordinary to drive through the London streets again, to feel the soft English breeze through the taxi window, to see the May sunshine on rows of Victorian houses, the blossom trees in the Hampstead front gardens. Everything was so familiar, yet we were seeing it with different eyes. It was as if we had lived another entire life in the seven weeks we'd been away.

To avoid the huge numbers of press who were apparently waiting at the hospital we had been asked to go in by a back door, where the Chief Executive's PA met us. We knew that a press conference had been arranged for us at 3.30 in one of the lecture rooms, and that the medical team who would be looking after Tom were to meet us first. Walking along the corridors, all the times I'd been here in the past came flashing back. This was where I'd brought the boys on occasion, where I'd come with Sophie when she'd broken her arm. The Royal Free was our local hospital and I was overcome with a sense of being on home ground. I felt so thankful that we had been able to bring Tom back to a place he knew, to enfold him here where his friends could have the chance to be with him, and – we would all have to accept it at some point – to say goodbye to him before he died.

The medical team were waiting for us in a small meeting room on one of the lower floors. As soon as we sat down I expressed my thanks to the hospital for having Tom, and for allowing us to take over one of their lecture rooms for a press conference. I felt awkward about this arrangement and wondered if it was usual. It had been made by someone in London whom we didn't know very well, and I had an uncomfortable feeling of being taken over, of somehow not being in control.

The doctors spoke quietly and sympathetically to us about Tom's medical condition, the need to do more neurological tests, run further scans. Then they began to talk about the importance of security, the need to have a guard on continuous duty outside Tom's ward, at least for the first few weeks, until things had 'settled down'. They were clearly somewhat apprehensive at the prospect of looking after such a high-profile patient, and it was only then that I began to understand what enormous public

interest there was in Tom's case. The doctors talked about the
extensive newspaper coverage there had been, and about reactions to the *Dispatches* programme. It seemed that Tom's story had
made an impact on people all over the UK.

As we entered the lecture room, I was aware for a moment of a
huge photograph of Tom projected on to a screen in front of us.
The sight of Tom's face in close-up threw me completely and I
stopped. There was a sudden loud clicking sound, and I felt
disorientated, very much taken by surprise, by flashing cameras.
We took our seats behind a table and when my eyes adjusted I
looked out at a sea of faces stretching to the back of the lecture
room. The place was packed, and people were standing inside the
doors. Waving microphones and cameras on rods were thrust
towards us.

'I'd like to ask Jocelyn. How's Tom?' called a voice from the
middle of the room.

It was such a simple, kind question, something that no one in
Israel had ever asked us. It made me feel that people really cared.
My voice was unsteady as I answered: 'Tom has a very, very
serious head wound. He is still in a coma, and sadly, he's unlikely
to recover. I'm afraid we must be realistic about that.'

'Nicola Woolcock from the *Daily Telegraph*,' said another
voice. 'What does the Israeli Defence Force have to say about
the shooting? I understand they've conducted their own enquiry.'

'On the basis of the evidence we've collected ourselves, the
report they've produced is a total fabrication,' said Anthony, with
great emphasis. 'We are conducting our own enquiry and we've
so far interviewed fourteen witnesses. We went out there with
open minds. We only wanted to discover the truth, but we've had
almost no cooperation from the Israeli army. What we do know is
that Tom was the third unarmed civilian to be shot in the same
area within forty-eight hours. The army seems to want to
intimidate and frighten people out of the area by a process of
terror. It is unaccountable and out of control.'

So now Anthony really had stated publicly what he thought of the field report. I wondered what Sherard would be thinking when he read the next day's papers.

'The army's so-called report consisted of twenty pages of very large print, and the majority of those were a history of the Israeli Defence Force,' I added.

There were numerous other questions. People wanted us to clarify what had actually happened on the day of the shooting, what we thought would happen next, whether anyone was likely to be brought to justice.

'And how have you both managed to deal with all this?' someone else asked. 'How are you feeling now? Do you blame yourselves for letting Tom go to the Middle East?'

How were we feeling? By this point I hardly knew. I could only think of seeing Tom settled in his new surroundings, and then getting home to Sophie and Fred.

'It's been a cruel seven weeks,' I said. 'We've been physically exhausted by all the emotion and the sadness of what's happened. All I can say is that I did what I could before Tom went to keep his eyes open to the dangers. Tom was someone who identified with other people's pain, and I'm enormously proud that he had this very strong desire to seek out injustice. We're extremely relieved to have him home and so grateful to the people who have helped. The support has been really staggering. Thank you so much.'

Finally it was over, and we took the lift to the seventh floor. Tom was lying in a corner of the Intensive Care Unit beside a large window that looked out over Belsize Park. Outside were the streets where he had walked, the houses of families he'd known all his life. This was where he'd hung out. This was his patch. The terrible underlying tension I'd felt every time I visited the Soroka Hospital melted away. Tom was here now, in his own place, among people who loved him. It felt so important that they would be able to come and share the precious time that was left. Though we had really no idea what would happen in the months ahead, I knew that being with Tom was all that really mattered now.

*   *   *

When Sophie opened the front door to us I hugged her and all the pent-up emotion and anxiety of the past days and weeks came flooding out. She had coped brilliantly while we were away, dealing with the press, fielding letters and enquiries, helping to set up a website in Tom's name. But she looked pale and very fragile.

We sat in the kitchen nursing mugs of tea, trying to anchor ourselves. There was so much catching up to do. Anthony described our meeting with the IDF and the progress of his investigation. I gave Sophie messages from Erella and various ISMers. Sophie told us of the huge support she'd had from her friends and even from the general public, amongst them journalists keen to keep the story in the public eye. And she told us how all Billy's mates had come round and cleaned and tidied his room before he got back. I knew we were all worried about Billy – too worried to say very much. We'd had word that he was filming the young soldiers' behaviour at checkpoints outside Nablus. So at least we all knew where he was and that the people he was with would be watching over him, knowing what had happened to his brother.

Our own friends had been amazing, dealing with bills, cleaning and servicing the car, organising practicalities. Sophie told us she'd also been contacted by Rachel Corrie's family in America, and they'd been talking and e-mailing. In particular she'd developed a rapport with Rachel's sister Sarah, who was slightly older than she was and whom she described as a 'wonderful person'. It had obviously been such a relief to them both to talk.

'Rachel's Mum Cindy told me that the day Tom was shot was the worst for her since the day Rachel was killed,' Sophie said. 'There were only three weeks in between and it was only 200 yards away. it was probably the same unit that killed James too.'

From all we'd read and heard about the Corries we had come to admire the dignified way in which they had dealt with their daughter's death, and especially the way they'd faced the subsequent smear campaign against Rachel and the ISM at home in

America. It seemed natural that I should make contact with Cindy, but I knew I couldn't do it yet. I wasn't ready to share that horror. What had happened to me? I thought. I was normally the kind of person who was able to go out to others, to feel their pain. I felt confused, as if I didn't recognise myself.

We rang Joe's home, where Fred had been staying, and spoke to Fred. 'Is Tom OK? Can I see him?' he asked immediately, and I could hear the little heartbreaking note of hope in his voice. Later, when he arrived home, he told us more about the scene at the airport, and the stir it had caused when he told the security officials rummaging in his bag that he didn't really know what was in it: 'My mother packed it.'

The phone was ringing continually while we sat at the kitchen table, and when we had talked ourselves out I went into the sitting room to listen to the messages. A harsh female voice immediately emanated from the handset. At first I couldn't believe what I was hearing. It was undisguised, obscene abuse. Tom was 'a fucking Nazi' and we were 'a load of fucking Nazi lovers'. I stood there in shock, and it wasn't until I heard the words 'I hope your fucking son will die a painful death' that I had the sense to put the phone down. I sat down on the sofa, feeling as if I had been violated, physically attacked. It was the kind of middle-class voice you might hear anywhere in north London, but there was something strangely familiar about it which I couldn't place. I decided to delete it. I hoped I wouldn't hear it again.

The rest of the tape was filled with supportive messages from well-wishers, including one from Afif Safieh, the Palestinian Delegate in London. When I phoned the number he had left I was immediately answered by Afif himself. He expressed his sympathy and concern, and asked if he and his wife Christ'l could come and meet us and visit Tom in hospital. The brief conversation with someone so warm and accessible, who seemed to understand our situation without my having to explain it, was like balm after that first appalling message. It was arranged that we would see them at the Royal Free at eleven o'clock next morning.

I sat alone downstairs for a long time after Anthony had left and Sophie had gone to bed, trying to put the day together in my mind, to make some sense of all that had happened. When I finally went upstairs I stood for a moment looking up at Tom's closed bedroom door. After Tom had left for Iraq I had had his room on the third floor redecorated and made into a bedsit, with a kitchenette and fridge. It was what he had always wanted – a place where he could boil a kettle, be a bit self-sufficient. I stood on the landing, knowing very well that the room was empty, that everything behind that door now was clean and bright and different. But in my heart Tom was still there, sitting in his old chair with his legs up on the windowsill, pen poised above the pad on his knees. '*Aren't you asleep, Tom? Want a cup of cocoa?*' He'd smile, pleased to be disturbed. '*Yeah. Thanks.*' I couldn't go in.

I wondered, yet again, whether I could have done anything to stop him going to Iraq. Probably not. Tom was someone who took calculated risks, the kind of challenging personality who gives an anxious mother nightmares. I thought of all the times I'd tried to stop him taking risks, tried to curb his enquiring mind to keep him safe. It was because I loved him so much, yet I realised that my caution has also been tinged with a kind of exasperation. Now I was beginning to understand my son at a deeper level, to see that he had taken risks because he was trying to know himself and the world better and because he hated injustice. I recognised that I had a hatred of untruth and injustice myself, which went very deep – we all did in the family. Now I was having to separate that out and learn to respect it in my son.

When we arrived at the hospital the next day we were met in the front entrance by Afif and Christ'l, and by a reporter from the *Hampstead & Highgate Express*. I warmed to Afif and Christ'l almost from the moment I saw them. Afif, with his ready smile, spoke eloquently and with genuine passion. Christ'l, fair-haired and elegant, was immediately empathetic. They both radiated wisdom and warmth and kindness, and I soon came to realise that they were a very special couple who were deeply loved and respected in diplomatic circles, not just in London but worldwide. They provided a link between three worlds – London, Palestine and Israel – and I would come to depend on them greatly.

We took the lift to the Intensive Care Unit and were standing around Tom's bed when we were met by the Senior Registrar, who led Anthony and me into his office. Since the previous day they had done more brain scans and neurological tests and the Registrar was at pains to tell us – as kindly as possible – that there was really no hope of recovery for Tom, or even any likelihood of improvement. We would ultimately have to decide what we wanted to do about Tom's future, he said, but meantime, of course, they would do everything they could to keep him comfortable and stable.

It wasn't as if we didn't know this already, but the little flame of consolation, the faint glimmer of optimism that I had felt on Tom's return to England and to the Royal Free was doused in a flash by these cool and realistic words. I was too weary, and it was all too raw. I wasn't ready to hear this again. When we re-emerged into the ward I could barely speak and Anthony was deathly quiet; he looked desolate.

Christ'l put her arms round me and Afif said: 'Come. Let's find somewhere quiet to sit down.' We found a café round the corner from the hospital and over coffee they encouraged both Anthony and me to talk. It was quite clear that Afif knew precisely what had happened in Gaza and it was like the shedding of a load to talk to someone of such obvious depth and maturity. He was not out to make political capital or to polarise the situation. He approached Tom's shooting as part of a much bigger picture. 'Just see this in terms of a fight for justice,' he urged. It was the way Afif and Christ'l expressed their humanity that was so striking – asking detailed questions about Tom, genuinely wanting to find out how we were, telling us about their own experiences, and giving us names of important contacts in the government.

Afif told us that he had been educated at the Ecole des Frères in Jerusalem, near the New Gate into the Old City, along with a group of friends that included the Palestinian writer Edward Said. Edward Said's was a name I barely knew then, though I remembered that one morning in Israel I had heard a voice on the radio speaking of the Middle East in such a poetic and insightful way that I had reached for a pencil and started taking his words down. The speaker was Edward Said, and after our meeting with Afif I began to search out his writings. They brought me a whole new awareness of the richness and resilience of Palestinian culture. So often the Palestinians are seen by the Western world simply as victims, as a hopeless, disorganised, downtrodden society, but reading Edward Said and talking to Afif I began to realise how utterly wrong this was.

'Under the worst possible circumstances,' Said wrote a few months later in an article on Rachel's Corrie's death, 'Palestinian society has neither been defeated nor has it crumbled completely. Kids still go to school, doctors and nurses still take care of their patients, men and women go to work, organizations have their meetings, and people continue to live, which seems to be an offence to Sharon and the other extremists who simply want Palestinians either imprisoned or driven away altogether. The military solution hasn't worked at all, and never will work. Why is that so hard for the Israelis to see?'

I had seen it, and I knew it was true. As we said goodbye to Afif and Christ'l that day, I had no idea what good friends they would become, or how they, and indeed the entire Palestinian community in London, would guide us through the minefield of the coming months. But I did know, just from that one brief meeting, that Afif didn't simply represent the Palestinian cause. He represented the best of mankind.

Ten days later we received a letter from Yasser Arafat.

Dear Anthony and Jocelyn Hurndall,

    Allow me my dear friends, to express my solidarity and sincere sympathy at these difficult moments that you are going through, due to the shooting of your dear son Tom. We believe that Tom was deliberately shot, in cold blood, by the Israeli army in Rafah two months ago, as he was defending Palestinian elderly, women and children. He was on a humanitarian mission in solidarity with our people, as part of an International campaign of peace by supporters from around the world, that supported the Palestinian people's just struggle to stop the vicious Israeli aggression and put an end to the Israeli occupation of our land and holy shrines . . .

Arafat had expressed the condolences that had been so lacking from the Israeli government and I was touched by the private sympathy and humanity of his letter. But I had mixed feelings. This was our son, our Tom; I didn't want him to become political capital however much I wished his shooting to highlight a wider cause. I didn't want him to be rewritten as a saint. Sophie said later that, as he lay there in a coma, it felt as though he was being torn apart by people on both sides of the conflict.

THIRTEEN

Although we were home, normality seemed light years away. But Fred bravely went back to school part-time. Anthony, who had been given an extension for presenting his evidence to the Judge Advocate General in Israel, concentrated on finishing his report. In Israel we had both been completely focused on Tom's tragedy and our concern for our children. Now back in London, Anthony and I saw each other, either at home or at the hospital, almost every day. There was still an overwhelming amount to discuss and we supported one another. But we were all of us out of our minds with pain. We were trying to think of one another, but the very nature of grief made it impossible. We all found it hard to talk about the one thing that was on our minds.

Each day I went to the hospital, and Fred often called in there on his way home from school and sat quietly by Tom's bed listening to music. Almost as soon as Tom arrived in England there had been a change in his appearance. The external wound in his head had more or less healed now, the seepage of spinal fluid had stopped and so, more or less, had the bleeding from his ear. Quite suddenly the terrible swelling went down, leaving a raw, exposed, sunken area above his left temple with a ridge of bone where a section of his skull had been removed. It was agonising to see Tom in this state, but to me it was of the utmost importance that I put these feelings aside. Tom needed us to be strong for him, to help him bear everything. The disfigurement did not detract from his innate dignity. When I was with him I felt an overwhelming need to cradle his head, to stroke it.

Anthony was as distressed as I was. His feeling was that Tom would not wish others to be distressed by the sight of his wound, and at first he felt it should be covered. But to me the greatest respect we could pay Tom was to accept him as he was, wound and all, to share his cruel disfigurement with him. I felt there was no reason why we or anyone else should be protected.

One Sunday afternoon when we came back from the hospital Sophie looked pale and somehow disorientated – but we were all feeling disorientated, so I didn't pay too much attention. On Monday morning we were standing talking in the sitting room before she went to work, and she suddenly said rather vacantly, 'I don't know where to go.'

I was astonished. This was Sophie, my highly organised daughter. What did she mean?

As I opened my mouth to reply Sophie crumpled and sank to the floor. Her eyes were closed and her face was ashen. I managed to lever her on to the sofa and tried to give her some water, but she didn't respond. When she came to she seemed confused, and our neighbour, a GP, advised taking her to hospital. So within an hour I had not one but two children in the Royal Free. She was discharged within a couple of hours but when I brought her home she was almost too worn out to walk upstairs. It was just an indication, if I needed one, of the extreme strain she had been under. It was some days before she felt ready to return to work.

Since Anthony and I had been in Israel engaged with the struggle to bring Tom home I hadn't realised the extent of Sophie's emotional and physical exhaustion. She had been running the campaign which had developed beyond an appeal to raise funds for Tom's return and was now carrying on as a form of tribute to him, concerned with highlighting the plight of the many threatened families in Palestine and demanding accountability within the Israeli army. The non-stop interviews were emotionally draining, and the shock of Tom's return to the UK (Sophie felt she had in some ways said goodbye to Tom already), combined with seeing the cruel change in the wound on his head, brought about a complete physical collapse: her body simply shut down.

Gradually friends began phoning and arranging to visit. We had to explain that there was a twenty-four-hour guard on Tom's room, and we would need to add them to a list of visitors. I loved seeing them when our visits coincided because they were all, had been, a part of Tom. Some of them, when they came, brought CDs of Tom's favourite music to play him, others wrote personal, spirited messages on the large sheet of wallpaper on the wall opposite his bed.

Among the first people to visit was Tom's friend Sam. He and his mother Ann both adored Tom – most of the time, that is – and Ann was probably one of the adults outside the family who knew him best, his faults as well as his virtues. Tom had spent hours in Ann's kitchen, laughing and discussing everything under the sun, with Tom asking about Ann's life, and acting the mature adviser. I, in turn, was – and am still – devoted to Sam. To me it was as though he represented the emotional side of Tom. A talented musician, Sam is a liberating personality, able to express his feelings and to talk about them in an unusually articulate way. But there were times, as they were growing up, when neither Tom nor Sam was easy, and Ann and I had often laughed and commiserated about the challenges of bringing up our loveable sons.

Sam told me later that he had been in Dingwall's, a jazz bar in Camden Town when he heard the news of Tom's shooting. 'I was standing next to the bouncer, and I got this call on my mobile,' he said, 'and someone told me I just cried out, really loudly, "Oh, something terrible has happened to my friend!" Then we all went up to Alex's house and sat watching the news.'

Ann described to me the first time she went with Sam to visit Tom. Several of Tom's friends and their parents were visiting that day. They had collected at Belsize Park tube station and walked up the hill together. They couldn't all go in at the same time, and there were people already waiting outside the ward, including

Anthony and two of Tom's fellow students who had come all the way from Manchester.

'When we finally got in and I saw Tom lying there, with that terrible, terrible wound, I burst into tears,' she said. 'Sam said, "Just a minute, Mum." He went off and came back with a cloth to cover Tom's head. Then he bent down and started mopping Tom's face, stroking his hands so tenderly, rearranging the bed-clothes, trying to make sure he was comfortable. He was so concentrated, so concerned, it was heartbreaking. He was talking to Tom all the time: "Man, it's been about a week since I saw you. Everyone's thinking about you. Look, my Mum's come to see you . . ." It was as if Tom was at home and they were having an ordinary conversation.

'Then Sam put on a CD he'd brought. It was that song he and Adam wrote for Tom called 'Sleeping on the Floor'. Suddenly above the music I heard this strange kind of wailing. It was Sam, he was weeping his eyes out. Then he took hold of Tom's wrist and started dancing. Tom's wrist was like a twig, so, so thin, but Sam just held on to it as if they were dancing in a group, just like they'd always done, and he went on dancing to the rhythm, singing the words, except that his voice kept breaking. It was completely abandoned and unselfconscious, but it was so angry too. It was as if he just couldn't accept what had happened to Tom. I felt he was saying to him, "Come on, mate, you've got to get out of this." I just sat there watching them, with tears streaming down my face.'

All Tom's friends were different, of course, but perhaps the person who caused me most concern was Tom's close and oldest friend Adam. Adam is a very different kind of character, wry, witty, thoughtful, clever, less of an extrovert perhaps. He and Tom had known one another since they were small boys, attended the same prep school, been lost on a motorbike in the Egyptian desert together. Their outrageous wit and banter had often had us all in stitches, and he was part of the close group that surrounded Tom. He knew very well how difficult it was to dissuade Tom when he made up his mind to do something – I'd heard him describe it in an interview. Adam happens to be Jewish, and I wondered, still wonder, how he is dealing with Tom's loss. But I understood something of how angry he was when I heard that he had confronted the Israeli Ambassador outside our local cinema in Belsize Park. He must have discovered that the Ambassador was due to watch a film, and he'd joined a small crowd of demonstrators. Although he couldn't get near because of the security police, he shouted out at him to go and see his friend Tom Hurndall. 'Go, Adam!' I'd thought.

For the most part, however, Adam's anger was unexpressed and I didn't know how to help, though I had tried to get in touch.

And then there was Alex, one of Tom's closest confidants. Alex had lost his own brother in a car accident, and I knew that this tragedy had devastated his family. Tom had attended the funeral, and had always kept a newspaper report of the accident, with a photo of his good friend's younger brother, stuck on his bedroom wall. The family had shown enormous empathy for us and for Tom. The loss of Tom would surely revive terrible memories for Alex, and I was worried about how he would cope. And there were other friends, too, whom Tom had loved, who I knew less well. I thought of them in their grief, and hoped they were not feeling isolated.

My own friends, I think, tried to hide their distress at the sight of Tom. Guy and Ann, the director of the English Chamber Choir and his wife, arranged during these early weeks to meet me at the Royal Free to discuss their idea of a Concert for Tom. Though they were very controlled – for my sake, I'm sure – there was no disguising their shock, and it was the same with all my friends who came to the hospital. I knew the depth of their concern and affection, and I was grateful for their tact.

One still, bright morning, some days after our return, I was upstairs tidying and I started walking, almost without thinking, up the stairs to Tom's room. Until then I had avoided those stairs quite consciously. Now something had shifted, some defence had dropped. But I stood for a while, bracing myself, before opening the door.

Sunlight streamed through the window on to the newly laid oak floor and into the little kitchenette with its clean white surfaces. Where Tom's old writing desk had been there was a new beautifully carpentered built-in desk, with folding doors designed to hide the mess. Down one wall were spacious fitted cupboards, where his crowded wardrobe had once been. The only recognisable thing was his old chair. Tom's room, as I remembered it, was no more.

The Saturday before the shooting I had spent the day clearing it ready for the builders to come in. Almost every inch of the walls and ceiling had been covered by Tom with photographs of his family and friends. It was as if he wanted to be completely surrounded by the people he loved, by everything that had happened in his life, as if to remember every minute of it. There were pictures of us on holiday in East Anglia, his friends taken at school, in pubs, scuba diving, up on Hampstead Heath, much more recent photographs from university, pictures of Tom and Kay on holiday in Luxor, and in Paris by the Eiffel Tower. There were fading colour photos of my parents taken at my grand-parents' much-loved holiday cottage on the Solway Firth. He had even found a photograph of Anthony and me sitting in a restaurant when we were engaged. It was a panoply of Tom's whole life. Painfully, lovingly, trying not to damage them, I had removed the staples and taken everything down. Now, standing in this unfamiliar room, this bright emptiness that should have been his to fill, all I could feel was the gaping hole of his absence. I couldn't find any meaning to it all and I moved aimlessly around the room, utterly bereft.

Eventually I got up and opened one of the new fitted wardrobes. There on the ceiling, which was still painted the familiar indigo blue, were some photographs I'd forgotten to remove. Tom's friends looked down at me, smiling, waving, making faces at the camera. A little bit of Tom was still there. That tiny remaining corner of his old room seemed as precious as some fragment of a medieval wall-painting. On one of the cupboard shelves was a stack of stationery, including a pile of the simple, buff, spiral-bound A5 writer's pads that Tom always had with him. I picked one up, saw him again in my mind's eye, with his feet up on the window-sill, pen poised. I leafed through it, gazed and gazed at it, wondering what he would have written on those empty pages.

On another shelf was a folder labelled 'Memories'. Some small, folded bits of paper fell out. On one was written 'Playing with Sophie when we were little'. On another 'When my mother says "Well done"'. It took my breath away, that sharp reminder that everything you say and don't say as a mother means something. *Oh Tom, did I say 'Well done' to you often enough? I pray that I did.*

Another buff folder held some English essays he had written at Winchester. There was a lyrical description of a ship at sea in the evening sunset with a glowing comment from his English master, a piece entitled 'A night out with the lads' in which he described how much he disliked drinking and how alien and 'out of it' he felt on such occasions. Underneath it were several more note-books, with dates on the front. Tom's diaries. I'd asked the builders to take everything down to the cellar, but Sophie must have brought them up again. The very sight of Tom's hand-writing affected me for days, and now, confronted with these diaries, I crumpled inside. Should I open them? The family had been at sixes and sevens over what to do about them, and we'd vaguely decided to put them away for a few years. Then it would be up to each of us to decide whether we wanted to read them.

Now I remembered that one day when I was at the Residence in Tel Aviv, Sophie had rung me, very excited, saying that she had found something beautiful that Tom had written. The date was November 2001. Tom would have been nineteen. The words jumped out at me:

> *What do I want from this life? What makes me happy isn't enough; all those things that satisfy our instincts complete only the animal in all of us. I*

want to be proud. I want something more. I want to look up to myself and
when I die, I want to be smiling about the things I've done, not crying for
what I haven't. I guess I want to be satisfied I know the answer to this
question. Everyone wants to be different, make an impact, be remembered.

Since we'd got back, people I'd met had often asked me, 'So
what was Tom doing in the Middle East?' I understood why they
asked, but there were times when something in me bridled, and I
found it difficult to answer. The implication from these often
rather comfortable people seemed to be that Tom's journey had
been just a young man's fancy, the kind of immature thing that he
would ultimately grow out of. Looking at this diary I knew what I
wanted to say: 'There are some people who don't just stay in their
comfort zone, who don't think that we're here in this world just
for ourselves. Tom was one of those. He was as pleasure-loving
and party-going as any young man, but he also wanted to record
the vileness of conflicts like this so you can sit in safety on your
sofa and know about them. *That's* why he was in the Middle
East.'

Some time later, a good friend sent me this passage from John
Ruskin:

The greatest thing a human soul ever does in this world is to see
something, and tell what it saw in a plain way. Hundreds of people
can talk for one who can think, but thousands can think for one
who can see. To see clearly is poetry, prophecy, and religion all in
one.

*   *   *

In Highgate, Anthony was still working desperately on the final
stages of his report. I knew he was frustrated at the length of time
it was taking, but it was extraordinary that he could do it at all in
the circumstances. I was keenly aware of how important this
report was for Anthony. It was part of his tribute to Tom. Into it
he channelled all his love and all his anger at the shoddiness and
injustice of what had happened. His honesty, his painstaking

pursuit of the truth, his determination to be even-handed, exposed the IDF's pathetic effort for the lying and self-serving exercise it was.

The tone of the report was calm and considered, the language clear and economical. It started by describing why Tom had been in Rafah and why the ISM had been in Salah El Din Street on that day, including the unprovoked shootings at the Abu Jabr house. It went on to give a clear picture of what had happened, based on the evidence of fourteen witnesses – nine ISM volunteers, two photographers, Khalia Hamra from Associated Press and the freelance photographer Garth Stead, and the three Palestinian witnesses, Mohammed, Amjad and Sahir. Neither the volunteers' nor the Palestinians' full names were given because, as Anthony tellingly put it, 'they are concerned at possible retribution from Israeli army and intelligence forces'.

Finally, point by point, it demolished the IDF's report, with all its inconsistencies and implausibilities, and Major Biton's attempt to defend it.

'The IDF acknowledge Tom was hit and taken to Soroka; that there was no other incident that afternoon,' Anthony had written. 'Beyond that their account does not tally in any way with the facts. Tom was shot in a different location, he was not exiting any building, he was not facing straight onto the security zone in front of the security wall, but behind a mound in a street eighty metres away. He was not wearing camouflage fatigues but an orange thigh-length jacket. He had no pistol. He was not pulled back into any building. He was not taken away in an ambulance. There is no similarity between the locations. The events described are two different events: one real and the other a fabrication.

'There is only one conclusion possible on the facts available. Given the admission that the commander was deliberately aiming at an identified adult, that no other adult was in view, and that Tom was wearing a clearly visible orange jacket, the conclusion has to be that the soldier shot Tom knowing his target to be either an international peace activist, who was part of an organisation

considered to be impeding the activities of the IDF, or a photographer recording such activities.

'General Eiland and the IDF chiefs of staff have sought to avoid
responsibility by a straightforward fabrication. Their version does
not accord with verifiable facts or with any possible interpretation
of those facts.'

The report was supported by witness statements, photographs
and clear location maps. It was cool, brilliant, unanswerable, a
veritable sword of truth, cutting cleanly through all the IDF's lies.

During these first weeks at home we became aware that many
concerned voices were being raised in Parliament over Tom's
case. In early June we received a letter confirming that the
Foreign Minister Jack Straw had agreed to our request for a
meeting. It reiterated the well-worn claims. 'The government,'
Straw assured us, had 'continually pressed the Israeli government
for a full and transparent enquiry' into Tom's shooting, and had
asked the Israelis to 'review their rules of engagement and to try to
avoid further civilian casualties in the future'.

Before seeing Jack Straw in mid-June we had a meeting with
Richard Burden, a Labour MP with a close and consistent interest
in the Middle East, during which we showed him this letter.
We were in the House of Commons when he challenged Jack
Straw's Parliamentary Under-Secretary to clarify what precisely
was meant in it by a 'full and transparent enquiry', and to reveal
what Israel's response had been to the request for a review of the
rules of engagement.

Around this time another Labour MP, Jeremy Corbyn, tabled
an Early Day Motion, signed by twenty-nine MPs:

That this House notes the shooting of 21-year-old Tom Hurndall
whilst helping Palestinian children escape gunfire from an Israeli
army watchtower in Rafah, Gaza; calls on Israel to conduct a full
military police inquiry into the incident; supports the calls from
Tom Hurndall's family for the Israeli military advocate-general to

start a prosecution against the Israeli commander who fired the bullet; and sends its support to the family of Tom, who is in a coma at the Royal Free Hospital from which he is not expected to recover.

The government response was predictably anodyne, but it was overwhelming to realise that there was a solid group of impressively well-informed and conscientious MPs who were behind us in our passionate struggle to get justice for Tom, and who were as appalled as we were by what the Israeli army was doing. We were deeply grateful, but I must admit that at this point the heartbreaking day-to-day reality of visiting Tom made the world of politics seem remote, and it was only later that I was able truly to appreciate all that was being done.

'Remote' was certainly the impression we had of Jack Straw when Anthony and I eventually went to meet him at the Foreign and Commonwealth Office. Or perhaps 'disconnected' would be a better word. Anthony was very clear that the purpose of this meeting was to seek Straw's support in holding the Israelis to account and calling for the soldier who fired the shot to be prosecuted. We appreciated that this was a delicate issue, but inwardly we were still smarting at the feebleness of the government's response, and the memory of Jack Straw's first statement after Tom was shot, in which he had metaphorically shrugged his shoulders with the observation that the Foreign Office had been telling British nationals not to enter Gaza. I remember Sophie shouted with outrage at that point and wanted to turn the television off.

While I recognised the need to discourage teams of people from entering the Occupied Territories and putting themselves and British diplomats at risk, somehow it seemed an inappropriate kind of statement to make directly after the shooting of a young man – and especially cold for someone with a son of almost the same age. I wanted Jack Straw to know that Tom was a thinking young man who had gone down there not simply on a whim, but to make a serious record of what was happening. I had brought along a small section of Tom's Rafah journals on Anthony's laptop, in which Tom described what he was seeing there, and his reasons for going. After all, I thought, if we're asking Straw to represent Tom's case to the Israelis, then it's important for him to have an idea of who Tom is.

We waited for what seemed ages in a high-ceilinged, dark-panelled room at the Foreign and Commonwealth Office until Jack Straw appeared and led us into his elegant office. After initial pleasantries, Anthony outlined our case and asked emphatically for government support.

When Anthony had finished speaking I opened the laptop and after a short explanation began to read from the journal. So absorbed was I in Tom's words that it was a while before I became aware of the pressure of Anthony's hand on my arm. I looked up and understood. There was something in Straw's expression that indicated that this was not appropriate, and I stopped immediately, feeling uncomfortable. But as we were finally ushered out amid further formal pleasantries, I was glad that I had done it. I was determined that Tom's voice should be heard. This was a human situation, and I knew that politicians, who take the enormous decision to go to war on our behalf, needed to be reminded of it.

Some good did come out of that meeting. Jack Straw passed us on to Baroness Symons, Minister of State at the Foreign and Commonwealth Office. This was a very different kind of encounter. Professional but extremely approachable, Baroness Symons was visibly moved when she heard the details of Tom's story, and clearly impressed by the weight of the evidence that Anthony showed her on his computer, including Garth Stead's photographs of the shooting. Soon after that she wrote a letter to Silvan Shalom, the Israeli Foreign Minister, informing him of our meeting, describing Anthony's report and the photographic evidence as 'powerful and disturbing' and urging the need for the Judge Advocate General to institute a Military Police Enquiry.

'You will know that this case continues to receive a great deal of media and parliamentary attention in the UK,' she wrote. 'I know you will agree that the family deserve full answers to their questions. Our Defence Attaché in Tel Aviv will be presenting the Hurndalls' evidence to the Judge Advocate General. I have agreed to see the family again when the Judge Advocate General has issued his report.' In other words – 'What your army has done is still under the spotlight here, and this family is not going to go away.'

Baroness Symons struck me as a very human person with an incisive and insightful mind, who was able to say difficult things in a challenging but acceptable way. We felt we'd found a real ally.

While Anthony was preoccupied with his report and with seeking the necessary legal advice to carry forward our demand for answers and recognition from the Israelis, and Sophie threw herself into the press campaign to keep the case alive, I spent my days at the Royal Free. It was the only place I wanted to be. As I woke each morning, my first conscious thought was how soon I could get to Tom. He had been moved from the Intensive Care Unit into an airy, light room on the neurological ward, and here his close friends came and went, most of them back from university for the summer. I realised that they were now looking for a response as intensely as we had done during the early days in Israel. Adam and Sam visited Tom together and sang and played to him. "We're sure he could hear us," they said. Often one or another of his friends would say to me wistfully, 'I'm sure Tom can see. I'm sure his eyes were following me.' Or, 'I'm sure Tom knows I'm there.' Kay, in particular, had a very stronge sense that Tom knew she was there, and had even moved his head to follow her round the room. To me it was a measure of his friends' love and longing, and of their disbelief. They simply weren't ready to accept the finality of what had happened.

I felt worried about Kay. She and Tom had shared so much and she was grief-stricken, but with her usual generosity she was now doing her best to take care of Fred, to whom she'd become very close. He would regularly go and see her after school, and they often visited Tom together. Cruelly, at around this time there was a fire at Kay's flat and she lost her computer with all Tom's e-mails on it, her camera equipment and many photographs. Though she did manage to rescue some pictures and mementos of Tom, she was devastated.

Though unnecessarily modest, Kay is a brilliant photographer, and she and Tom had been close for about a year – ever since the day he'd walked into the Hampstead photography shop where she was working. They'd travelled together, spent weekends in Paris, walking the streets till five in the morning, intoxicated with the excitement of it, missing the train home because they were having such a good time. Kay, who is quite a tomboy, had a picture of them sitting side by side on a parapet in Montmartre. They'd climbed over some official barrier to get there and they were gazing serenely out from this eyrie, relishing their secret view of Paris. They'd travelled to Egypt together in 2002, and among the photos they brought back was one of Tom playing chess on a boat going down the Nile, legs stretched out on deck, his head bent slightly to one side in an attitude of fierce concentration as he considered his opponent's next move. Tom would always play chess with anyone who was willing.

Kay would later describe to me how they'd been resting on a bench outside a temple in Luxor and had been ambushed by a group of children.

'It was too much,' she said. 'There were at least fifteen of them, and they were all over me, asking me for my ring, my earrings, my pen – they were ready to grab anything. Tom just loved it, he thought it was really amusing, and he was down on one knee taking photographs. One of the little boys actually took something out of my pocket, and I got quite angry, but Tom said, "Oh don't. They're only kids." He was always so sympathetic. He loved kids.'

It hadn't always been easy for Tom's girlfriends. I knew that some of his friends had tended to close ranks against them. When I looked at the messages on the whiteboard in Tom's hospital room – 'Come on, get off your arse, Hurndall!', 'Wake up, mate!' – the photographs of Tom and Sam and Ollie hamming it up in *Reservoir Dogs*-style trilbies and dark glasses in some north London street, it brought the atmosphere of their friendship back to me with unbearable sharpness, like an overheard phrase of music, or the drift of a familiar scent. It was a mixture of intelligent talk, and teasing, and exuberant physicality – talented young men, growing up and full of life. Many of Tom's friends, perhaps more especially the girls, confided in him because he listened and understood.

Love affairs and female friendships had had to take place alongside this closely guarded inner male circle. So I was aware that Kay avoided the boys when she came to see Tom, as did his first girlfriend Libby, and I realised how isolated they both must be feeling.

Gradually we were getting to know the staff at the Royal Free. As time went on, we could see that the obvious love and admiration surrounding Tom, the visits and messages, were helping them see behind Tom's shattered body to the person he had been. During the long heavy hospital hours, one of the things we did was to fix photographs to one of the walls. I was so anxious that the staff should see him as a real person rather than simply as a body, and now they could see a fuller Tom, more dimensions of him. One of my nightmares was that when I was not there to interpret for him they might not understand the small signals I had come to recognise, and I felt that knowing him better might help.

I became very attached to one very special West Indian nurse – I wish I could remember her name, but at that time my mind was so confused and overloaded that many things slipped away. She was of medium height, with a distinct physical presence, and everything she did and said had a spiritual quality. She looked beneath the surface of things, and I remember her saying to me very gently one day: 'I can feel that Tom is a most unusual person, and I know he has done something great that will be remembered.' She gave me such comfort. In hospital everything tends to be reduced to the physical, and I was so grateful to talk to someone who recognised and acknowledged Tom's spiritual side.

I think it may have been this nurse who first told me about *Romeo and Juliet*, a play that had always had a particular resonance for Tom. It must have been on the syllabus at Winchester, and – much to my disapproval at the time – we'd noticed one day that he had a tattoo on his wrist. It was a stylised heart surrounding the words 'Defy the Stars', and he explained to us that it derived from a speech by Romeo in which he challenges fate with the words, 'Then I defy you, stars!' For Tom it summed up a whole philosophy of taking responsibility for your own life. He wanted to live every moment on his own terms. That philosophy affected everything he did, and it was clearly one of the things his friends remembered most about him, and wanted to acknowledge, for it seemed to go to the core of who he was.

And so a group of them had been coming to the hospital when no one else was there to perform *Romeo and Juliet* around Tom's bed. I think it consisted of Adam and Sam and a couple of others – Antonia, one of Tom's close female friends, and a very sensitive young man called Daniel whom I know Tom confided in and respected, and who was actually in the process of converting to Judaism at the time Tom was shot. ('Daniel,' Tom had written in an e-mail from East Jerusalem, 'you and I need to sit down and talk when I get back because being around activists 24/7 and being in Palestine is seriously messing with my head and I need someone I trust who knows about the situation to help me sift through all this mess out here as this is my first time doing this and it's getting really hard to be objective, plus some of the stuff I've been seeing is pretty heavy and it's just making me lose it.')

Performing the play took several visits, and there seems to have been a certain amount of musical accompaniment, with Sam on guitar. 'Yes, there really was quite a noise,' one of the nurses told me. 'At one point I had to come in and tell them to be quiet.'

I don't think the Royal Free had ever seen anything quite like it. All of Tom's friends, in their own particular ways, were paying tribute to him.

For all of us that early summer was both a precious and a painful time. We knew that there must be a limit to the limbo of Tom's existence, but we couldn't yet bear the thought of letting him go. Though we knew that Tom was never going to recover, we had no real idea of how long he was likely to continue as he was, or how we were going to deal with it.

I remember sitting in the garden and talking things over with Anthony and Sophie. I thought seriously about whether I could bring Tom home and look after him myself, but was this wholly unrealistic? My career had centred round working with various kinds of disability in school, but I had no direct experience whatsoever of looking after a severely disabled person. It was hard to imagine caring for Tom in his old room on the third floor, but could we perhaps convert the basement into a self-contained flat and have help from a series of carers? Or should we look around for suitable long-term homes? Converting the basement would be beyond our means, but we might make it part of our claim for compensation from the Israelis.

In July I attempted to return to work; but it was a post that required all of me and more, and I couldn't manage it. Half of me wanted to try to return to normality, but the other half knew I couldn't. Things simply weren't normal. Anthony looked drawn, pressured as he was by the need to finish his report and the need to resume his legal work. I felt pressured too, emotionally drained and physically depleted. I was dismally aware of my failure to respond to all the letters of sympathy from friends, and from the hundreds of other people unknown to us who had written and sent donations. I lay awake at night worrying about it and about Billy out in Nablus.

There were huge demands on Sophie too. She was interviewed by the media and spoke at university student unions around the country: given Tom's age, a great many students felt passionately about his plight. Tom's first and much-loved girlfriend Libby, who had influenced him profoundly, spent months organising a spectacular Peace Festival at Nottingham University to celebrate his life. She later told me what an impression Sophie had made in her address. 'Sophie spoke to the students in a way that most of them had never heard anyone speak before. To see a girl near enough their age standing up and speaking with that passion and clarity was something. She was of their generation and she gave a sense of how powerful people can be. So many things came out of that day. It gave an opportunity for a huge number of students to take part in something political.'

Yet though Sophie was managing to do all this, I knew she was in a fragile state.

So once again we put the matter of Tom's future on hold.

What disturbed us all was the question of whether Tom was in pain. No one seemed able to give us an answer to this – perhaps because there wasn't a straightforward one. We were told at various times that he felt no pain, and that he had no 'understanding' of pain. But occasionally he would make a sudden jerky movement, or turn his eyes upwards as if trying to connect with something or someone, and it was impossible then to believe that he had no feeling. I know we were all terrified by the spectre of 'locked-in syndrome' – that Tom might be able to see and hear but unable to communicate.

On 25 June, Anthony and I attended a meeting of the Ethics Committee at the Royal Free to discuss Tom's future treatment. We were welcomed by the Chairman, a consultant psychiatrist called Dr Geoffrey Lloyd, and introduced to the other members of the panel, which included a consultant neurologist, the director of nursing and the hospital chaplain. They asked sympathetically how we were coping. It was hard to answer such a question without breaking down, but I managed to say that I was trying hard to understand what had happened and wanted to ensure that something positive came out of all this suffering. Anthony added that we felt we had come to know

Tom at a deeper level during the past ten weeks by reading what he had written. They encouraged us to speak about Tom and why he had been in Rafah, and Dr Lloyd asked us how we saw his further treatment.

'I'm just trying to think very hard what Tom would have wanted,' I said.

'And what do you think Tom's own view would have been?' asked Dr Lloyd gently.

I thought about all the things Tom had said and felt about living life to the full. *'Without happiness, pain is only a passing thing of interest, and without pain, what is happiness?'* That's what he'd written in his Rafah journal. Now he could feel neither. That acute intelligence, that engagement with life, was gone.

'I'm sure Tom wouldn't want to survive in his present condition,' I said. 'What we wonder is, whether he is suffering at all.'

Dr Lloyd thought for a moment. 'You can be certain Tom is not suffering,' he said, 'but given the nature of his injuries, there's very little prospect of any significant recovery. We're ensuring he has adequate nutrition, but he's likely to experience further infections, and the question is how actively we should treat them – with antibiotics, for example.'

This was something we had discussed with Sophie. Though she could not bear to come and see Tom, I knew that he was constantly in her mind and she was haunted by the thought of how his life might end. She had particularly wanted me to ask how long he would survive if he got pneumonia.

'That's a very hard question to answer,' said Dr Lloyd. 'Tom is still physically strong, and he might overcome it. But I think it's likely that complications would develop.'

Another thought that haunted all of us was that Tom might recover sufficiently to become aware of his condition. 'I couldn't bear that,' Anthony said. 'I would prefer him to remain as he is than have him suffer.'

Dr Lloyd told us that the likelihood of such a recovery was very small.

'There is no question of our withdrawing supportive care,' he said finally. 'The only question is, how actively you would like us to treat any infection that develops.'

'I don't think Tom himself would want to be treated, and I think many of his friends feel he wouldn't want to go on existing like this,' said Anthony. 'In fact the whole family is agreed about it.'

'So you're at one on this,' said Dr Lloyd.

I thought of Fred. I knew he was still hoping against hope that Tom would recover. Neither of us felt Fred should have to be involved in this decision. It would be too painful for him, and the panel agreed.

'So I think it's clear,' said Dr Lloyd, 'that if Tom develops an infection you would not wish us to treat it.'

What other course of action could there be? This decision seemed to bring us one step closer to a resolution for Tom, though I could hardly bear to think of what it would actually mean, or how prolonged this process would be.

Quite frequently now when I came home at night I found another hateful phone message. It was the same voice spewing out the same vitriol – filthy, abusive stuff about our being 'Nazi-lovers' that would have upset me more if I hadn't known, with utter certainty, that we were none of us racists, none of us anti-Semitic. We were emphatically not out to polarise the situation, or to get the Israeli people. This was not what our campaign was about. We were only interested in bringing the Israeli army and their government to account. It went without saying that both sides had suffered tragically. The Palestinians were the victims of the victims. But the casual shooting of civilians, the brutalising apartheid that was being practised on the Palestinians now could never be the answer. It could never be in the interests of either side.

Since I was a small child in Mauritius I had known what it felt like to be on the outside. My whole life and my career in education had been bound up with the effort to include those who exist on the margins, looking in. I knew that I mustn't allow my belief in my own integrity to be shattered by this disturbed and paranoiac woman. But I was also aware that inwardly I was balanced on a knife edge, and after a while I did call the police. They took the matter seriously and eventually traced the calls to two phone boxes in Belsize Park, though they were unable to identify the caller. It was shocking, somehow, to know that she was only down the road.

What a contrast these calls were to the understanding letters we received from thoughtful Jewish people who were clearly tormented by what was happening in Israel. As the parents of one of Tom's friends wrote to us: 'As you know we are Jewish and although not religious we have always been proud of our heritage. It is this which makes it so difficult for us to express ourselves to you. We share your view that the manner in which this whole matter has been treated by the Israeli authorities is reprehensible. It may be the Israeli way but it is most definitely so un-Jewish. The central tenet of Judaism is the concept of justice and that it must not only be done but be seen to be done. The barbarity of the last few years shows how far these standards have been eroded.'

It was just one of the many hundreds of letters we received at this time from all over the UK. They came from friends, and from well-wishers we'd never met, from people who had known Tom – teachers, fellow peace workers, the staff of the Jessops camera shop in Manchester where he had worked while studying – and from people of all nationalities who had simply read about him in the papers. These, and the love with which our friends surrounded us, helped us carry on. But inwardly I could feel only bleak despair. As another of our friends wrote: 'What a world we live in that this should have happened to such a brave, beautiful and principled young man.'

FOURTEEN

For some time now we'd known that Tom had left his big main rucksack in Amman, where he and Nathan and Michelle had stayed in a small hotel together before entering Israel. They gave us the hotel's name, and at some point Anthony had phoned its owner, Mr Al-Kayyali, who had assured him that the rucksack was there and that he would keep it safely in his attic until we could arrange for it to be collected.

Michelle told us that Tom and Mr Al-Kayyali had played a lot of chess together, and later Mr Al-Kayyali gave his impressions of Tom to a journalist from the *Camden New Journal*, who happened to be in Amman. 'He was, what can I say, a pure man, only thinking of others,' he said. 'He was shooted after saving one little child, he went back to help another one. He wanted to help the Palestinian refugees in Jordan and worked for the Red Crescent in the camps. So pure, so good!' Knowing the mischief that always surrounded Tom, and remembering how blue the air could be on occasion with his anecdotes at the supper table, I wasn't so certain about that last sentence. But Mr Al-Kayyali went on to say, 'You felt he knew the value of human life', and I certainly agreed.

From time to time the thought of the uncollected rucksack pushed its way to the front of my consciousness. In the event Mr Al-Kayyali solved the problem for us. In early July a photographer called Michael Burke phoned. 'I have your son's rucksack,' he said. 'The proprietor of the Al-Saraya Hotel in Amman asked me to bring it over to the UK for you. I'm so very sorry about what happened. Could I bring it round?'

We sat in the kitchen with Tom's big black rucksack on the floor between us. It became difficult to breathe. I could hardly bear to look at it. The last time I'd seen it it had been standing in Tom's room, ready and packed on the evening before he left for Baghdad. Now it was returning home with someone else. I felt betrayed. It should have been Tom sitting there on the sofa, telling me about Amman and the Al-Saraya Hotel, and the journalists who apparently hung out there on their way to and from Baghdad. 'Mr Al-Kayyali was very cautious about giving me the rucksack,' Michael Burke said. 'He wanted to be certain I would deliver it to you in person.'

When he'd gone I sat looking at the rucksack. I thought of all the places it had been with Tom, all the roads he'd walked along; all the bridges he'd crossed. He'd flown with it, taken it on trains, carried it through customs. I could see his tall rangy figure, slightly bent forward by its weight, smiling and holding up his hand to wave as he disappeared into the crowd. Tom had carried that rucksack everywhere; it was part of him. Now it seemed to me like an old friend that had let him down, and I wanted to grasp hold of it and say, 'What the *hell* were you doing? Tom always looked after you. Why didn't you look after him?' I felt angry with the ISM, too. What was this policy that had allowed Tom to confront bulldozers and tanks so soon after he arrived, thirsty and tired, from Jerusalem. *And why were you in such a hurry, Tom?* At that moment all my pent-up anguish came to the surface, and I could feel only fury at what Tom had put us all through.

I put the rucksack on the sofa and very slowly started to unzip the pockets. More unused little writer's notepads; pens. In one pocket was a photocopy of his passport, a list of emergency addresses of embassies, maps, cards of journalists and other people he'd met, details of places to eat and stay copied from the Lonely Planet guide. Every eventuality covered.

In another was a list of the human shields who were going to Baghdad, with James Miller's name on it, and an information sheet. It contained instructions on vaccinations and what to take:

money, clothes ('the Iraqis tend to dress well and would appreciate if we did also'), water purification tablets, a penknife . . . It was
the kind of list anyone going on an expedition might receive. But
this wasn't just an expedition:

> We have all decided, individually and for our various reasons, that
> this human shield action is an appropriate response from respon-
> sible human beings to the irresponsible threats of aggressive
> governments.
>
> There are significant risks for all of us taking part, and you
> should carefully consider the potential consequences before com-
> mitting yourself to this action. But if you're like many of us, you
> recognize a greater danger lies in our acquiescence in the face of
> injustice. And the more who recognize the absolute danger of
> doing nothing, the more will act toward making this world one
> they are proud to have made.

Tom, I now knew, *had* considered the potential consequences,
been prepared.

I unzipped the main compartment. In it were clothes – a single
sweater, T-shirts, some boxers, a few of pairs of baggy cotton
trousers. I knew that Tom sometimes concealed his notebooks
and pens by wearing a pair of short trousers with big pockets
underneath another pair. I remembered Nathan telling me how
he had patted him down to test the system out. Tom may have
been idealistic but when it came to dealing with hostile officials he
was also savvy. And he'd always been an economical packer. Kay
told me he'd been through her rucksack when they were preparing to go to Egypt and reduced the contents by about two-
thirds. 'It was partly because he knew he'd have to carry it for me,'
she said, laughing. 'But also he just knew I wouldn't need it all.'

So this, and the little canvas bag that he'd had with him in
Rafah, contained all he had taken to last him two to three months.
Automatically I started taking out the clothes, looking at them to
see if they needed washing. Wrapped in a T-shirt at the bottom

was something hard. Two more reporter's notebooks. I opened one, and there in front of me was Tom's careful writing: *'21st February 2003. It wasn't what you would expect as we came in to land. Thick cloud sent the intermittent flashes from the wing thudding back up the fuselage . . . Amman, Jordan . . .'*

With a lurch of the heart I realised that here were the missing pieces of the jigsaw: Tom's diaries covering the first part of his journey from the moment of his arrival in Amman with the human shields. . . .

Also at the bottom of the rucksack, written on a piece of lined paper and wrapped around a CD, was a note dated 22 February addressed to me – his final communication to me, now one of my most precious possessions. In it Tom asked me to forward the CD, containing a piece he'd written on the human shields, to the editor of *Pulp*, the Manchester Metropolitan University student magazine. He went on: *'. . . just so you know, I'm still in Amman and it's Saturday night. We're leaving on Monday morning and should be there in the evening and we have accommodation already set up. Everything is going great & the people all know exactly what they're doing. See you soon, love Tom.'*

'Everything is going great.' I sat for a very long time, not reading, just thinking about him, gazing from time to time at the notebooks. Such modest looking notebooks, yet the even writing on their pages held Tom's thoughts, a part of his mind. They seemed almost too precious to open. I remembered how I used to say to him, before he travelled anywhere, 'Tom, are you organised, do you know what you're doing at the other end?' Finally I phoned Anthony. 'Do you know what I've just found?' I said.

On a beautiful evening in early July we gathered in St Marylebone Parish Church for the Concert for Tom. It was one of those early summer evenings one dreams of – warm, serene, still. Late sunshine flooded in through the high windows, gilding the wood of the pews and falling in golden pools on the floor.

Anthony, Sophie and I sat in the upstairs balcony, watching people arrive. ('Please don't sit at the front. If we see you it will

make us cry,' my friends from the choir had said.) That was a
relief. Both Anthony and I feared that this concert might undo us.
Fred sat below with Tom's friends. Looking down, it seemed as if
the stream of arrivals would never end. Soon the church was
packed, with people filling the balcony, too – there must have
been at least five hundred. Many I recognised, but very many I did
not. I so wished Billy could have been there, but he was still in the
West Bank. We'd heard very little from him, though self-
addressed packages had been arriving from time to time. As he'd
promised, TFH had been 'keeping an eye' on him, and the
founder of the ISM had been in touch. But I was still worried stiff.

So much love and thought had gone into the preparation of this
concert. Ann and Guy, the members of the choir with which I had
sung for so many years, and Tom's close friends had all contributed.
As we sat waiting, the sound of Van Morrison's 'Brown-Eyed Girl'
wound its way round the church and up into the vaulting. Then
Sting's voice singing 'Shape of My Heart' and 'Fields of Gold', and
Sinatra's, and the Eagles'. Adam and Sam and Alex had put together
this selection of tracks Tom loved. It was the vibrant music that had
filled our house, so difficult to hear now.

Then the English Chamber Choir filed in, all my friends who
had surrounded me with such affection and support, and the
concert proper began with Bach's beautiful setting of Psalm 117,
Praise the Lord.

It's hard for me to convey the quality of that evening. Music
speaks with its own voice, touching us in a way that is beyond
words, and that is why I had been fearful. It was the first time since
the tragedy that I'd truly opened myself to it, and I wasn't sure I
could bear it. Yet for me the whole experience turned out to be
one of consolation, of being enveloped by love.

All Tom's friends were there, and many of them took part – an
astonishing array of talent led by Sam and Adam, both now doing
degrees in music at Leeds. It made me smile just to think of El
Loco, their band. Tom had been an occasional manager and
roadie of El Loco.

Tom's long-time friend Simone, a violinist, gave an exquisite performance of Massenet's 'Meditation' from *Thaïs*. Laura, a member of the choir, sang 'On My Own' from *Les Misérables*. That was a must. Tom had loved *Les Mis* and had seen it several times. Then there was 'Era' by the French composer Eric Lévi. In 1995 the choir had recorded it at Abbey Road Studios under Guy's direction, and Tom had played it often, really loud.

And none of us will surely ever forget Sam on trumpet, accompanied by the renowned jazzman Eddie Harvey, playing Gershwin's 'Summertime'. It wasn't just a piece Tom had loved. As Sam played it, it was a lament for a lost friend, a cry of grief and loss and longing for times past that left us all stunned and tearful, and then – despite the request in the programme not to clap – spontaneously applauding. Nor shall I ever forget the sound of Adam's beautiful, steady voice as he sang, with such tenderness, the Eagles' 'Hotel California', with Sam accompanying on piano. As requested, we all joined in: *'Voices calling from far away . . . Some dance to remember, some dance to forget . . . You can check out any time you like, but you can never leave.'*

There was music from the Russian Orthodox tradition: Rachmaninov, Tchaikovsky; John Tavener's exquisite *Song for Athene*, written in memory of a young Greek girl killed in a road accident in London. I was completely absorbed, uplifted, and I know Anthony was too. It was strange, but I wondered what Tom would have made of it all.

And how fitting it seemed when Rageh Omaar – so familiar from his reporting of the Iraq war for the BBC – rose to read from Tom's journals. Truthful, passionate, angry, these were dispatches from a war zone. It was as if Tom was speaking to us directly, telling us about that last journey of his, from the moment he arrived in Amman with the other human shields, through the sandstorms and hardships of the refugee camp in Jordan, to his final days in Rafah, his first encounters with the monstrous bulldozers of the IDF, and the attacks on Dr Samir's house.

Rageh read clearly, with enormous feeling, and I wondered what his thoughts were. Tom, I sensed, would have greatly respected Rageh's journalistic savvy and the breadth of his experience as a foreign correspondent.

Later, Rageh wrote a moving piece about the Concert for Tom in the *Guardian*. It was called 'Company of a Stranger', and in it he described how he had several times visited the block of flats in Baghdad where Tom was staying, to interview the human shields – 'I may even have passed Tom on one of these occasions. Who knows?' Of the concert he wrote: 'It was both intimate and moving to hear the songs that made Tom Hurndall happy and, for me, a reminder that we sometimes don't realise the connections we have with people whom we think we do not know.'

That evening was full of connections, interweaving many different strands of Tom's life, like some beautiful fabric wrapped round us to warm and comfort us. His friend Antonia read from his e-mails, with their wry, affectionate, often playful messages to his friends softening the horrifying descriptions of what he was seeing: '*Hi! Another update. I'm now in Rafah, a few hundred metres from the Egyptian border. Within a couple of hours from our ride getting in, I had been shot at, shelled, tear-gassed, hit by falling brick/plaster, "sound" bombed, almost run over by the moving house called a D10 bulldozer, chased by soldiers and a lot else besides . . . on the downside: I didn't get a good night's sleep because I kept getting woken by the machine-gun fire that echoes around the area at night . . .*'

And Peter Best, a friend from the choir, eloquently read Tom's poem 'All the way along this line', in which Tom wrote of struggling to gain 'some semblance of control' over his own life:

> '*To find this focal point I must find a clear path*
> *Not only patches or clearings in the forest . . .*
> *Growing in maturity is facing what must be done,*
> *Not just responsibilities, as I am starting new*
> *And choosing my cards, not running from them.*'

At the end of that evening it was hard to express what I felt. I tried to thank everyone, but the speech I made seems terribly inadequate to me now.

Afterwards we all wandered over into Regent's Park which, through a contact of one of the choir members, had been kept open especially late for us, and sat on the grass in the balmy evening, eating the picnics we had brought. Surrounded by the quiet talk of friends, and of the many hitherto unknown people who came over to speak to us about Tom, I felt comforted and at peace. The horrors of the past two months receded briefly. As I sat watching the sun sink in a ball of fire behind the Nash terraces, somebody put a hand on my shoulder. It was the very special nurse who had given me such support during our visits to the Royal Free. 'When I heard about the concert, I had to come,' she said. 'I shall never forget Tom.'

One morning a few days after the concert I woke early, as usual, but feeling there was something different about the house. When I went downstairs there was no sign that anything had changed: the hall was empty; in the kitchen everything was as before. I was out in the garden at about ten o'clock when I turned suddenly at an unexpected sound and saw a tall figure at the garden door. It was Billy. *Billy was back*. 'Hello, Mum,' he said simply, smiling his sweet smile. I ran towards him and hugged him and hugged him, weeping, barely coherent with relief. I had been worried out of my mind about him, though I understood that we all had our own ways of trying to come to terms with what had happened. 'Don't you *ever* do that again,' was all I could say, over and over. I was hugging him for about the tenth time when Fred came up behind us, grinning from ear to ear, and snatched a photograph.

Oh! The relief at having Billy safe home again. He'd arrived back at Heathrow late the previous evening and had gone straight to the hospital, carrying his backpack and the rest of his luggage, to see Tom. That was Billy. No fuss, straight to the point. But I was immediately struck by the change in him. He had become far more outgoing and demonstrative, more self-confident and, as we were soon to discover, extremely well informed. As we all sat round the kitchen table later that day I could see that he was wanting to spare me some of the details of what he'd seen. With his new video equipment he'd been filming soldiers at the West Bank checkpoints. All he would say was that a lot of the footage was 'pretty distressing'.

He didn't have to tell me. I'd already read reports from the Israeli human rights organisation B'Tselem, so I knew a lot of it, and it made me incandescent − Palestinian women in labour prevented from getting to hospital, forced to give birth at checkpoints, sometimes losing their babies as a result; men and women kept waiting for hours in the hot sun for no good reason, unable to get to work; young children taunted and then fired at if they retaliated by throwing stones; university students subjected to verbal abuse on their way to university; the tyres of cars fired at if their drivers happened to lose patience after waiting hours and speak impolitely to the checkpoint soldiers.

Billy had shot many hours of film, which he'd sent on ahead of him − those were the regular packages that had kept arriving.

'Weren't the Israeli security suspicious that you had a video camera and no film?' Sophie asked.

'Oh, I had film on me,' said Billy. 'I'll show you a bit.' And he did. It couldn't have been more innocuous. It showed an adorable kitten, which Billy had filmed somewhere near Nablus.

'I think they may have been a bit surprised, but what could they do?' he said, grinning wickedly.

With all the relaxation of hindsight I thought that I needn't have worried. Billy would have taken care of himself, so organised, practical, always thinking ahead. I remembered him, as a thirteen-year-old, spending six summer-holiday weeks tiling the downstairs loo. He was absolutely determined to get it right, and he made a perfect job of it. With no training whatever he'd designed and built elegant fitted cupboards in the house when we moved. Billy's the person anyone who needs something doing always comes to. He's always been a problem-solver, brilliant at science at school. I hoped he was eventually going to follow that clever scientific brain of his. But at the moment we were all just getting by as best we could.

Having Billy back, with his understated humour, his dependability and thoughtfulness, it felt as if the sun had suddenly come out. I could see that he was especially aware of the need to be there for Fred. They'd had brushes in the past, when Fred had borrowed Billy's tools and hadn't returned them, for instance, but now Billy was adopting a more protective, fatherly role, and we felt concerned that it was a responsibility he didn't need at this point.

Yet I could tell from the way he spoke that beneath his apparently equable exterior Billy was extremely angry. Tom's shooting had politicised him, awoken him to the reality of what was happening in Israel. This, I thought, was the effect that such a family tragedy, such an injustice, could have on a young man – but how much more so if that young man was a Palestinian seeing his home destroyed, members of his family humiliated and shot. This was the way to breed enemies.

FIFTEEN

The long hot days of August came, and with them utter, blind exhaustion. We had been home for nearly three months now. I felt finished, played out, as if I was dragging myself along an interminable, dark tunnel without end. I had a sense that the family was fragmenting, each of us locked into our own particular nightmare, but I felt powerless to gather us together. As Cardinal Basil Hume so beautifully put it, 'Grief cannot be shared because it is mine alone'. We had always talked, and we still did, but now there were boundaries, no-go areas, things none of us could really bear to discuss. One of these was what we were going to do about Tom.

I couldn't concentrate on anything unless it was to do with Tom. Everything distressed me, as if I were missing several skins. When the end of term came I wondered whether I would be able to return in the autumn.

Anthony's completed report had now been delivered to the Foreign and Commonwealth Office, and Jack Straw had undertaken to forward it to the Judge Advocate General in Israel via the Embassy in Tel Aviv. Since this was a military matter, would it be TFH who delivered it? The thought was somehow comforting. So, in an exhausted and rather fatalistic frame of mind, we waited to see what would happen. Our hopes weren't high.

As part of our legal campaign to get justice for Tom, we, together with our lawyers, made a bid that summer to have the then Israeli Minister of Defence General Shaul Mofaz arrested under the provisions of the Geneva Convention when he visited London for a meeting with Tony Blair.

Our legal affairs in the UK were now being dealt with by Imran Khan, an eminent London solicitor well known for his human rights work on such high-profile cases as that of Stephen Lawrence. I took to Imran greatly. He was dark, slight, elegant and very quick, and had a concentrated depth to everything he did. To apply for an arrest warrant, however, we needed a barrister, and so, on a boiling summer day, we found ourselves in Furnival Chambers off Chancery Lane talking to the distinguished QC Michel Massih, who had pioneered the concept of prosecuting Israeli war criminals and had handled some of the most high-profile cases in the UK. His work in this field had established that under the Geneva Conventions Act, the UK had a positive duty to prosecute those suspected of committing grave breaches of the Geneva convention. We believed we had a good case.

Michel was a complete contrast to Imran. Silvery-haired, bewhiskered, larger than life and resplendent in a wonderfully flamboyant bow tie, he was theatrical, often outrageous – Imran told us he frequently had the courtroom in fits – but cut straight to the point. I later learned that he was part of the able and enlightened Palestinian community in London we were just beginning to meet through Afif and Christ'l, and, like Afif and Edward Said, had been educated at the Ecole des Frères in Jerusalem. He and Imran, and Michael Mansfield, who would later represent us, did a great deal of human rights work for which they took no payment – something for which we shall be eternally grateful to them.

Next day Anthony, Sophie and I sat in the stifling courtroom in Bow Street to see Michel make an application for a warrant to arrest Mofaz. Behind us sat a row of dark-suited men who were clearly from the Israeli Embassy.

The legal argument, which was not in effect rejected by the District Judge, was that there was evidence that Israel had a policy of targeted assassinations and that the Army committed several breaches of the Geneva Conventions with impunity. The defence team had presented the court with a well documented dossier detailing the various breaches of the Conventions and which supported our case that the murder of Tom formed part of a pattern of behaviour by the Israeli army.

The Judge took time to consider the issue overnight. Next day he dismissed the case not on the basis of insufficient evidence linking Tom's murder to Mofaz, but on the technically narrow point of 'immunity of a minister of state'.

But our action did create ripples, as did our attempt to arrest another member of the Israeli Government when he visited London – the Prime Minster Ariel Sharon. Those both inside and outside the Palestinian community who, like us, were filled with indignation at the brutality of IDF operations, were appreciative of what we and this powerful legal team had done.

That August I read voraciously on the Middle East. The news from Gaza was appalling – a four-year-old Palestinian boy shot dead and two other small children injured by the army; another eight-year-old shot twice in the head as she walked down the street with her mother in the Khan Younis refugee camp to buy a packet of crisps; a twelve-year-old girl shot in the head by random IDF fire while sitting at her school desk . . . It was the slaughter of the innocents. The heartbreaking list went on and on. The Palestinian Centre for Human Rights reported that at least 408 children had been killed by the Israeli army since September 2000, mostly in the Gaza Strip, in Khan Younis and Rafah. And the IDF command didn't even feel it needed to justify or explain. The excuse trotted out repeatedly was that the children had been 'caught in crossfire'. We knew what that meant. As one journalist commented: 'The Israeli army's instinctive response is to muddy the waters when confronted with a controversial killing.'

I thought of Rafah and couldn't get the women's faces out of my mind. We too had suffered loss, but all through our time in the Middle East we had known we could leave. We had something better to go back to – a decent home, the possibility of work, the support of friends, properly equipped hospitals. Yet these women who had seen their children injured and murdered were trapped in intolerable conditions in the open-air prison the Israeli occupation had created. Even if children survived, the crippled Palestinian health service was no longer equipped to treat them. Physicians for Human Rights, a group of Israeli medical volunteers who went regularly into the Occupied Territories to bring medicines and give medical aid, reported that many Palestinians could now only get the care they needed at Israeli hospitals, but needed special permits to go to them and were often refused when they arrived.

I was terribly anxious too about Amjad and Mohammed and Sahir and the ISMers still hanging on in Rafah, despite the vicious attempts in Israel to smear the organisation's name and push them out. Billy had received an e-mail from Amjad in his fragmented English.

> hi billy
>
> how are you, i hope you are okey, also my freind here say hi, hi from injured Palestine to our friend in London. Please don't forget we all time thinking about people who's suffering also as us, all my friend and family know about Tom.
>
> I know you can do more than us, you can write, you can speak. About us, the condation is very hard, they are killing us every day, they never don't.
>
> My love to your family.

It was signed simply 'sad'.

Yes, we could write and speak. The media were still following Tom's case closely, Anthony was regularly quoted in the press and I gave interviews to the *Evening Standard* and BBC *Woman's Hour*, trying to draw attention to the atrocities in any way I could, while making clear my empathy for the Israeli victims of suicide bombers. But by the early weeks of August I felt I could barely carry on. I was on automatic pilot, struggling through the days. Coping but not coping. The only moments of respite I seemed able to find were at the old thatched cottage on the Essex/Suffolk border which Anthony had inherited from his mother, Gwen. Except for a brief time when Anthony and I had first separated, she and I had been close, kindred spirits, and it was soothing to be there among the things she had loved, walking round her garden with the Harwich Estuary glinting in the distance, trying to recall the hundreds of conversations we'd had, wondering what she would have been saying to me now.

I remembered so clearly sitting with her in that garden when Tom was a little boy, talking with some exasperation about his need to explore and challenge and always be on the move, his naughtiness which I found so wearing – the 'come and get me' look on his face when I called him, his insistence on climbing higher up a tree than I wanted him to go. Gwen heard me out sympathetically, and then she said, with absolute conviction: 'Don't worry. Tom's going to do something special with his life you know. You'll see, Jocey.'

Now I would arrive in the evening, and for an hour or two the quiet of this isolated countryside would soothe me – until I went to bed and the haunting would begin again: images of the Soroka Hospital, of those desperate pockmarked streets in Rafah, of Amjad and Sahir, covered in blood, struggling under the weight of Tom's body – I had reached that dangerous stage of emotional fatigue where I had lost the ability to sleep. Even at the cottage I was always half-awake, on the alert for a call to say that something had happened to Tom. I felt guilty for every moment I wasn't with him to interpret his needs, to protect him as I hadn't been able to do then.

Close friends, full of concern, suggested that a holiday might help. Their apartment in the Pas de Calais was free. Why not go there for a couple of weeks? But now we were confronted with the need to find another place for Tom. The Royal Free had made it clear from the start that he could stay there only temporarily – we had always understood that it was an acute hospital with no long-term beds. It was clear that bringing him home would be impossible, and, though we had been looking, we hadn't so far found a feasible nursing home. Since we had no idea how long Tom might survive, it was hard to know what we were looking for.

At last we were offered a bed by the Royal Hospital for Neurodisability in Putney. It had once been called the Royal Hospital for Incurables. I imagined what it must have been like to be a patient entering a place with such a name. At least sensibilities had moved on to that extent, I thought. It was a great deal further away than the Royal Free, but when we visited I was impressed by the dignified old building with its large, light, airy rooms and by the fact that this was a specialist hospital where everything possible would be done for Tom.

Yet the thought of seeing him moved once again was more than I could bear. My eye, my mind, my heart had been on Tom every moment of that fearful journey from Israel, and I felt less able to cope now than I had done then. And there was something so final about this move. Rationally I knew it was the right thing to do, but in my heart I felt we were abandoning him to this faraway place and I couldn't bear the thought of it. I was torn between the longing to shut myself away somewhere where there were no demands, and guilt at the thought of leaving. Anthony and I talked about it and we decided I should go to France. So, during the second week of August, Fred and I set off in the car, and on one of the hottest days of the year Anthony travelled in an ambulance to Putney with Tom.

The apartment was large and cool and very French: high ceilings and pale grey paint; terracotta tiles on the entrance hall floor, a big double front door with a knocker in the shape of a hand, a bay window looking out to sea. In the quiet you could hear the sea licking the shoreline. Half-buried in the sand of the dunes below were the concrete remains of old Second World War sea defences, all broken up now, with bits of rusted metal sticking crazily up. They reminded me of Gaza. Everything reminded me of Gaza.

We had been coming to this apartment almost every year since Sophie was six. As time went on we'd arrive in a car laden with bikes – or skateboards, or rollerblades, whatever was the sports fad that year. There was always the bliss of familiarity, the magic of that first morning when we would wake, relaxed in the unaccustomed quiet, and the children would run barefoot straight out on to the beach, or up the village street in search of their friends. The same group of them, mostly French but with a few English children thrown in, was always here in August. There would be days of blackberry picking, and pancake parties at different houses, and lying in the swing seat at the back, reading, or simply dreaming, gazing up at the sky. So safe. That seemed another world now. A golden age.

Before long Fred's French friends, Guillaume, Clement, Eugénie, were knocking at the door. They knew what had happened to Tom – one of them had even done a project about the shooting at school. The tragedy had been talked about in France. But they were too young to understand why Freddy didn't feel like coming out with them, didn't want to go and play football, run among the sand dunes, or climb about on the old concrete sea defences as they had always done. He preferred to stay quietly indoors. They called every day – 'Où est Freddy?' – and hung about outside in a warm and friendly way, never giving up.

I spent much of the time swimming in the cool water or walking barefoot along the beach to Cap Gris Nez. At least my senses had time to regenerate a little, but I was utterly without energy, still, I see now, in a state of shock. All I could do was worry – that Tom might be in pain and no one at the new hospital would be able to read the signals, that no one would notice if he had cold hands or feet, or if he was too hot and needed a fan. I fretted that there would be no one there to explain things to them, as I would have done. Anthony assured me that he was in excellent hands. But in the end I was desperate to get back.

I found him lying in a spacious, airy room, with light streaming

in through two vast Georgian windows. Immediately I came
through the door I could see that something was terribly wrong.
One side of Tom's body was moving and jerking convulsively in a
way I had never seen before. I went quickly over to him and took
his hand. It was burning. I felt his forehead; that was burning too.
His face was contorted as if he was in agony. He must have a
severe infection. Was that the reason for these dreadful convul-
sions which gripped his body and shook it, over and over,
ceaselessly, exhaustingly? There seemed to be no one I could
ask. Down the corridor I could hear the medicine trolley doing its
slow rounds. Eventually I managed to find a nurse.

In my fear and anguish, my words came tumbling out. 'Look at
him,' I pleaded. 'How long has he been like this? You can't just
leave him in this terrible state. You must give him something. I
know he's in pain. You've got to do something.'

She seemed taken aback. 'Please wait,' she said. She went away,
and I sat holding Tom's burning hand, stroking his forehead,
talking to him quietly, soothingly, as one does to a sick child –
*Tom, my darling, my darling, it's Mum. I'm here. Don't worry. I'm here
now, Tom, and I'm going to see you're all right. Mum's here, darling.* I'd
no idea if he could even hear my voice, but I wanted him to feel
my presence, perhaps sense the familiar tone.

After an age the nurse returned with the duty doctor. 'Can you
please give him something,' I said. 'I know my son, and I can see
he's suffering.'

The doctor looked at me searchingly. I had not then understood what a delicate ethical issue the giving of pain relief to
terminally ill patients is. It was carefully explained to us later that
once a patient has been given morphine, the body acclimatises to
the drug and needs larger and larger doses for it to be effective.
This in turn raises issues about the ending of life. But all I could
think of now was helping Tom, and I knew, absolutely knew,
that he was suffering.

'I think it's probable that he has no sense . . .' the doctor began.
I couldn't bear it. 'I don't care,' I said. 'If there's the slightest

possibility he's in pain I think it's inhuman not to give him something.'

So Tom was given an injection, and gradually his face relaxed and the awful jerking subsided. It was a difficult beginning, nobody's fault, and was not typical of our relationship with the hospital staff, whom I soon came greatly to like and respect. With hindsight I can see that they had not yet had time to get to know Tom, just as we had not had time to get to know them. But driving back across London that night, through the crowds drinking on the pavements in the West End and the late-night theatre traffic, I wanted never to go away and leave him again.

Meanwhile, Danny and Erella had arrived for a visit. Erella and I had been phoning and e-mailing, and despite her positive approach to life I was always conscious of the unspoken message that underlay so much of what she said and wrote: 'I want to get out of here. But where can I go?' A number of people I'd met in Israel had said the same. So we had invited them to come and stay at the cottage, and I went on ahead to prepare before Anthony drove them down.

It was a thrill to see them arrive as the car swept through the gates and round the circular drive, but I found Erella, normally so bursting with warmth, in a bad way. She and Danny had been detained at Ben Gurion airport for four hours while Erella had been put through what amounted to an interrogation. Their luggage had been searched with a toothcomb, then 'lost', and she couldn't see properly without her disposable contact lenses. She was still smarting from the insult to her dignity.

'They even went through my hair,' she said, raising her hand to her long grey hair which she wore up in a bun. 'It was disgusting.'

This came on top of an aggressive security interview two weeks before they left.

'They kept on asking me why I wanted to support people who were not Jewish. "It is interesting that in your case only Palestinians need support," one of them said. They kept trying to push me into saying I was against the Jewish people.'

'And what did you say?'

'Well, this young man went round and round in circles, trying to force me to incriminate myself, until eventually I lost patience, and I said very loudly: "Now listen to me. You have hurt me very much. I am a Jewish person. This is my country, but I am everybody's friend, whatever their nationality. I am a bereavement counsellor, and if I see young people in need I support them, wherever they come from." Then I looked straight at him and said: "If you continue like this, I shall leave the room." '

When Erella throws down the gauntlet it is impressive.

'And what did he do?'

'Well, then he did stop,' said Erella. 'But at the airport they still went through everything. It was humiliating. What must it be doing to these young people that they are being taught to treat their own citizens in this way? It's sick, it's paranoiac. They are damaging themselves as much as they are damaging us.'

After a few days Erella began to recover as the peace of the cottage and walks in the countryside did their work. She and Danny both fell in love with the light, the wide skies and the broad, open fields of East Anglia. It was their kind of place. It was very hot, and we all sat in the shade and talked, or made lazy excursions to Constable country, to Flatford Mill and the little villages around, where we ate cream teas or drank long glasses of beer in pub gardens. I thought of the kibbutz and the way Erella had saved my sanity, and I was so grateful to be able to give her some kind of respite in return. It was a brief and lovely interlude, a break for both of us from the other fearful things that crowded in. But we knew it was merely an interlude. After they left I found a card from Erella and Danny. It said, 'You have a piece of Heaven'.

It was much more difficult now for Tom's close friends to see him – the journey across London took an hour and a half by car, and longer by train and bus. But there were other people who made contact that summer. Ned, who had been at the Hall School in Hampstead with Tom, phoned me asking if he could come round. At thirteen he and Tom had gone on to different schools and their ways had divided, but being friends so young had left a bond. Ned had just come down from Oxford. Now he sat on the floor in the sitting–room, clearly aghast. He had asked to see Tom's journals and he was both moved and appalled by what he was reading. From time to time he would stop and run his hand through his hair, gazing out of the window, as if seeing the scenes Tom was describing. He stayed all day, and over lunch he questioned me about Tom's motives for going, the conversations we had had before he left. Clearly the journals caused him to think very deeply, not only about the situation in Gaza but about the Tom he had known and the altogether more complicated person the journals revealed. 'I do wish I'd seen more of Tom,' he said as he left.

A friend of Tom's from his house at Winchester phoned to ask if he and two others could come and visit Tom in Putney. I met them in the reception area, three exquisitely mannered, attentive young men in suits and ties. I couldn't help thinking of Tom's London friends, 'the boys' I was so fond of, with their closeness and streetwise humour. Tom had such a wide variety of friends. I remembered these young men, and we sat and talked for a moment about what they were doing now. One of them had gone into the City, the others were just finishing at university. It moved me greatly to see them again and I could see Tom in each of them.

After a while I led them down the hall and through the big room where groups of people with varying degrees of disability were watching television, some making unintelligible noises as they watched. For anyone not used to spending time with severely disabled people the sight was disconcerting, but the boys were open, sensitive, empathetic. When we reached Tom's door the three of them hesitated, as if not wanting to intrude.

Tom was sitting upright, supported in a wheelchair. I knew this was almost more disturbing than seeing him lying down. One day, quite early on, I'd walked through Tom's door and very nearly collapsed. He was sitting on a special bed wearing a T-shirt and tracksuit bottoms, supported by two physiotherapists, his unseeing eyes gazing straight ahead. For some time I had not seen Tom sitting up, and the shock of it had been intense. The physiotherapists explained that it was better for his lungs if he sat upright. They were also testing to see if he had any residual sense of balance – I can't really imagine why. I sat there wincing as they gently moved him this way and that, looking for any sign of coordination or response.

The physiotherapists were sensitive and caring, but I sensed his distress, and it was as much as I could do not to rush at them crying 'Don't, oh please don't.' It was such a relief to me when he was back in bed. After witnessing a number of assessments and physiotherapy sessions I asked if he needed to be put through any more. I knew that the hospital was simply doing its best to understand Tom's condition, which was essential to making further decisions, but there seemed so little point in putting him through physiotherapy when he had so much to bear already, and when there was no hope.

Now I beckoned the boys to come in, and they stood round him. They didn't feel they had to say anything, but their shock and sadness were plain. One of them touched him gently. These were young men who had known Tom when he was active, funny, challenging, full of life. They'd played football together, sat in class together, enjoyed loud music. Now they looked down at the wreck of the person he had once been, and I could see they were remembering. Each of them had known him well. They were a part of him, and he was a part of them. The relationship was clearly still there. And yet Tom wasn't. I was moved by their visit and filled with an agonising sense of loss – Tom's loss, the loss of possibility.

Late that summer, too, we met Rachel Corrie's parents for the first time. We had dinner together in a homely Italian restaurant off Sloane Square, and it was an emotional meeting. As Sophie said afterwards: 'They're the only people I know who really understand. Losing a member of your family in a freak accident is one thing, but it's another to have someone you love deliberately murdered by a soldier who's quite certain he's going to get away with it.'

Cindy and Craig Corrie were on their way back from a memorial ceremony for Rachel in Rafah, near the spot where she had died. They had stayed in Dr Samir's house – the house where Tom had slept and which Rachel had died protecting – and they described how they had all been sitting quietly having a meal when the IDF drove a bulldozer straight at the house. It was a piece of outright intimidation. 'They knew we were there,' said Craig, 'and they went on doing it until I phoned the US Embassy. The noise was unimaginable. And these poor guys in Rafah have to go through this all the time.'

As to the IDF 'report' into Rachel's death which had entirely exonerated the army, Craig said in his measured way but in a voice unsteady with anger: 'They said the doctor who did the autopsy said that her death was probably caused by tripping on debris or perhaps by being covered by debris. Well, that statement is not in the autopsy. They must have gone back to get that statement, and of course I would like to ask the doctor how many times he's seen somebody with I've forgotten how many broken ribs, breaks in her spinal column and crushed shoulder blades and cut lungs just from tripping.' The Corries had been told the report was secret, only to discover that the Israeli government was covertly distributing it among members of the US Congress to prevent an independent investigation.

I found Cindy and Craig deeply sympathetic. We shared so much – the loss of our children, shock at our unexpected treatment by the Israeli government and by the governments of our own countries, a determination to bring this tragic cause to the attention of people in the West. Above all, we wanted to do something tangible for the people of Rafah, and especially the children. The Corries told us of a Youth and Cultural Centre in Rafah, providing health care and activities for the children in the refugee camps, which was to be named after Rachel. We talked of our hopes of setting up a learning support project for disabled children as a memorial to Tom.

They shocked us with descriptions of the persecution they had suffered in the US following Rachel's death – the personal attacks, the anonymous letters and phone calls, the smearing of Rachel's name by the media and on pro-Israeli websites, the vicious attempts to discredit the work of the ISM. By comparison we felt we had been lucky. For us, the British media had been a channel of communication and by and large had treated us with consideration and compassion. And, whatever our feelings about the official government line, we knew that a substantial body of MPs was behind us. Even the obscene phone caller had been silenced after I'd managed to break into the stream of abuse to say: 'When you give me your name we can have a mature discussion. But I don't talk to people who aren't prepared to give me their name.' After that the calls had stopped.

Later that week we took the Corries to see Tom. I remember the loving atmosphere they created, the gentle way Cindy bent to touch Tom's shoulder, the care and attention with which they looked at the photographs ranged round the room. Cindy had brought a photograph of Rachel, which we put beside Tom's bed. She told me: 'When Tom was shot I just felt like Rachel had been killed all over again.'

I was gradually getting to know the staff at the Royal Hospital and the hospital routines. Three or four days each week I drove there, knowing that I would come back home in the evening utterly depleted. Being there tore my soul, yet it was where I wanted to be. I slept fitfully, waking every few hours, lying waiting for the daylight when I knew I could get into the car and go to Tom. I felt his need calling to me, his utter dependence and vulnerability drawing me, much as the need of a newborn child keeps its mother in a constant state of semi-wakefulness through the night. I wanted to do everything for him, protect him, cherish him, care for him. I learned from the nurses how to cut his nails, how to pat his forehead very gently, how to clean his teeth while the nurse held the suction tube. I cut his hair, which still grew so thickly around the terrible wound.

I spent long hours sitting beside him, gently massaging his feet and the stiffening fingers of his long hands. Sometimes I talked to him about the happy times we'd had – the mischief he and Billy had got up to in France, climbing high up on the old rusting sea defences when I'd told them not to – Tom's defiant side. And the days at the East Anglian cottage when they rode together round the garden on the motor lawnmower with its chunky trailer, collecting firewood, or helped Anthony chop up a fallen tree and store the logs in the woodshed across the lawn. *Tom, can you remember when you first went to school – the Montessori school in Ashley Road? Sophie loved it, but you just wouldn't sit still on those little squares of carpet to listen to Lucy, that lovely teacher of yours. And you wouldn't do what you were supposed to do with the wooden bricks. You wanted to glue them together. When Lucy closed the school she gave each of you a present, and yours was a bag of bricks, with the message: 'Dearest Tom, these are for you to do with what I would never allow you to do. Love Lucy.'*

Often I put music on the CD player and sat listening as the sound of Bach or Mozart or Sinatra or Sting filled the room. I had read somewhere that hearing was the last of the senses to go. One day at the Royal Free one of the nurses had helped me place my arm beneath Tom's shoulders, and I had cradled him through the whole of *Les Misérables*, tears blinding me as I remembered how the music would go on the minute he fell out of bed. Now as I cradled him, I could feel his bones digging into my arms, he was so thin. And all the time I told him how much we loved him, how proud of him we were – of his bravery, his humanity, his hatred of injustice. *Tom my darling, this terrible suffering of yours has not been wasted. You saved those little children's lives in a place that has become known for the taking of life. People all over the world will remember you and thank you for what you've done.*

Sometimes I just sat quietly, gazing out of the big windows at the well-kept gardens outside. Familiar snatches of poetry, of hymns, of things I'd read to comfort myself, ran through my head.

'Do not go gentle into that good night . . . Rage, rage against the dying of the light . . .' Those were words that Tom knew and had read aloud at his grandmother's funeral.

Sometimes I sat simply struggling to conjure up Tom as he had been, to enter into that magic realm of memory where the past is as vivid as the present. It was not that I could not remember things he had done. I could recall them by an effort of will, but somehow the colour had been drained from them, the intensity had been wiped away. And without such memories, what would I have left when Tom was gone? I tried to explain this to Anthony. 'I'm sure it will all come back in time,' he said reassuringly.

Anthony was able to come to the hospital most days. He would often come late in the evening, giving me the chance to go home and get some rest. Billy came regularly too, as did Kay, and Fred often came with Anthony or me. But still Sophie could barely bring herself to visit. For her I knew there was no point, since she didn't believe Tom had any consciousness at all.

Someone who did come to the hospital was Libby. When Tom was eighteen he and Libby had been in an intensely close relationship and she had continued to be an important person in his life. Libby had been at boarding school when they met and the fact that the relationship was a little clandestine had been part of its charm. Tom, the romantic, would drop little parcels off at her front door – some sweets, a minidisc of their favourite songs he'd compiled for her, a rough sketch. I think her parents were anxious at first about the visits from this tall teenager, but they soon came to realise that Tom didn't drink or do drugs and would always return Libby home safely. Now her father was always with her when she came to the hospital.

Libby's memories of Tom were so vivid. She told me that on their first date he'd taken her to one of the ponds on Hampstead Heath at night. He'd brought two sleeping bags, some candles, wine, and hot chocolate for when it got cold. 'We spent the whole night talking until the sun came up over the pond and we could see its smoothness like glass,' she said. 'Needless to say, he had me hook line and sinker after that. I thought he was wonderful.'

Sometimes they'd hop over the wall into the local park at night, dodging the park wardens, playing on the swings. At the beginning it was all lighthearted fun, but in the end the relationship became too intense to last. Yet for Libby he was always a rock. If he knew she was upset he would stand quietly at the end of her road. 'It was the most beautiful thing anyone has ever, ever done for me,' she said. 'It gave me such protection and peace of mind. One night it was snowing and he was just standing there, in his long dark coat, blowing on his hands. I can picture his silhouette against that little bit of wall any time.'

Now, for all of us, the change in Tom's appearance was shocking. It was as if his whole being had sunk in on itself. We were convinced he was in pain. And yet his young man's body was strong, unable to give up. I wished his death could be quick and merciful, yet how could I let him go into that place where I could not follow? *Lord, now lettest thou thy servant depart in peace . . . Tom, my darling, how are we ever to let you go?*

SIXTEEN

When Tom was first shot we'd been told that he was unlikely to survive the night. Since then the time had expanded to another day, another week, another month, another year even – nobody really had any idea how long. But as October came, and the old trees in the hospital gardens began to lose their leaves, I became aware of a shadow, something intangible that told me death was approaching, however slowly. When I got home from the hospital at night I paced about, unable to rest, possessed of a kind of desperate, unreal energy. There was so little I could do.

My close friend Julia urged me to come away with her for a week to the Scilly Isles. At first I was doubtful. 'What if something happens?' I said. 'What if Tom suddenly gets worse?' 'Then we'll come straight back,' she said.

So in the end I went, and it was perhaps one of the most important decisions I made at that time. That week enabled me to gather strength, both physically and emotionally, to clear my mind a little, and to regain some slight sense of the person I had once been.

We stayed on St Agnes in a guesthouse run by a warm and intelligent young couple who took great pains to make us comfortable. From my bedroom I could see a brilliant white lighthouse against the skyline, and each morning I woke to the golden sunshine of an Indian summer, the screaming of gulls and the distant sound of the sea.

I was overwhelmed by the wild beauty of St Agnes. The island is joined to another tiny island, called Gugh, by a sand-bar, and

Julia and I would often walk there at low tide and stand gazing into the turquoise blue water, so clear you could see the white pebbles on the sea floor. One day we went to the lush subtropical gardens on Tresco and I could feel myself drawing peace and strength from this salty old garden, with its steps and statuary and distant views of the sea. Everywhere on these islands I found beauty, and there was barely a moment when I did not think of Tom. I phoned Anthony regularly and he told me Tom had a temperature, which was not at all unusual, though it worried me.

Sometimes Julia and I would walk over to the other side of St Agnes, to Wingletown Bay, where the huge Atlantic breakers crashed on jagged black rocks far out to sea, and I would lose myself in the inevitability of the sea's movement, its vastness, its force. No one stood a chance against that gigantic swell, those tons of unrelenting water. The scene that kept flashing before my mind's eye was the first chapter of *Jane Eyre*, in which Jane hides from her bullying stepbrother behind a red velvet curtain in the drawing room bay window and pores over Bewick's *History of British Birds*, with its wonderful engravings of seabirds and ship-wrecks on wild coasts. The sight of the great rolling breakers made me think that mankind is very small, and that the forces of good have to speak very loud if they are to be heard. I felt the shortness of life – not only Tom's, but the brief time any of us has on this earth. It made every action seem important, the responsibility to be a force for good, however small, vital.

When we returned home there was still no word from Israel about an enquiry. It was almost six months now since Tom had been shot. Anthony was frustrated, and Sophie and Billy were angry. At the end of September, Sophie and Billy had both made fiery speeches at an 'End the Occupation of Iraq' rally in Trafalgar Square, and while I was away they had written and delivered a letter to the Israeli Ambassador in London, describing the family's 'anguish and deep disappointment at the lack of response to their request for a fully transparent inquiry into the shooting of Tom'. 'We do not accept,' they wrote, 'that there can be a reasonable excuse for delaying or refusing such an inquiry which, under the norms of international law, the family have every right to expect.'

The news from the Middle East was worse than ever. Twenty people had been blown up in Haifa in a suicide bombing by a member of Islamic Jihad, and Israeli reprisals followed swiftly – not only against Syria, which was accused of harbouring terrorists, but against the Palestinians penned up in the Gaza Strip, always an easy target when Israel had a point to make. On 10 October at midnight eighty Israeli tanks, accompanied by military bulldozers and helicopters, burst into the Rafah refugee camp and began shooting, shelling and demolishing homes and firing gas grenades. As the Palestinians fled, eight people, including three children, were killed and sixty-five injured. Some people were so badly wounded they had to have limbs amputated. Two of the children had their heads blown off. By the end of the incursion 120 homes had been demolished and 1,500 people left homeless.

The IDF had cut off Rafah's electricity and water supplies, and the whole of Gaza was under closure. Access routes to Israel and Egypt were sealed, and all main internal roads were closed, so that ambulance drivers were being forced to carry critically ill patients over rough, unpaved back roads. Anyone trying to avoid the checkpoints was fired on, and it was reported that the army had opened fire on Palestinian medics attempting to help the wounded.

The official pretext, as usual, was that the army was looking for tunnels used by arms smugglers, but a few weeks before, on Kol Israel Radio General Samiya of the IDF Southern Command had been more honest. The army's aim, he said, was to totally rase all houses and structures within a strip of 300–400 metres of the Egyptian border so as to create a *fait accompli* and ensure that this evacuated strip remained under Israeli rule in any permanent agreement.

On 13 October we received an e-mail from the ISM in Rafah:

It is now six months since the horrific day when Tom was shot and your suffering continues, as does the suffering of the Palestinian people. Rafah has just been invaded by Israeli occupation forces and Yibnah and Block 'J' were sealed off. The place where Tom fell was occupied by the tanks of the army responsible for shooting him. Just today, 19-year-old Zuky Alshareef was shot in the neck and killed in Kir Street in the same place as Tom. Tom has become part of this land. He will never be forgotten. His memory will live on in Rafah's children. We wish you strength and courage and hope that you will take comfort in the thought that justice and peace must, eventually, prevail.

More e-mails arrived from Amjad. His English made them hard to decipher, but we understood that his home had been demolished and the family were sleeping on a school floor. Yet they kept going back. It was the only home they knew, and besides, they had nowhere else to go. On 20 October Amjad wrote to tell us that a nineteen-year-old neighbour had gone back to look at his own derelict home and had been shot in the head by the IDF.

When this happend I was home [Amjad went on] and I took him by a car of my friend to elnajar hospital. He is died now. I think you will ask why I was home: because I miss my home and I went to see it with my father, but my father told me I dont want to leave my home. Never I cant leave my home. He is told me this is my house I came to from Bet Daras in 1948, how can I leave my house, and I see him starting to crying and I left him.

The thought that Amjad's father had now been violently driven from the home to which he had come as a dispossessed refugee in 1948 was unbearable.

Mohammed e-mailed to tell us he had gone to look for Dr Samir and his family and had been shocked to find their house abandoned. All the doors and windows had gone and a channel about four or five metres wide had been dug all the way round it. Frightened people in the neighbourhood told him that on the last day of the invasion the army had told the family that if they didn't leave, the house would be demolished on top of them. After the horrors of the preceding days, this must have been too much even for the lion-hearted Dr Samir.

I felt a white-hot fury at what was being done to the people of Rafah, and the resounding silence from the Judge Advocate General on the subject of an enquiry into Tom's shooting, despite consistent pressure from our lawyer Avigdor Feldman in Tel Aviv, only made me more furious. I wrote a letter to Tony Blair which Sophie and I delivered personally to Downing Street, asking for a meeting, and urging him to challenge US support for Israel's actions.

How loud do I have to shout [I wrote] and what language do I have to find to say that this is unacceptable in a civilized society? Mr Blair, I am asking you to challenge Mr Bush's support of this deeply immoral regime which is cruel beyond human understanding and which I have seen for myself at first hand: the illegal demolition of houses, the destruction of olive groves, the process of depriving people of the possibility of earning a living, the closure of checkpoints, the cutting off of water and electricity, curfews, humiliation, terror . . . so it goes on. In short, the dehumanization of a people. Mr Bush's statement that 'Israel has the right to defend itself' says it all and clearly demonstrates views that collude with the perception of Israel as the victim. If ever there was a level of aggression that far outstrips justification and provocation, then here it is.

I wrote to everyone I could think of – the editors of newspapers, sympathetic MPs such as Andrew George and Frank Dobson, even to Cherie Blair. Surely, as a mother herself, I thought, and someone involved in defending human rights, she must be as appalled by this inhumanity as I was. As Christ'l pointed out, the Prime Minister's wife had recently met some Israeli victims of suicide bombings, and meeting me might help to provide a counterbalance. I also agreed to appear on a BBC TV discussion programme called *Hard Talk* in which I was asked some searching questions about Tom's motives for being in Rafah, and what had happened since. I found such appearances an ordeal, but fortunately, perhaps, I was in a state of such controlled fury that I was able to forget my nerves. All I had to do was to think of what Tom had lost and it gave me an unearthly energy.

The programme made me think even more deeply about Tom, and why he had been in the Middle East. I knew he had gone as a photojournalism student, eager to witness and photograph what was going on. But there was more to it than that. It was Tom's nature to seek the bigger picture, to understand and share other people's experiences. You could see it in his eyes from a very early age, in the way he carried himself, which was sharply observant but somehow unassuming.

In fact at this stage I didn't manage to meet either Tony or Cherie Blair, from both of whom I soon received cautiously phrased letters. But after *Hard Talk* I received dozens of e-mails and letters of support, many from distressed Jewish people living in this country. 'I am a mature man and an ex-soldier but I feel like crying with shame, anger and humiliation at the Israeli government's atrocious and unforgiveable treatment of your family,' wrote one.

Please believe me when I tell you that there are many, many thousands of Jews, such as myself, in the UK and Europe and even in Israel itself who abhor the policies and actions of the Sharon administration.

After the Second World War, the decimated remnants of European Jewry had a dream, as did Martin Luther King, that all men are born equal. In Israel, that dream has turned into a nightmare so horrific that it can well provide the spark – and may indeed already have done so – that will lead the entire world into another era of darkness.

Then out of the blue, in the last week of October, we heard from the Foreign and Commonwealth Office that the Judge

Advocate General in Israel had ordered a military police investigation into the circumstances of Tom's death. It was not what
we had hoped for, which was an immediate criminal prosecution.
Once again, it seemed, the army was about to investigate itself,
and we were not surprised when we learned from Avigdor
Feldman, our lawyer in Tel Aviv, that his request to see the full
report of the enquiry when it was completed had been refused on
the grounds that it was 'confidential'. 'But I do assure you that in
the circumstances an enquiry like this is quite unprecedented,' said
the man from the Foreign Office.

In the same week we received a cheque for £8,370 to cover the
cost of Tom's repatriation, accompanied by a letter from the Israeli
Ambassador reminding us that this sum was made 'as an *ex-gratia*
payment and without any admission of liability by the State of Israel
or the Ministry of Defence as to Mr Hurndall's injury'. It represented only a fraction of the cost of bringing Tom home, but I paid
the cheque into the bank and waited for it to clear so that I could
transfer the money to the Thomas Hurndall Fund bank account.

I could barely believe it when, a week later, I received a letter
telling me that the cheque had bounced. 'Insufficient funds' was
the reason given. It was so improbable, so absurd almost, that it
was hard even to be angry. I wrote a letter which was published in
the *Guardian*, suggesting that, since funds were so tight, perhaps
Israel should channel less funding towards the construction of
illegal 'security' fences and the development of remote-control
bulldozers and more towards the rebuilding of wantonly destroyed Palestinian homes.

The response from the Embassy was not an apology, but an
attempt to cover up with a public statement that the cheque had
already been cashed – the implication being, I suppose, that we
were trying to pull a fast one – plus a long defence of Israel's policies
in the Occupied Territories. After some chilly communication the
cheque was finally re-presented and cleared, but, as in all our
dealings with Israeli officialdom, the incident left a bitter taste.

*   *   *

I felt at this time that I was leading parallel lives – the public one and the intensely private and painful one that continued day by day at the hospital. In a way, one fuelled the other. Tom's nightmare was ongoing, yet there was so little I could do to help him that I think the despair and distress I felt were translated into a determination to make a difference anywhere else I could. I wrote e-mails to Amjad, and was relieved when I heard from the ISM that money had been raised to enable his family to rent a flat. Amjad himself was desperate to get out of Gaza – who wasn't? – and his e-mails were becoming increasingly depressed. '*If any body can help me just send me massage, love from your sun Amjad.*' It was heartbreaking. His ambition was to come to England and we wanted to help him, but I knew this was more than I could cope with just now.

The whole family was feeling the weight of Tom's suffering and we were all responding differently. I could see the pressure of it in everyone's eyes. Sophie had decided to move away from home to live in a friend's flat, and I had to accept her need for distance. I thought often of the old days, when all the children were at home, and how easy affection had been. I remembered Billy plaiting Sophie's hair as she sat at the kitchen table, the ribbing and the laughter. I remembered how Sophie used to say to Fred, 'I love you more than the stars and the moon and the mountains.'

Fred was quiet and sad and when we were not at the hospital he spent a lot of his time in Tom's room, which seemed to give him comfort. Billy, in his usual practical and thoughtful way, had decided he would transform Fred's old room at the back of the house to make it more inviting. He'd taken out the ceiling to give it greater height, installed three roof windows and built on a little balcony. Now he was building a platform bed. It was a wonderful piece of work, fun and imaginative, and it tore at my heart to see the way he was trying to take care of Fred.

Anthony and I were both spending more and more time at the hospital. All I could do was to sit with Tom, holding his hand, gently dabbing his face, talking to him, hoping that the warmth of my body, the sound of my voice, the smell of my perfume, the tinkling of my bangles, would somehow reach him and comfort him in his prison. During those long hours I told Tom everything. I told him what was happening to the family and to his friends, and about what was happening in Gaza. I told him about our meeting with the Corries. I told him about the letter I'd just received telling me that the Students' Union at the London School of Economics had recognised what he had done by voting him its Honorary Vice-President. I told him how much we loved him and admired him and talked of him, and that he would always, always, be in our hearts. I told him these things not because I believed he could hear me, not because I needed to pour my heart out, but out of love and a feeling of deep respect for him and what he had done. I wanted to do everything right for Tom.

His breathing was very shallow now and his bones were visible beneath the translucent skin. Often he jerked his head, his hands clammy, his forehead damp with sweat. We were all certain that he was in pain, that this could not go on. At first I had thought of Tom as being in purgatory, in a kind of no-man's-land between life and death. But purgatory, I remembered having studied Dante's *Il Purgatorio*, was a place where you had a chance to gain something, a step on the way to something else. Dante's ideas of the relationship between celestial influences and human responsibility made me think of Tom's tattoo. Tom had already been engaged by such ideas, but he could never pursue them now. This was not purgatory, it was hell – *L'Inferno*.

The hospital was aware of our deep distress, and it was arranged that Anthony, Sophie and I should have a meeting to discuss Tom's future care and the likelihood of recovery with Patti Simonson, the hospital social worker, and with Professor Andrews, Director of the hospital. By this time Anthony and I both believed that, as parents, we had a serious responsibility to speak for Tom, to ask that he should not go on suffering. It wasn't that

Tom simply had no quality of life; it was worse than that, it was a totally negative quality. The gift of life had come to seem even more precious to me during the past six months, but I knew that Tom's condition was not life.

Patti explained to us carefully that, though consultation with the family was crucial, the decision to allow Tom to die was not ours to make. Nor did it lie in the hands of the hospital and the Primary Care Team; it rested with the court.

Professor Andrews, a kindly, greying man with an encouraging manner, was clearly aware of how difficult this meeting was for us. Like Dr Lloyd of the Royal Free's Ethics Committee, he asked us: 'What do you think Tom would have wanted?'

I told him of the passage in Tom's journals where he describes, in brave and unsparing detail, what precisely would have happened to Rachel Corrie as she was crushed by an IDF bulldozer, and says that with such a maimed and unrecognisable body he would not have wanted to survive. We discussed whether this passage might constitute a kind of advance directive, and Professor Andrews asked us to send it to him.

As we sat at the table in Patti's office in the hospital on that warm November day, everything around me seemed very distant and unreal. I was asking whether my child should be allowed to die. A part of me could not believe that this was happening, and yet I knew that if we asked that Tom should be kept alive it would be not for him, but for us.

Yet I had no idea, before this meeting, of the legal complexities that this would involve. Firstly, we were told, an application would have to be made by the Primary Care Trust to the Family Division of the High Court to withdraw food and hydration from Tom. Under British law there could be no merciful injection. Since Tom was breathing on his own, there was no life-support machine to turn off. This application would have to be accompanied by a report on his condition from an independent medical expert, and by a witness statement from someone speaking on Tom's behalf. If the application was granted, Tom would be moved to a house in the hospital grounds and we, his family, would be able to live there with him until he died. We would have to watch him die of thirst.

I remember Anthony looking at Professor Andrews and asking, 'How long is this likely to take?', and Professor Andrews replying, 'Normally ten days to two weeks.'

We all sat gazing at him, unable to speak. 'Isn't there *any* other way?' I said finally.

'No, there isn't. This is where British legislation stands,' he said. He was clearly a humane man in a painful position. This was a high-profile case, and the hospital could not afford to put a foot wrong. But the idea that we had to put Tom through this agonising process in the year 2003 seemed barbaric, incredible. Why could the law not acknowledge that increasing doses of morphine would probably kill him anyway, and agree that his misery should be ended now? I tried to imagine what it would be like for Fred – for all of us – to watch Tom die of dehydration. All I could say as we left was: 'Professor Andrews, if you ever want me to speak publicly in favour of giving a lethal injection, about the need for all this to be done differently, then I will.'

Short of taking Tom to a country like Holland or Switzerland, which seemed unthinkable in his condition, there appeared to be no other way. So the hospital set wheels in motion, and a week later, in the presence of Anthony and Sophie, I made a witness statement on Tom's behalf to a sympathetic young lawyer, Kiran Bhogal, setting out my belief that it was 'not, in the existing circumstances, in Tom's best interests for him to be given life-sustaining medical treatment measures (including ventilation, nutrition and hydration by artificial means)'. It was a long and very personal statement, and in it I strove to give as full and truthful a picture as I could of Tom's present state and an interpretation of what his own wishes would have been. 'What I am clear about is this; that this is not what Tom would have wanted,' I said. 'I am trying to meet his wishes even though in my heart I would always want him to be there. To be mature and rational I need to let Tom go for Tom's sake.'

Anthony, Sophie and I had agreed what Tom would have wanted beforehand, and we all signed. As we left the solicitor's office I was overwhelmed by the weight of what we had just done. I said to Anthony, 'I feel as though I've just killed Tom.'

It was horrifying to see the *Evening Standard* headline a few days later 'Let Human Shield Boy Die'. The press had got hold of the story, and the *Daily Mail* and other national newspapers trumpeted the fact that we were applying for permission to 'turn off Tom's life-support machine'. I was devastated. It felt like the grossest intrusion into something deeply personal, as if my innermost soul had been invaded, and I paced the house at night, distraught, unable to sleep. Suddenly all our anguish was public property, the agonising decision we had made reduced to a few crude and simple sentences. Soon we began receiving letters from the pro-life lobby. On the whole they were polite, but I was sickened by their holier-than-thou tone. These were from people, I was certain, who had never experienced the pain of seeing their child in Tom's condition. For whose sake were they asking us to keep him alive? To me it felt like arrogance. The hospital, too, was unhappy with this unwanted publicity.

As October turned into November we felt we were living in a state of suspension, simply hanging on, waiting for the inevitable, but not knowing how or when it would happen. Everyone was beginning to think of Christmas preparations. All I had in mind was that this would be our last Christmas with Tom.

The twenty-seventh of November was a day I had been dreading: Tom's birthday. He was twenty-two. It was a family tradition on birthdays and special occasions to have a hydrogen-filled balloon bearing a special message floating above the kitchen table, attached to the fruit bowl. The last time I'd bought a balloon for Tom had been the previous September, on the day he was going off to university. I remembered rushing out and coming back with one in the shape of an enormous champagne bottle with the message 'Good Luck Tommo' on it. It had been such a happy day, full of anticipation. We'd all sat down to coffee and croissants, with Tom – typically – still filling out his university bank form. Then, etched into my memory, was the picture of Tom and Billy hugging and hugging as they said goodbye like a couple of young bears, exuberantly lifting one another off the ground in a rocking motion.

Today, on this saddest of birthdays, I'd gone to the Party Shop, the same shop I'd been going to for years to buy a balloon for Tom. I chose one in the shape of a star, with the words: 'To dearest Tommo, with all the love we have. Mum, Dad, Sophie, Billy and Fred.' As I walked across the hospital car park carrying the balloon I met Anthony walking with Tom's godfather Max, who was just leaving. It was always warming to see Max. We had all been friends since university. He was part of our life, our past, a cheering, positive presence. But that day there seemed very little to say.

Tom was looking extraordinarily peaceful. Winter sunshine flooded in through the big windows and he lay in a kind of halo of light. He was so frail now he seemed hardly there. I kissed him and tied the balloon to the foot of his bed. Then I lit a candle, and put some framed verses from the Koran sent to him by a Palestinian organisation on the shelf behind his bed.

Outside the Foreign Office that evening, at a candlelit ceremony to mark Tom's birthday organised by the London branch of the ISM, Sophie and I cut a cake decorated with the words 'Blessings to Tom'. There were balloons and banners tied to the railings, supporters sang 'Happy Birthday', and the police and Foreign Office security guards stood tolerantly by as Foreign Office staff leaving work were offered symbolic pieces of cake.

I had dreaded this part of the day most of all – I think we all had, fearing that we wouldn't be able to hold up in public. But in fact we felt cheered and buoyed up by all the kindness and support. There were crowds of young people there, including

Raph, whom we had got to know well at the hospital in Be'ersheva and who was now working in London. Afif and Christ'l came, warm and supportive as ever, and so did our solicitor Imran Khan and other members of the Palestinian community. As Fred said thoughtfully, when asked by someone how he felt: 'I'm not really upset about today. I'm kind of happy. It seems strange and I've been thinking about why, but I'm not too sure.'

After the cutting of the cake we moved on to the LSE, where Sophie was taking part in a discussion panel. I was presented with an engraved glass panel on a stand marking Tom's Honorary Vice-Presidency of the Students' Union. As I rose to express my gratitude everyone stood in tribute to Tom and applauded. It was deeply moving.

The evening ended with the screening of two films – *Human Shields*, which followed the experiences of the ISM in Rafah and Tulkarem in the weeks after Tom's shooting, and Sandra Jordan's *The Killing Zone*, her horrific Channel 4 documentary covering the day Tom was shot. Sandra was there, and it was extraordinary to see her again in this very different setting. We had shared an experience in Gaza that few other people could understand. But before the films were shown I stole away. I couldn't watch.

SEVENTEEN

We all wondered how we were going to get through Christmas. In the end Billy, Fred, Anthony and I decided to go to the cottage, while Sophie arranged to spend it with her friends in London. It was the first Christmas we hadn't all been together. The cottage had always been a place of comfort and consolation for us, but as we prepared for Christmas it was hard to find consolation anywhere – even in all the loving thoughts and messages that poured through the letterbox. The world seemed drained of hope and colour.

As I shopped among the Christmas crowds, carol singers were singing of 'peace on earth and mercy mild'. But where was the peace in the world? Where was the mercy? I couldn't make sense of anything. I went about automatically, preparing food, writing cards, wrapping presents. It all seemed entirely without meaning.

We drove down to the cottage on Christmas Eve, unpacking the car in the clear frosty air, making up the beds, lighting the fire, chopping wood, going through all the familiar rituals, trying to keep ourselves busy in order not to think too much. On the news we heard that the Israeli army had again raided Rafah, killing at least ten people and destroying more than one hundred homes, some, reportedly, with the residents still inside. Mixed in my mind with all the comforting images of Christmas – the stable, the holy family, the shepherds and the wise men, all set against the traditional, peaceful background of the Holy Land – were ghastly pictures of what was happening there now. I thought of Amjad and his father and their demolished home, and homeless Dr

Samir, whose children Tom had so loved. And I thought of Tom arriving in Jerusalem, walking into the Old City and seeing young children in the street fighting one another viciously with sticks. As he'd written in his journal: '*Now I'm here at the heart of the Holy Land and the reason I am here is because of war. This place is saturated with anger, resentment and frustration. You can feel it in the air.*'

We had heard no more from Kiran Bhogal, the young lawyer who was dealing with the hospital's application to end Tom's life, since the application was before the court and we were due to attend a hearing in January. But as I went through the motions of Christmas I was thinking all the time about how I could help the family through the ordeal that was to come. I wanted Billy and Sophie and Fred to be able to associate Tom's dying with some kind of beauty rather than with pain and horror. I thought of lighting candles, buying lovely flowers. But in the end I knew I would be trying to make something beautiful out of something barbaric that should never be happening – something deeply uncivilised and grossly disrespectful, not just to Tom but to all those close to him. Tom was going to die, one way or another, but our other children would have to carry on, and I felt deeply concerned about the effect all this was going to have on them.

That Christmas neither Anthony nor I went to Midnight Mass. It was something from which I normally drew spiritual strength, a feeling of togetherness and continuity. But this year there were too many other people's needs to consider.

On Christmas Day we got up early and Anthony, Billy and Fred drove to London to see Tom, while I stayed and cooked Christmas lunch. At about three o'clock they were back, very subdued. Anthony said that Tom was breathing badly and seemed feverish. The dosage of morphine had been increased now to every four hours. We managed to get through lunch and then wrapped up warm and went for a walk along the darkening lane, gasping and stamping in the icy cold. After that we got out the board games and played Risk and Scrabble in front of the fire until it was time to go to bed, trying not to remember the fun of past Christmases – the laughs, the banter, the outrageous remarks, the sheer bursting life when Tom had been with us.

Back in London on 30 December I read that the IDF had shot five more Palestinians in Rafah, one of them a young man carrying the coffin of his brother who himself had just been shot. The radio informed me that George Bush had 'strongly condemned' the actions of the suicide bombers who had killed four IDF soldiers at a bus stop just outside Tel Aviv.

Next morning the phone rang early. It was the Foreign Office, with news that an IDF soldier had been arrested for Tom's shooting. When interrogated, he had confessed to knowing that Tom was an unarmed civilian. He had not yet been charged, but the Foreign office would keep us informed.

That evening, as I sat with close friends in front of the fire, listening to the church bells ringing in the new year, I was seized with fresh outrage at the thought of the Christmas carnage in Rafah, at George Bush's complicity in Israel's barbarous actions, at the silence of our leaders. And I thought of the words of Edmund Burke: 'All that is necessary for the triumph of evil is that good men do nothing.'

Occasionally people had suggested to me that I'd become 'politicised', but for me this was a wider issue than politics. It was to do with morality and human values and our responsibility towards each other. By this time I was studying the Israeli/Palestinian conflict with a passion, and everything I'd read and seen told me that the Israeli response was cynical and disproportionate. Anthony and I had both reached this conclusion quite independently and by different routes, and for both of us it had been reached with great internal struggle. With all the clarity of youth, Sophie and Bill had reached the same conclusion far sooner.

Now, towards midnight, I sat down and poured out my feelings in a piece which appeared that week in the *Guardian*.

When will those responsible accept that it is illegal to collectively
and obsessively punish a whole community? [I wrote] Does Tony
Blair regard the children of Palestine as children of a lesser God?
Does he accept that his inaction is tantamount to complicity in the
process of destroying any peace initiative in the Middle East? Mr
Blair, you now know that a British citizen has been shot in cold
blood while trying to shepherd children from the live bullets of an
IDF sniper. Are you now ready to openly condemn these actions?

Each day now we could see that Tom was growing weaker. He
had developed pneumonia and his breathing was laboured and
shallow, however many times his chest was cleared. The morphine was having less and less effect, and he shifted restlessly as if in
pain. I sensed as I sat beside him that he had now entered a
shadowland, a place nearer to death than to life. Yet the will to
live in his young body was so strong, it still could not surrender. I
could only pray O God, release my child.

On the first Monday in the new year I asked one of the doctors
how much longer he thought Tom had.

'I don't think it will be very long now,' he said.

I asked what that meant.

He thought carefully and then said, 'About a week.'

It had taken so long to reach this point, we had been told so
many different things at different times, that the calm, precise
answer came like a blow. For some months now I had felt almost
beyond tears; now I felt dislocated from the world, hurled into a
bottomless black morass which sucked me down. I longed for
Tom to be free of all this horror, but I could not imagine a world
in which he was not physically there, in which I could not see him
and touch him. And in such a little time, I would have to face that.
This was the very worst. All the manifestations of his physical
being seemed so precious now – the T-shirts and tracksuits piled
up neatly on the shelves, his toothbrush, his shampoo, the small
possessions we had brought with him to the hospital.

Billy and Fred came often – Fred pale and accepting and

terribly brave. Sophie came, and Kay, Libby and Antonia. I called
one of Tom's little inner group of friends, 'the boys', and
explained that we were close to losing Tom. When they visited
they stood looking at him in a kind of loving disbelief, still
somehow unable to accept that the Tom they had grown up with
and hung out with could be leaving them in this way. I racked my
brains to think what my other responsibilities were – who else
should I be telling? What would I live to regret if I didn't do it
now? But everything outside the hospital room faded into
irrelevance. I could really only think of Tom.

On 12 January Anthony and I were both with him in the
afternoon. Anthony was standing beside the bed and I was sitting
with my hand beneath Tom's arm when I felt a kind of energy in
his body, and something changed in his face, which was illumi-
nated almost with a look of recognition. Anthony saw it too. It
was as if, with an enormous effort of will, Tom was summoning
up all the last energy he had to be with us. Though his eyes were
unable to focus, I had the sense that he was looking down at me as
I sat in the chair beside him. I just kept holding him and repeating,
'Look, Tom darling, this is Mum. We're here. Mum and Dad are
here. We love you very much. You're doing so well. Well done,
Tom, well done, darling.' And I do believe – perhaps I want to
believe – that at some level there was recognition.

That evening when we got home there was a message from the
Foreign Office to say that the soldier who had been arrested for
Tom's shooting had been charged with aggravated assault. He was
also being charged with obstruction of justice for shooting Tom
and then seeking permission from his commander to kill him on
the grounds that he was carrying a gun. A second soldier was
under arrest for allegedly corroborating his account.

Next day, 13 January, was my birthday, and I went to the
hospital early. Anthony and Fred had been there through the
night. I leaned over the bed and put my face beside Tom's on the
pillow so that I could hear the beating of his heart, feel the quick
rise and fall of his breathing. How often I had soothed him like

this when he was a small child, unable to sleep. I told him about
the soldier, and I promised him that we would make sure justice
was done, that we would hold the army's chain of command to
account. I told him that all his suffering had not been in vain and
that what he had done had touched and inspired people across the
world. I told him what a good person he was. And again and again
I told him how proud we were of him and how much we loved
him.

*Oh Tom, my darling, you must go now into a place where I cannot
follow. I must let you go, but you know that in my heart I will never leave
you. You'll be at my shoulder, always. You are my son; my child.*

Billy came and we went to the canteen where, with great
sweetness, he gave me a card and a birthday present – a little
Walkman for me to listen to music on. It was so typical of him to
remember. With all the surrounding trauma my birthday seemed
so unimportant, but it was deeply touching to me that he had
thought of it. We went back to Tom's room and Billy put on
some of Tom's favourite music. Anthony phoned to say he would
come in the evening. We sat there all day, with Billy holding
Tom's hand in his quiet, peaceful way.

By late afternoon I sensed that Tom had reached some turning
point, and I knew that I must tell Father Hubert, our local parish
priest. Father Hubert was an old friend. He had known Tom since
he was a child, had prayed for him, said Masses for him, though
Tom had stopped going to church years ago. I knew Billy
wouldn't like it – Billy and Sophie had both rejected Catholicism
in their teens – but in my distress it was all I knew how to do. It
had nothing to do with my own faith. I needed the comfort of
Father Hubert's spiritual presence. Tom, I knew, had been a
spiritual person, though not bound by any creed. He had been
inclusive, respectful of everyone's beliefs. Now I wanted Father
Hubert to bless him on his journey, to help me let him go.

When I phoned Father Hubert he was about to say Mass, but
he put everything aside and at 5.30 he came. This wonderful
eighty-year-old had made the long journey by tube and on foot

from the station, and when he came into the room his presence was like a benediction. I felt his immense strength and calm. There was no need for words. When he arrived Billy left the room abruptly. This made me so sad, but I understood, and I hoped that one day Billy himself would understand.

Father Hubert said nothing, but he took my hands in his firm dry ones and held them. He stood for some time looking down at Tom with great love. Then, from his small bag he took out a prayer book, and another for me, and in his strong quiet voice began the prayers for the departing: *'I commend you, my dear brother, to almighty God, and entrust you to your Creator. May you return to him who formed you from the dust of the earth . . .'*

He made the sign of the cross with oil on Tom's forehead, beside the livid wound: *'Through this holy anointing may the Lord in his love and mercy help you with the grace of the Holy Spirit. May the Lord who frees you from sin save you and raise you up . . .'*

The beautiful, enduring words were like a bell gently tolling in celebration of Tom's life. I stood looking down at his dear face, so closed now, so remote, and felt a deep thankfulness for the twenty-two years we had had him with us. And such pain as I have never felt before or since, and such loneliness.

It was dark when Father Hubert left. I wanted to drive him to the station but he wouldn't hear of it. I walked with him to the main entrance, and again we stood silently with my hands in his before he disappeared into the night.

I walked back along the quiet corridor. The canteen was closed, but I sat down in it and took out my mobile phone. I knew Anthony would be here soon, but there were other people I felt I should send messages to – people who needed to know that Tom would not be with us long. I was just starting when the phone rang. It was one of Tom's nurses. Almost without hearing what she was saying I picked up my things and fled up the stairs and along the corridor towards Tom's room.

The nurses were standing round his bed. I flung my coat on the floor and ran towards Tom. Someone put a hand on my arm, and I heard someone else say: 'He's gone.'

I stood looking down at my dead child. And I knew that I was also looking at a young man who had lived a worthwhile life, and whose heart had been in a good place. Whatever his human frailties Tom had essentially been a deeply good person, a courageous person who had risked himself for others, and who had made a difference. And all I could say was, 'Well, done, Tom. Well done.' Over and over I kept repeating it as I held him. 'Well done, darling, well done.'

The nurses must have wondered why I was saying it but I couldn't explain. I was thinking of that precious little bit of folded paper in his 'Memories' file on which Tom had written: 'When my mother says "Well done".'

III

LONDON – ASHKELON

MAY 2004–AUGUST 2005

EIGHTEEN

On the morning of 10 May 2004 I stood in the courtroom of the IDF Southern Command at the Kastina Junction Military Base near Ashkelon, about sixty kilometres from Tel Aviv. It was the first day of the trial of the soldier who had shot Tom. I'd arrived in Tel Aviv from the kibbutz the evening before and been driven down to the base early that morning with Neil Wigan from the British Embassy. It was a bleak place, a cluster of low, functional buildings set in scrubby desert land on the outskirts of the town of Ashkelon and surrounded by a high wire fence. Outside, in the dried-earth parking lot, we'd met up with Karin Loevy, an able young woman lawyer from Avigdor Feldman's practice who spoke fluent English and would be attending the whole trial. Since it was a criminal military trial she would have no direct part to play and nor would we. But to us she would be a vital link, keeping us informed on all the legal issues. The trial could last many months, we'd been told, since the court would convene quite spasmodically, sometimes for only one or two days a month.

I had been adamant that a member of the family would be present on this first day, and it was agreed I should go. It was a statement. I wanted the IDF to know that we were still on the case, that we were watching them, and that we weren't going to go away.

It was a small, wood-panelled courtroom. I couldn't have been more than a few yards from the accused soldier when he was led in. Though he had not been publicly identified, I knew that his name was Sgt Taysir Walid Heib, that he was a Bedouin, and that he was twenty years old. He entered with a strange shuffling gait and I was shocked when I heard the clunk of leg irons. He was in uniform and handcuffed to another soldier, a woman who looked even younger than he was. In fact none of the small group guarding him looked more than nineteen or twenty. Although he was so close to me, I didn't meet his eye, then or at any other time during the trial. Though I was conscious of what I was doing, it was an almost instinctive reaction – an indication, however slight, to the defence lawyers and above all to the whole Israeli Defence Force that we were convinced he was only a tiny cog in a much bigger wheel.

We had asked to see the full evidence of the military police investigation and the IDF had responded with a three-page summary that raised more questions than it answered. But we knew from what Taysir had been telling the press that the full evidence contained crucial transcripts of statements about IDF rules of engagement made under questioning by him and his fellow soldiers. It was possible these transcripts might shed light on a whole culture of random killing in an army that had declared itself 'the most moral army in the world'. We were determined to see the full evidence, and we were ready to take our case to the Supreme Court if necessary.

In many ways Taysir was an ordinary looking young man. He had strong Bedouin features, with what appeared to be a scar down one cheek and another on his forehead. When the leg irons and handcuffs were removed, he slouched on a chair between his guards. There was none of the professional formality between them that I would have expected. This was a military trial, and it all felt very much 'in-house'. Occasionally he and the guards would exchange a remark in Hebrew, and even laugh, like any group of teenagers. It was hard to believe they were in court, and that the case was one of manslaughter.

I looked at the soldier from my place at the front of the courtroom with a strange mixture of feelings. Here was the man who had shot my son – knowingly, the evidence indicated, a sniper taking aim with cool precision through his telescopic sight. Here was the man who had lied, who, we now knew, had made five conflicting statements in an effort to save his skin, and had finally attempted to withdraw his confession.

I thought, too, that he was a boy who had been given too much leeway by his commanding officers, functioning within a culture that, in a literally unwritten and unspoken way, seemed to give out the message that it was acceptable to shoot unarmed civilians in cold blood. A pawn in a much larger and more terrible system designed by people much further up the military hierarchy. Who was he, I wondered; where had he come from, what was the track that had taken him to that desolate guard post on the Egyptian border? I didn't just feel anger and contempt. I had a powerful need to know who this young man was, what were the factors that had brought him to this point, what had gone through his mind as he pulled the trigger. The immorality of such an act was incomprehensible to me, but I desperately wanted to understand.

The defence and prosecuting counsel were already in court and Karin pointed them out to me. Hila Gurney, the IDF prosecuting counsel, was quite a severe looking young woman, dressed in military uniform with her hair scraped back. I guessed she was only in her twenties, and wondered how someone so young could be acting for the prosecution in such a politically sensitive and high-profile case. Her assistant, Oren Lieber, looked pleasant and even younger. But from the moment Hila spoke she came across as competent, alert and highly professional, with a confident but not overconfident presence. However, we already understood the limitations of her brief. She was here simply to establish the guilt or otherwise of this particular soldier, but nothing beyond that. There would be no discussion of any wider issues, of how much responsibility for Tom's shooting should be borne not just by this single soldier, but by the chain of command. Indeed, as I was to discover, whenever anything came up that was remotely connected with the army's rules of engagement – or 'national security' as it was called – we would be required to leave the court.

The main defence lawyer, Ilan Bombach, seemed a very different kettle of fish, a puffy-faced, self-important looking man in a civilian lawyer's black gown, whose bleached-blonde miniskirted fiancée sat not far from us casting vacuous glances at me.

The three military judges entered and took their places on a raised dais behind a low wooden bench-desk. The charges against Taysir were read out: manslaughter, obstruction of justice, submitting false testimony, obtaining false testimony, and unfitting behaviour. Another soldier had been arrested on a charge of giving false testimony on Taysir's behalf, but there was no sign of him, and I presumed he would be having a separate trial.

As the charges were read out Taysir sat sprawled on the bench, occasionally crossing and recrossing his legs, looking deeply bored. His entire body language indicated what a waste of time he thought all this was, and that he was certain he was going to be cleared. And why should he think otherwise? The IDF chain of command supported its soldiers, did it not? No indictments had been made against the driver of the bulldozer which had killed Rachel Corrie. No soldier had been called to account and prosecuted for the killing of James Miller. And since the beginning of the Second Intifada thousands of Palestinian civilians had been shot and injured by the army without the soldiers' behaviour being seriously challenged by the IDF itself.

The main issue under discussion that day and the following one was whether the statements already made by Taysir under questioning were admissible as evidence. He was now claiming that these statements, which had led to his indictment, had been made under duress.

He spoke only to confirm his name and rank; the exchanges were between the defence and prosecuting counsel, and we saw very quickly what the pattern was to be. Hila's approach was quick, economical and to the point, whereas Ilan Bombach's was slow, pedantic and overblown. He read laboriously from his sheaf of notes, questioning the minutest details: how many breaks had Taysir been allowed during questioning, for precisely how long, what exactly had he been given to eat, how much water had he been allowed . . . the list went on and on *ad absurdum* until the main point was lost in repetitions and technicalities and even the judges seemed exasperated. Bombach was clearly clutching at straws as he saw each objection calmly and directly countered by Hila.

In fact what seemed to take up much time in court was the fact that Taysir had previously been convicted on drugs charges, something the IDF seemed to take more seriously than killing a civilian. It was also claimed that Taysir could neither read nor write Hebrew and had a poor grasp of the language. His comprehension was also poor, due to a learning disability, and he was therefore confused about the rules of engagement.

The court's noisy air conditioning made it hard to hear, the sound of Bombach's irritating and insistent voice with its circular questioning was draining, and it was a relief to us all when the lunch break came and we could go outside. Journalists asked for my reactions. I thought about Taysir and his appearance in court – pathetic somehow, as if he was incapable of grasping what he'd done, or the gravity of the situation. Some of the Israeli press had already dwelt on the fact that he was an Arab, a Bedouin – basically one of Israeli society's outcasts, as I was beginning to understand – i.e. not 'one of them'. They implied that Tom would never have been shot by an Israeli Jewish soldier, but we were far from convinced. As far as I was concerned this soldier had been trained by the IDF, was operating under their rules of engagement and was their responsibility. And I could only say what I had already said on the BBC *Today* programme – that we hadn't come this far to attend a show trial, that we believed there were systemic problems within the IDF, and that there were still many questions to be answered.

★   ★   ★

At the end of two interminable days of objections from Bombach, the court was adjourned for a month to consider the admissibility of Taysir's evidence. I had spent the two nights of the trial in a hotel in Tel Aviv and now, as ever, I was grateful to be driven further south to the kibbutz by Neil Wigan, where I was to stay for the next ten days. My eyes felt as if they had sand grains in them, and my head throbbed from the strain of trying to take in what was going on in court at every level. I'd felt like a sea anemone, receiving sensations through countless filaments. I knew it was going to take some time to make sense of all these facts, issues and impressions.

What a relief it was to sit once more with Erella in the green haven of her verandah, with the smoke from one of her roll-ups rising lazily in the evening air. People naturally unburden themselves to Erella, and I found myself going over with her once more the terrible time after Tom's death, when all the family's pent-up anger rushed to the surface and I felt most of it was directed at me. For all of us our grieving had been stalled by everything else that was going on. Now for the first time our loss had begun to seem like a reality. It was a time of insanity. Everything seemed out of control. It's still hard to think about, but it is part of Tom's story, part of our desperate individual battles to come to terms with his loss.

Now I felt the need to look back to what I believed I'd given Tom. It was easy to remember the mistakes I'd made, the things I would have done differently. But at least I felt that I had not tried to make him into something he was not. I'd had faith in him, encouraged him to search for his star. '*Much of the morality I hope I have I believe comes from your example . . . my decision to help out in a refugee camp is a result of the ideals you and other people gave me.*' Tom had written that in his Middle East journal. It was a surprising but comforting thought.

Next day, as we sat down to the customary delicious meal of salads and fruits in the kibbutz's communal dining room, Erella introduced me to a pleasant, serious looking man in his late thirties who lived on the kibbutz and was currently doing research for a Ph.D. on an aspect of Jewish Thought. His name was Ehud. It emerged that he had been a refusenik and had spent time in an Israeli prison for it. There, he told me, he had met three Bedouin soldiers, members of the same unit in Rafah in which Taysir had served. I asked what he knew about this unit.

'Well,' Ehud said, 'the Rafah unit is different because it's a Bedouin unit, so it's not made up of conscripts. Legally, being Arabs, Bedouins are not obliged to do military service, so these are volunteers, people who have made up their minds to be professional soldiers.'

'Why on earth would a Bedouin want to fight for Israel considering how Israeli society treats them?' I said.

'They hope it will bring them some sort of social acceptance, prove that they're "good" citizens,' said Ehud. 'Basically they do it to better themselves.'

'And does it?'

'No,' said Ehud. 'They're still discriminated against when they leave the army, and some of their own people despise them, because they're shooting their own brothers after all. They're confined to this special unit and it's treated very differently from the rest. There's no progression; a Bedouin could never, say, become a pilot. Normally combat units rotate – they do a few months in one area and then they're moved to another front. But the Bedouin unit doesn't rotate. It's been in the Rafah zone for years. It's really the worst zone because it's right on the Egyptian border. The place is absolute hell.'

Ehud reflected for a moment and then went on: 'Soldiers like the one who shot Tom probably come from the poorest Bedouin villages in the north, the unofficial ones not recognised by the government – no water, hardly any electricity, walking several kilometres to school for a few years and then leaving school early. Soldiers like these are not seen as human. They just serve the army's purposes. Their life has little value.

'The three Bedouin soldiers I met in prison were all there on drugs charges. But what can soldiers do with this horrible routine – being shot at and shooting all the time? If they want to preserve their sanity it's very logical they will use drugs as a form of escape. From what I heard in prison it's absolutely routine.'

'There seem to be longer sentences for using drugs than for shooting Palestinians,' I said.

'The army doesn't mind if soldiers shoot Palestinians,' said Ehud. 'They're just "doing their job". If they're charged it's always said that it "happened in a war zone", or that the victim was "caught in crossfire".'

After talking to Ehud, I couldn't sleep. There was something so disturbing, so barbaric about what I had just heard. More than ever now I was convinced that Tom was the victim of a victim, that it was the people, the policy-makers, who had put Taysir in this position who should be on trial in the courtroom in Ashkelon.

As ever, the news coming in from Gaza was appalling. Seven IDF soldiers had been killed in Rafah, and in revenge forty-five homes had been bulldozed and more than forty people killed. In what seemed an unbelievable act of barbarity, Rafah's little zoo had been flattened by IDF bulldozers, the animals butchered or crushed.

'People are more important than animals,' the zoo's co-owner was reported as saying. 'The zoo was the only place in Rafah where children could escape the tense atmosphere. There were slides and games for them. We had a small swimming pool. Why would they destroy that?' The destruction of the zoo and its animals had particularly angered Billy.

As usual the official explanation was that the army was hunting down Palestinian fighters and weapons-smuggling tunnels running under the border from Egypt. But the zoo was away from the border, in the al-Brazil district. An IDF spokesman put the devastation in Rafah down to 'explosive devices' activated by terrorists. But that was not the story that eyewitnesses or foreign correspondents told.

Israeli aircraft were now flying low, using sonic booms to

terrorise civilians in the Gaza Strip. Women were giving birth prematurely, people were having heart attacks, suffering burst eardrums. It was equally shocking to read of Israeli complaints that these sonic booms could be heard in some parts of Israel, frightening children and keeping them awake at night.

I received a devastating e-mail from Amjad. On 13 May, at 2.30 a.m., Amjad's mother had been knocked unconscious by an explosion very near his home and he had taken her to hospital. When he returned, the electricity had gone out all over Rafah, and there was shooting 'from everywhere' – the tank, the tower and an Apache attack helicopter flying overhead. Amjad went to look for the group of friends who had been with him and saw them near a local supermarket. But then, he wrote,

> I saw the Apache sent to them a bomb and I was very stressed and I went quickly but where are they? I did not see them head or face, just I saw some hands here, some heads there, it was the first time for me to see like this. I tried to carry some from there but I wasn't strong. I tried to be but I didn't. Today morning I was thinking about them, and I blacked out and was taken to hospital and now I can't move normally and am afraid and worried, today my friends, tomorrow it may be me. Where is the justice? I want to let everyone know about the martyrs.

Amjad listed their names and ages – eight young Palestinian men blown to bits, some of them Amjad's schoolfriends. The oldest was twenty-three.

I had last seen Amjad in London, not long after Tom's death. During that period his e-mails had been becoming more and more desperate and eventually, with the support of the Labour MP Jeremy Corbyn, I had written a letter to the Consulate in Gaza offering to sponsor Amjad and inviting him to stay. Though I was barely functioning at the time, I felt it was the least I could do.

Within days of his arrival Sophie and I had taken him to a meeting on the Israeli occupation of Palestine held in a committee room at the House of Commons. We were anxious for him to know that there were people in England who cared about what was happening in Rafah, and wanted to do something about it. At the end of the meeting I had introduced him to the assembled MPs and everyone had risen to their feet and applauded him.

When we got outside into Parliament Square Amjad had let himself go, punching the air in a gesture of irrepressible excitement and triumph. By then it was quite late, but there was no curfew, no fear of snipers, no military helicopters flying overhead. Amjad's expression said it all. It was the first time he had walked down a street without fear. Next day, he'd set off into London on his own and simply walked and walked. He'd wanted to experience every moment of his new freedom, to live it, breathe it in.

But within days the contrasts and contradictions were too much for Amjad and he'd become increasingly angry, disorientated and disillusioned. 'They do nothing but talk. We die, they talk,' he would say furiously when we watched the news. In the week before Tom's funeral he'd decided to return home. It was painful to watch his struggle to make this decision – one I felt he shouldn't have to make. But it was the only life he knew.

Now I couldn't bear to think of him, grieving and terrified. Amjad, who so longed to take hold of his life, but who had such an impossible life, who could easily, even now, be dead. I rang him on a poor connection from the kibbutz. As he answered, I could hear shooting in the background. He told me he was out in the street near his house. I knew that street well.

'Please, go back inside, Amjad,' I implored him.

'It's no good,' he shouted over the noise. 'It make no difference inside or out. Inside they shoot at you too, or bulldoze your house with you in it.'

He sounded distraught. His father and mother were both ill – how could one be well in a situation of such stress? Anything I could say was wholly inadequate. 'I miss you and your family so much,' he said several times. And 'I never stop thinking about London.'

'Dear Amjad, please take care. Keep safe,' I begged him as we said goodbye. But it seemed an empty thing to say.

An Israeli withdrawal from Gaza and from some of the West Bank settlements was being discussed under a new plan proposed by Ariel Sharon. Erella took me to a demonstration in support of withdrawal in Rabin Square in Tel Aviv. It was a huge gathering, about 150,000-strong. Erella pointed out to me groups from various Israeli peace organisations – B'Tselem, Machsom Watch ('Women Watching at Checkpoints'), Peace Now, Ta'ayush ('Living Together').

It was an impressive gathering, but when the official speakers, who included the former Prime Minister Shimon Peres and a retired Israeli general, took the platform, what struck me most was that for them this withdrawal plan really seemed to have little to do with the Palestinians. It was all about what would benefit Israel. Where, I thought despairingly, was the human feeling, the justice, that would take the concept of withdrawal much further and ensure the Palestinians had equal human rights, access to water, and freedom from fear? I felt I learned a lot that day about the mentality of those in power in Israel.

A few days later we went in coaches to a much smaller demonstration in the Negev, at the Kissufim checkpoint not far from Rafah. This was a protest against the recent horrible incursions and killings in Rafah, and the atmosphere was very different – infinitely more human. Members of the Israeli Parliament, the Knesset, were there, and it was a pleasure to bump into the human rights lawyer who had so generously lent us his flat in Be'ersheva. People spoke spontaneously, and at some point someone handed me a microphone and I talked briefly of what had happened to Tom and of his desire to build bridges, of the challenge of bringing the IDF to account, of my pity for the sufferings of both the Palestinians and the Israelis, and of the need to search for true reconciliation.

*   *   *

Afif had put me in touch with a member of the Knesset, Dr Ahmad Tibi, who represented the Palestinian interest, and towards the end of my stay on the kibbutz I went to Jerusalem to meet him. His car collected me at the hotel, and I was driven up the winding streets to the Knesset, a monolithic flat-roofed modern building set on one of the hillsides on which Jerusalem is built.

As soon as his assistant pushed open the door of Dr Tibi's office, I could see he was a man firing on all cylinders. A television at one end of the room was on, and proceedings in the Knesset competed with the news on Al Jazeera, Sky and numerous other cable channels. Dr Tibi, a powerful looking man in his fifties, was speaking on the phone as he sprang up to meet me, and to my astonishment he said something into the phone and then handed it to me, saying, 'It's President Arafat. He would like to speak to you.'

I was mildly taken aback. I asked him how he was – at that point he was incarcerated by the Israelis in the Muqata, his compound in Ramallah – and he said something like 'Complex times!' He told me how sorry he was about Tom, and that he had a picture of him on his wall. 'You are doing great things in the UK, speaking out,' he said, 'and I want to thank you.' I wasn't sure how I felt. We'd been uncomfortable that Arafat had claimed Tom as a martyr for the Palestinian cause, but at another level I understood it as an act of desperation. It was a way of drawing attention to an unbearable situation, which seemed to be what martyrdom was about.

After Dr Tibi and I had talked a little, his secretary took me into the Knesset's main chamber. I suppose I was expecting the relatively controlled atmosphere of the House of Commons, but as we came though the door I was hit by a babel of angry voices. Members were on their feet shouting and screaming at one another, others were moving about the floor. Was it always like this or had I just chanced upon a moment of madness? There must surely have been more rational voices struggling to be heard, but it seemed like a marketplace. At one point Dr Tibi's secretary made a scoffing noise and I asked her why. Pointing out one woman Member of the Knesset she said, 'She's just said that the Palestinians are not human beings.' And at my shocked look: 'Oh yes, it's said all the time. Sometimes these right-wing MKs call the Palestinians cockroaches.'

When Dr Tibi moved to the dais, he welcomed me and spoke about what had happened to Tom. Realising I was in the chamber, an Israeli journalist came up to me and began asking me how I felt about suicide bombers. I could tell there was a hidden agenda here, for as soon as I condemned suicide bombing unequivocally, and expressed empathy with Israeli victims, she lost interest and moved away.

My departures from Israel were always intense, vulnerable times and I was grateful next day for the presence of the Israeli driver from the British Embassy who would always wait and see me through the various security procedures until it was time to board the plane. On this occasion we had passed smoothly through several when suddenly we were surrounded by a group of officers from Israeli Security. The next hour was one of the most unpleasant and intrusive I have ever experienced. A woman took my handbag and briefcase from me without a word. Absolutely no explanation was given and, as ever, no one made eye contact. My luggage was fetched back from the aircraft hold, and everything was taken apart. Fingers were rubbed along every hem and seam of my clothing, wrapped presents were unwrapped and examined, every item of my make-up was opened and minutely inspected, my Chanel perfume held up and observed from every angle. Oddly, someone asked me if my hairdryer was working and as I'd used it that morning I replied, 'Yes, it is.'

In a back room everything, including my jewellery, was sorted into boxes. My shoes were taken away from me, and I was told I was going to be body-searched. I objected, but the driver, who had stayed with me, said: 'Just go along with it. Let them.' 'What possible reason could they have to behave like this?' I said. He leaned towards me and said with emphasis: 'They say these instructions have come from the very top.' Realising I could easily miss my plane, I gave in. But when the woman had finished going through my hair I couldn't contain my fury. 'It's not enough that you kill my son,' I said. 'You behave like this with a mother?' They stared back with their trained, impassive gaze. But I thought I detected a flicker of embarrassment on the face of the young woman who had searched me. It seemed I was being given a very clear message by the authorities. 'We don't want you in Israel, and we're going to make things very uncomfortable for you if you come.'

In the grand scale of things the incident was unimportant and back home I quickly unpacked my bag. It was like revisiting the scene of a violation. It took me a few days to realise that my hairdryer was broken and that the pad on which I had noted the contact details of many people, and on which I had made crucial notes about the trial, had mysteriously disappeared.

There was a terrible hollowness at the heart of the house now which couldn't be filled. I was worried about every member of the family but felt powerless to intervene, and I was struck once again by the loneliness of grief. We all have choices as to how we respond to death, and what transformation we undergo – W.B. Yeats called it 'a terrible beauty' – and to a degree we were energised, taking up the cause of justice for Tom and for others who had suffered. Much of the time we tried to clutch at ordinary life from within the political and media furore that surrounded us. Anthony concentrated on a new project, developing a way of improving access to justice. Sophie seemed far away, wrapped in a cloak of self-protection that I felt unable to penetrate, while Fred was grieving in a silent, withdrawn way that broke my heart. Billy I could see had in some way been given a new direction by our tragedy. Just as I distracted myself from the pain of it by trying my best to use it to influence events, he too was preoccupied with what was happening in Israel. He was thinking of moving away from home to live with friends and I knew how much Fred would miss him.

Seeing one another only seemed to add to the pain. When we did get together, what seemed to comfort us most was sharing memories of Tom. It helped, too, when other people talked to us about him – his old friends, his new friends, anybody who had known him. It was as if we were all having to re-create Tom for ourselves, to build up a picture of him that we could hold on to. For us and for Tom's friends, putting together all these different memories somehow helped us to get closer to him, to know him better. Tom's friends had been incredibly important to him. *'I get paranoid sometimes, as does everyone,'* he had written in his diary, *'but there is nothing better than knowing how much my friends care about me. It is an incredible feeling when I suddenly realise what good friends they are, that they love me as I do them, and that I'm worth it.'*

I found comfort in talking to Mohammed, who had arrived in London at about the same time as Amjad and was now applying for asylum – his work in Rafah as a Palestinian peace activist made it far too dangerous for him to return. In his intelligence and self-awareness Mohammed reminded me of Tom. He had already succeeded in getting out of Rafah to spend four years away from his family studying for a degree in Bangladesh – an incredible achievement – and now he was hoping to study engineering in England. To me he was a vital link with Tom's last days in Rafah. He had been one of the last people to see Tom alive.

Thoughtful friends would ask me how we were. I didn't want to burden them, although I did confide in a few close friends, and in Erella, of course. With Erella one barely needed words. I'd learned from her that the most truthful thing to say was 'I am all right at this minute.' Inwardly it was frightening. Tom was with me night and day and I found myself remembering the small, sometimes quite mundane things. I saw him taking off his black and red biker's jacket as he walked into the house and throwing it over the banister. It was so stiff and heavy it invariably fell off.

'Hang it up, Tom,' I'd say. How often had I said that? I saw him harnessing his energy as he got ready to sprint – it was one of my loveliest memories, Tom ran like a gazelle. I remembered the time in Cornwall when he and 'the boys' had noticed some seals swimming about in the water near the jetty where they were standing. Everyone was aghast when Tom jumped in among them. Afterwards I asked Tom why he'd done it and he'd simply smiled and answered exuberantly: 'I wanted to swim with seals.'

NINETEEN

At the beginning of June the military judges in Israel were still considering whether the evidence given by Taysir was admissible in court, and we waited to see when the trial would be resumed. Billy was keen to attend it. But Peter Carter, the Deputy Ambassador, had taken me out to dinner when I was in Tel Aviv, and at the end of it had said: 'I have to tell you that Danny Carmon at the Foreign Ministry says Billy will not be given permission to enter Israel.'

'On what grounds exactly?' I asked.

'They're not explicit, but I imagine they're thinking about his trip to the West Bank,' said Peter.

I was outraged. 'Would it be possible to arrange a meeting with Danny Carmon?' I asked. 'I've got several things I'd like to discuss with him.'

As indeed I had. There was the matter of compensation and damages, still unacknowledged and unsettled. There was the question of openness and transparency, a promise so often made by Israel but never kept. There was the matter of a formal apology from the Israeli government – something they seemed to feel was of no importance. And now there was this insult to Billy. The whole family felt affronted.

So once again I'd found myself at the Ministry of Defence with Peter, confronting Danny Carmon, whose smooth and smiling presence I remembered from our meeting with the IDF a year earlier. I put my points to him and was met with the customary diplomatic stonewalling. When it came to Billy he simply refused

to give me specific reasons for his exclusion, and I found this
extraordinarily callous.

'It's important to Billy to attend this trial; it should be taken as a
moral right,' I said. 'For him it's part of coming to terms with
Tom's death, and excluding him is just a further cruelty. It is
unacceptable that you do not give reasons.'

But it was no good. Carmon simply took refuge behind the all-
purpose phrase that he had 'taken note of what I'd said'.

Billy, of course, was furious when he heard the news, and was
all for setting off for Israel as soon as the trial resumed. Both he and
Sophie felt that if he was turned away the resulting publicity
would be making a point, but I was horrified by the idea. After
my experiences with Israeli Security, I had no illusions. I felt sure
they would have no compunction in targeting Billy. They had
repeatedly shown that they did not care that we had already lost a
member of the family, and I was adamant that, for Billy's own
protection, his decision needed to be taken with the knowledge
and support of the FCO and our Israeli lawyers. For a while I was
on tenterhooks, but fortunately Billy's innate common sense won
the day, and he decided not to go.

The trial resumed briefly in mid-June. Over the phone Karin
told me that the courtroom was packed with pro-IDF activists,
who arrived in busloads waving Israeli flags and placards reading
'Save Our Soldiers' and 'No Human Shields in War-Zones'.
They were there at the instigation of the Israeli Law Centre,
Shurat HaDin, which was organising a legal campaign on behalf
of Taysir and his family. Karin told me that Shurat HaDin's
vocal Director, Nitsana Darshan-Leitner, was telling the press
that the trial was a farce. 'Hurndall's family reached out to
British officials and human rights organisations to apply pressure
on the Ministry of Defence to in turn put pressure on the IDF
to find a soldier to blame and they chose this soldier', she was
reported as saying. There was more poisonous propaganda from
her about the terrorist activities of the ISM and the bias of the

British press. On 16 June the court was again adjourned after further arguments about the manner in which Taysir had been questioned.

At about this time an all-party delegation of British MPs and a member of the House of Lords – Huw Irranca-Davies, Crispin Blunt and Baroness Northover – visited Rafah, and on their return reported with shock that they had been shot at by the IDF, only yards from the place where Tom had been shot. 'It is absolutely appalling,' Crispin Blunt told the *Guardian*. 'If Israeli soldiers are prepared to do this to people who are clearly with the UN it is no surprise that so many Palestinians have been killed. This demonstrates that the Israelis do not want witnesses to what is happening in Gaza and the West Bank.'

To me, privately, he said: 'I can understand why Tom did what he did. There were children playing at that spot when we were there.'

July and August dragged by with very little for Karin to report. On 23 September the court reconvened and the commander, or *Magad*, of Taysir's regiment was called to the witness box. According to Karin he spent most of his time trying to defend himself and Taysir. He argued that if Tom had been standing where the prosecution claimed he was, the bullet that shot him could not have come from the watchtower – a line of houses would have intervened. The implication was that the shot had been fired by a Palestinian, or possibly, as the commander also implied, by a Palestinian disguised as an ISMer.

That particular watchtower, we knew, had since been moved by the IDF to another position, and before this we had been refused permission to view it from the inside to check for ourselves the line of vision and confirm one way or another the assertions now being made by the commander, despite Anthony's repeated requests. However, it soon became clear that the map he produced in court had been out of date even at the time Tom was shot, which undermined his evidence.

*   *   *

That same month I came face to face with Tony Blair. We met at a dinner hosted by the seventeen Arab League Ambassadors at the 2004 Labour Party Conference in Brighton, which the public service union UNISON had sponsored me to attend. I had been invited to the dinner by Afif, who was sitting with Christ'l on the Prime Minister's table, and after dinner he beckoned to me and to David Freeman, a lawyer with a close interest in the Middle East, and introduced us to Cherie Blair. When she tapped her husband on the shoulder and he turned and gave me his strong, firm handshake I came straight to the point, telling him I was very hurt that he hadn't yet publicly condemned the shooting of Tom.

He looked at me with light, glass-blue eyes that couldn't seem to decide whether they were looking at me or beyond me, and raised his hands and shoulders in a helpless gesture as if to say 'I didn't know I was meant to'. We talked for a few more minutes about Tom and the conclusions he was coming to in the days before he was shot. Blair listened attentively, but I found his gaze disorientating because I couldn't gauge its focus. Later, as he left the room, he looked back and nodded to me. No words, but a gesture of acknowledgement.

And while the West remained silent, in Rafah the horror continued. On 5 October a thirteen-year-old girl called Iman al-Hams was shot dead as she walked to school. An internal IDF 'debriefing' immediately after the incident found that the company commander who shot her 'had not acted unethically'. 'Anything that's mobile, that moves in the zone, even if it's a three-year-old, needs to be killed', he was recorded as saying.

It turned out that Iman had not been shot once only. Soldiers from the company told the press that the commander had 'confirmed the kill' – an appalling IDF phrase meaning that he'd pumped her body full of bullets from close range. Only after this disclosure, and the soldiers' release of a communications tape showing that another soldier had warned the commander that the victim was 'a little girl' did the IDF promise a military police investigation. And what would that lead to in terms of a conviction, I wondered cynically.

In November Dr Chapman, the pathologist who had conducted Tom's autopsy, travelled to Israel to give evidence about Tom's medical condition. According to Karin, Dr Chapman was a model witness: clear, concise and extremely polite. A colleague of Ilan Bombach had by now taken over and his defence team were crudely attempting to prove that he had not followed the procedures laid down by the Royal College of Pathologists during the post-mortem, and were questioning his report. Their information had been gleaned from the internet. Dr Chapman courteously pointed out that he had contributed to the drawing up of these particular procedures. They were trying to break the causal link between the shooting and Tom's death but the questioning was clearly going nowhere, and the judges cut it short.

Karin also described one extraordinary incident. There was a break in the hearing while the commander who had shot Iman al-Hams appeared briefly in court. Taysir apparently lounged in his seat talking to his guards and chewing gum. At some point the prosecution asked him not to chew gum, at which he let out an earsplitting screech and rushed from the building. The guards ran after him and he was brought back. He was rude and sulky, like a spoilt child wanting to make an impression, said Karin.

In December Taysir took the stand. Karin told us his answers were so absurdly contradictory it was obvious he was lying. Although he was a crack shot – we already knew he had won an award as a marksman – she felt he was a person with a very poor level of comprehension. The judges did their best to get him to open up about what had actually happened, but he kept returning to what he had *reported* had happened, almost as if he couldn't tell the difference.

Taysir had at first said that he'd seen someone in uniform running towards the lookout post, and that he hadn't fired at him but 'far away from him just to frighten him'. He'd never had him in his telescopic sights. After the shot he'd seen him fall, but not as if he'd hit him. Then he claimed that he had fired ten centimetres from Tom's left ear but that Tom had moved.

Under further questioning he admitted that he had lied in his original testimony – that the person was not wearing a uniform. But he could not bring himself to say that he was actually wearing an orange vest – just that he had 'something round his neck'. He had not attached any significance to this.

The prosecutor then asked why, if it was not important, he had lied to the military investigator about what Tom was wearing. Taysir had no answer.

He said that after firing the shot he had turned away to do something with his gun, and when he looked back there was no sign of the person. He admitted that he had then phoned his commander – after he had already shot Tom – and told him there was someone in uniform with a weapon coming towards him, and asked for permission to shoot, which was given.

'So you gave a false report to the company commander?' the prosecutor had asked.

'I did not give a false report,' he replied. 'He might have had a weapon under his clothing. People fire freely there. The army fires freely in Rafah.'

After that, he said, there were no more shots. He knew he had not hit Tom – it must have been someone else. Asked why he had lied, he said it was because he was afraid and under pressure. His testimony was utterly confused.

What was clear was that Taysir was trying to emphasise that he had only been doing what was expected of him. He said his commanders had told him, and everyone else, to shoot anyone in the area they called the security zone, between the houses and the watchtower. It was standard procedure. 'I did what we were told, and that is that everyone entering the security zone must be taken out.' I was concerned that no one seemed to have pointed out that Tom was, in fact, a considerable distance outside the security zone when he was shot. He knew the dangers only too well.

When asked if he knew the rules of engagement Taysir said he hadn't discussed them with his superiors and hadn't seen them. 'In any case they are written in Hebrew and everyone knows I have problems with Hebrew.'

In early January we heard from Karin that Pinhaus Zuaretz, the brigadier in charge of the Southern Gaza district, was about to give evidence, and the defence were planning to play their trump card by calling their own medical witnesses. I knew I had to attend. I was also anxious to see Amjad and to bring news of Mohammed to his family. So I applied for a permit to go down to Rafah again. This time I planned to go alone.

I flew into Ben Gurion airport on a grey January day. It felt very much like flying into London on a winter's day, except that the ground was parched dark by the heat of summer. That day it looked muddy and the runway was wet. Rivulets of rain sparked across the mud-splattered port window, and I thought of Tom's description in his journal of his arrival in Amman: '*It wasn't what you would expect as we came in to land. Thick cloud sent the intermittent flashes from the wing thudding back up the fuselage, penetrating only a few metres, and the ground was only a wall of mist. You could see the raindrops momentarily frozen in their horizontal paths.*'

In those few words he'd said it all. I was seized by a deep sadness, which shocked me by its sudden onslaught. I told myself it would have been strange if I hadn't felt vulnerable arriving in Israel. And I knew that in the past months I had barely been able to grieve. It had been impossible at home – there were too many distractions, too many responsibilities. I'd found myself intentionally looking for activities to deflect the pain, knowing full well what I was doing. Now suddenly I was alone, and face to face with my grief.

At my hotel in the centre of Tel Aviv I was given a room with a view of the sea. The overcast, rainy sky merged with the dark water, and you could barely see the horizon. I stood looking out at the waves, my head already filled with troubling questions.

How was I going to deal with the coming days in court? Could I ever forgive Taysir for what he had done? I wished the pounding water would wash through my head and give me some relief.

I left the hotel and crossed the main boulevard in search of a restaurant. As I sat down the news was on and I could pick out the word 'Falestini' used over and over again. I knew it was the Hebrew word for Palestinians. As I left, Don McLean's 'American Pie' was playing in the background:

> . . . *Singin' this'll be the day that I die, This'll be the day that I die* . . .

I couldn't get it out of my head all evening. Many a time I'd heard this track emanating from Tom's room.

I woke at 6.30 and when I drew back the curtains the dawn was bright and fresh. The sun shone on the rocks, which were golden brown with seaweed, and the water spilled over them, glossing them momentarily as if with a clear varnish. There was blue sky over the windy sea. Near the shore the water was a pale khaki, broken only by explosions of white spume, but further out it changed sharply to a dark, dull indigo, as if a line had been drawn across the water. The wind caught the surface, flinging the spray joyously back, and I watched, comforted as always by the sea's mysterious rhythms.

At 8 a.m. the Embassy car arrived to collect me. This time I was accompanied by Adam Sambrook, the Hebrew-speaking member of the Embassy staff who had been attending the trial with Karin. On the way to Ashkelon I asked him what his impression of the soldier was, and of the defence team.

'Well,' he said, 'he's brighter than his lawyers are trying to make out, but certainly not the sharpest tool in the box. One of the defence's claims has been that he was too thick to understand the rules of engagement. As you've seen for yourself, his lawyer was really pedantic, but now they've brought in someone else.'

'What the hell,' I said, 'were they doing putting someone who couldn't understand the rules of engagement in charge of a lookout post in a heavily populated civilian area? Had they even tried to brief him?'

'Good question,' said Adam. 'They also claim that he doesn't speak very good Hebrew, but it's certainly as good as mine.'

As we walked into the courtroom we met the prosecution lawyer Hila. Apparently Taysir had not shown up that day. He had been on 'home leave', and no one knew quite where he was – not even the military police. It seemed extraordinary to me that someone accused of manslaughter should be allowed to go home in the middle of his trial. The defence were clearly embarrassed, and even the judges seemed at a loss.

The court rose to give the defence a chance to try to get in touch with their client. When it reconvened Hila whispered to us that apparently Taysir hadn't known the court was sitting today – he had expected to be contacted. There was further discussion about whether the trial could go ahead without him. The defence had been planning to call a medical witness, Dr Lazary, to challenge Dr Chapman's testimony. But after prolonged discussion, the judges announced that they had no authority to hear evidence without the accused being present, and the court was adjourned for a further two weeks.

Erella had invited me to stay with them at the kibbutz, and Adam and the Embassy driver took me there and dropped me by the now familiar pathway in the grounds. It was late evening by the time we arrived, and I walked slowly along the path in the velvet dark, drawing in deep, refreshing breaths of balmy air which carried the scent of herbs and new-mown grass. As I mounted the steps to Erella's apartment, I could hear the faint notes of the Moonlight Sonata. Danny was playing the piano. After the courtroom at Ashkelon the kibbutz felt like a haven, and I stood for a moment at the top of the steps, thinking how lucky I was to have found it, how fortunate to have the friendship of Danny and Erella, before the door opened and Erella enfolded me in her arms.

As always we sat up late, talking of the trial, of the situation in Gaza and the West Bank, of the isolation Erella herself so often felt, and of Tom. 'It's very rare,' I said at one point, 'that people can both feel the pain, the emotion of a situation and at the same time stand back and observe themselves objectively in that situation. Tom seemed to be able to do that.'

'It's the basis of meditation,' said Erella, 'to break down the barrier between the observer and the thing observed, to both actively meet your feelings and simultaneously stand back from them. Emotions are both strong and impermanent, so it's a very difficult thing to do. That's why Tom was so unusual.'

Later, speaking of Israel's actions in the Occupied Territories, Erella said passionately: 'It's so difficult. I am someone who sees what's going on, and I am facing such loneliness because of it. It's the price I have to pay for seeing: terrible loneliness. I've had it for most of my life – it's not as if I've just woken up after a certain number of years and discovered my country is lying. I've known it for a long time. It makes me sick.'

Next morning, Erella told me she had had a dream. She was with a group of people standing next to a very poor man who had a little tray of goods for sale. He kept reaching out to them desperately, trying to sell them something, but Erella was the only one of the group who noticed. No matter how hard she tried to draw their attention to the vendor they completely ignored him. Erella woke in tears. That dream, we agreed, seemed to be not only about Erella, but about Tom – about all those people who have the imagination to feel others' pain, who do not turn away from it, and the anguish they feel because others refuse to see it. And of the loneliness that can bring.

One evening, after a supper of Danny's famous roasted vegetables, for some reason I asked Erella and Danny about the Hatikva, the Israeli national anthem. It was a moment I shall never forget. They both began quietly singing and though I didn't know the Hebrew words, I joined in and hummed the tune. The solemn anthem spoke of courage and dignity, and hope for a peaceful homeland. I wondered what had happened to Israel, and to that courage and dignity and desire for peace, which had come out of so much suffering. Now, Erella told me, she could hardly bear to sing it – she felt too disillusioned.

I was still trying to get a permit to go down to Rafah. By the end of January I'd heard no more, and I spoke briefly to a young lieutenant at the Erez Crossing over an indistinct, crackling line. I tried to explain my movements – the necessity for me to be in Tel Aviv the following week so that the Embassy could take me to Ashkelon for the next stage of the trial, my anxiety to return to London as soon as the next stage of the trial was over – on 9 February an exhibition of Tom's photographs organised by Anthony with the assistance of Kay and others was to open at the Frontline Club, the foreign correspondents' club in Paddington. The bleak but predictable response from the lieutenant was that my permit application had not yet been processed.

The court reconvened for the umpteenth time in the first week of February. Adam Sambrook met me in Tel Aviv and drove me down. This was the day on which the defence called their first 'independent' medical expert witness, Dr Lazary, and his appearance in court was an experience I shan't forget.

Dr Lazary was a small, bumptious man whose views seemed to take no account of the facts contained in Dr Chapman's painstaking post-mortem report. His claim was that Tom's death had nothing directly to do with the shooting – that he had died as the result of major negligence on the part of the British hospital. In fact he believed, he said, that the negligence was so severe that it actually amounted to criminality.

It was hard to sit and listen to this poorly informed man talking on so smugly and confidently, and it was difficult to follow the drift of his argument. He appeared to have no grasp of the progress of Tom's condition following the shooting – what he was describing bore no relation to what I had actually observed, sitting at Tom's bedside, month in, month out, and from time to

time it was all I could do to stop myself getting up and telling him
how it had really been. He seemed unable to produce any real
evidence to back up his claims. How, I wondered, could he
possibly suggest that there was no causal connection between the
shooting and Tom's death when we all knew that the bullet had
destroyed a large part of Tom's brain?

I sat there tense with fury. But when we reached the point
where Dr Lazary began to imply that the family had been
complicit in Tom's death – I think it was even suggested that
we might have put a pillow over his head – and that had he, Dr
Lazary, been looking after Tom he would probably have recov-
ered to the point where he was able to communicate, I could only
shake my head in disbelief. I could stand it no more. I rose and left
the courtroom, my high heels audibly clacking on the bare floor.

I stood outside shaking, unable to stop the tears. Adam came
and joined me and we sat down on a bench. At one point I
glanced back into the court, to where the soldier was sitting. He
was watching me, and for a split second our eyes met. It was the
nearest thing to human communication we had during the course
of the trial. Eventually Karin emerged. 'Don't worry,' she said.
'The judges were not impressed with Dr Lazary. I don't think his
testimony has been much help to the defence.'

Towards the end of the day a further witness was called by the
defence – an impressively bright and articulate young soldier who
was in charge of the IDF's maps. His brief had been to establish
whether there was a line of vision between the watchtower and
the point where Tom was standing when he was shot, and he had
been given several sets of coordinates to work from. His evidence
was highly technical, but I understood that the coordinates, which
he had been given by the defence team itself, indicated that there
was either no line of vision, or only a partial line of vision between
those points and the watchtower. But it emerged in court that
none of these coordinates represented the exact point where Tom
had fallen.

However, among the documents the young soldier had been

given was a photograph of Tom lying on the ground beside the distinctive lump of concrete. This had enabled him to establish accurately the point where Tom had been standing when he was shot and he had taken it upon himself to work out a further set of coordinates. These calculations proved beyond doubt that there had been a clear line of vision between Tom's position and the watchtower.

This was a vital piece of evidence for the prosecution, and I was deeply touched by the young man's honesty and integrity. It seemed that the defence team had scored yet another spectacular own goal.

When I got back to the kibbutz I found that my permit for Rafah had come through. Erella and Danny were away, but Ehud called in and I told him about the trial and about my plan. He looked apprehensive. I rang Anthony.

'Is that really a good idea?' he said. 'Do you have to go down to Rafah now? If you do you're probably going to miss the opening of Tom's exhibition.'

'I know,' I said, 'but it's something I have to do while I'm here. I've promised Amjad. And I want to see Mohammed's family. Mohammed's cousin has said he'll meet me at the border. And I have to visit the site again.'

'Well, just be careful . . .' said Anthony doubtfully. But I could tell he wasn't happy.

One of Anthony's particular interests is photography and it had seemed natural that he should stay in London to finalise arrangements for the exhibition while I attended the trial. The effort he had put into this exhibition was a measure of his care and love for his son. The opening would be a big moment, and I felt hopelessly torn. Yet I knew it was important that I make this journey.

I spent the night in Be'ersheva and next day took a taxi to the Erez Crossing, stopping at a small flower shop to buy two bunches of flowers. It was raining and there was very little traffic on the roads. When we reached the high metal gates of the crossing I got out and paid the taxi driver, and suddenly all the strain of the previous days hit me. Before, I'd always been protected, with a member of the Embassy staff to see us through. Now I was just another person on foot. Flowers in hand, I walked towards the low checkpoint building.

I knew that inside it there were three channels – civilian, diplomatic and VIP. I ignored these classifications and walked up to the desk. Behind it I found the usual group of laid-back eighteen-year-olds, slouching and chatting, supremely unconcerned that anyone might be waiting. They already had my details and I had a contact number at the Embassy to ring, but even so I felt a little knot in my stomach, a lurch of uncertainty about whether they would let me through. There were very few people about. The soldiers looked at my papers without much interest, and after a few minutes indicated that I could proceed.

I walked on, through another door, past what looked like cattle pens where a few Palestinian men were standing huddled together waiting, and into a long tunnel with a corrugated-iron roof, lit by a few dim bulbs and the grey light from a long gap high up in the concrete wall. The floor was earth, and at intervals off to the side there were areas filled with rubbish. It was a horrible place. There was no light at the end of the tunnel, and I walked on into the freezing dimness, carrying my flowers. Then suddenly the tunnel curved, and round the bend I could see a distant light and a figure, a Palestinian guard. As I approached, the figure took on more definition, and out of this desolation came a welcoming smile. The feeling of warmth and relief was overwhelming.

Mohammed's cousin, also named Mohammed, was waiting for me, and we took a taxi along the now familiar road, through Gaza City and the bleak rubble of the Khan Younis refugee camp. Amjad had been adamant about wanting to come to the Erez Crossing to meet me, but I remembered how we had been shot at at the Abu Houli checkpoint, and knowing what a perilous flashpoint it could be, I felt worried about him. 'Please don't come. It's dangerous,' I insisted. He'd taken a lot of persuading, and I knew he was a little hurt.

When I met him in the Palestinian Progressive Youth Movement's sparsely furnished little office, he greeted me shyly. We weren't in London now. He looked somehow calmer and more mature. But he was still the same old Amjad, with his sweet boyish smile and zest for life, and that sense he always gave me of a compassionate spirit triumphing over suffering. It was good to see him, and before long he had relaxed and was asking me about Billy and Fred and Sophie and Anthony, and inviting me to lunch with his family.

I knew immediately we entered Amjad's house that this visit from his London friend was a significant event. We sat on mattresses in Amjad's room, which I was told he had tidied specially for the occasion. The family all smiled and made a gentle joke of it. 'He's thrown everything into the cupboards,' said his father, a delightful older man with the same warm brown eyes as Amjad.

His mother and sisters were hard at work in the kitchen, bringing in huge dishes of rice and pungent smelling chicken with coriander. His father asked me about London, and told me how he had worked for the British under the Mandate, and come to this house in 1948. 'Now it has been made good again, and I am happy,' he said. From time to time he would pick out a particularly choice piece of chicken and place it thoughtfully on my plate saying 'Have a bit.' I was wet and exhausted, my feet were freezing, and my back was aching from the unaccustomed position. But inwardly I thought I had rarely felt such human warmth as I felt in this desolate place.

After lunch I gave Amjad's mother one of the bunches of flowers I had brought. Then Amjad and I walked together to the place where Tom had been shot. I'd notified the army that I was coming, told them I'd wear an orange scarf around my neck so they could identify me from the watchtower. At intervals I phoned the IDF number and they would ask me sharply, 'Where are you now? Which road?', and I would try to describe our position among the bombed-out buildings. If anything it all looked worse than before. It seemed incredible that people were still actually living here.

We approached the barrier of rubble and the huge block of concrete. As always, beautiful children were running up and down the mound, jumping and laughing and calling to one another. Amjad and I stood together for a moment, simply looking. Then I laid the other bunch of flowers in the place where Tom had fallen, where I thought his head would have been. The group of lovely children stood together around the spot. Our eyes met and they smiled.

We were silent as we left, but after about twenty yards Amjad pointed out a derelict looking building riddled with bullet holes. 'School for deaf people,' he said. 'Are they still using it?' I asked. It was hard to believe. 'Many deaf people in Rafah,' said Amjad. 'From the bombs and planes making boom,' and he put his fingers in his ears. How good it would be, I thought, to be able to do something for this poor school.

There was now just time to see Mohammed's family. His mother and his four sisters welcomed me like a long-lost friend, pressing food upon me and thanking me over and over for helping Mohammed. Under the terms of his asylum, Mohammed could not return to Gaza for several years, and I saw from the look in his mother's eyes how much she missed him. She gave me some special seeds for making tea that she knew Mohammed liked, and I tried to describe a little of his life in London, and how he was.

It was hard to leave, but it was beginning to get dark and I knew the Erez Crossing closed at eight. Mohammed's cousin was to come back with me, and Amjad insisted on accompanying us as far as Gaza City, where he said he would stay with friends. When it came to it, it was difficult to say goodbye – I had learned so much about him and his life. So I pressed his arm, and he quickly got out of the taxi, waved and disappeared into the night.

It was completely dark when we reached the Erez Crossing. I

said goodbye to Mohammed and showed my papers to the Palestinian guards who were sitting in the open behind a rickety looking trestle table at the entrance to the tunnel, attempting to keep warm with a small cooking ring on an extension lead, which hissed as the raindrops hit it. One of them picked up the phone and there was a terse conversation with the soldiers on the Israeli side. Then they bade me a friendly goodbye and I started down the tunnel.

It was empty and eerie. I tried to walk as purposefully as possible, to give myself courage. I could hear dripping water. Wires without light bulbs hung down. The only light came from the glare of the watchtowers through a gap along the top of the tunnel twenty feet or so up. I rounded the bend – put there to prevent Israelis and Palestinians shooting at each other from either end – and there, suddenly, in front of me were huge steel gates, about fifteen feet high. Through the bars I could see the cattle pens I'd spotted on my way out, and more huge steel-barred gates beyond. I pushed at one of the gates in front of me, but it didn't budge. I stood there feeling increasingly angry – not because I was wet and cold and tired, but because the whole thing suddenly struck me as so outrageous, so arrogant, so unnecessary. I stood there for a good ten minutes. I could hear voices in the distance, and from time to time I called out 'Hello! Is anybody there?'

Eventually a rasping voice over a loudspeaker said, 'Wait!' Then, 'Push the gate.' I pushed it but nothing happened. 'The other one,' came the irritable voice. Nothing happened again. 'No, the other one,' from the exasperated young voice. It was completely disorientating. I went back to the first gate, pushed it, it opened, and I went through.

Now I was in a kind of cage with an electronically controlled and locked gate behind me and a gate in front of me, and steel pens at the side. The voice came over the loudspeaker again, but this time I couldn't understand what it was saying, so I just carried on walking until I was taken up short by an order: '*Stop!*' This was followed by something else, but still I couldn't make it out. 'I can't understand you!' I said to the loudspeaker, naively imagining someone could hear me. But no – this was a one-way conversation. Eventually I deduced what they wanted and took my coat off. Another faceless order was shouted. I put my arms out and turned round. Then I was told to walk forward.

Now I was up against another set of massive gates. I rattled them, but they didn't open. I called out 'Hello!', but no one answered. Eventually a young soldier appeared, sauntering towards me, taking his time. I was furious. I could have been his mother. 'Can't you just open the gate?' I said. He said nothing, simply handed me a glove through the bars without explanation. 'What's this for?' I said. 'This isn't the way to treat people. You need to explain.' I was carrying a plastic bag with the seeds Mohammed's mother had given me, and a tracksuit for myself that she had insisted I take. He pointed to the bag and said: 'Put this glove on and rub it round the things in that bag. Then give it back to me.'

I was fuming, but did as I was asked. Another, more mature-looking soldier joined us. 'Look at me,' I said. 'Do you honestly think I've got something in here that would harm anybody?' Neither of them said anything, but the older soldier looked slightly apologetic.

By this time I was aware that an elderly Palestinian man had come up behind me. I looked back at him, but he gazed down at the ground, avoiding my eyes. I felt desolate for him. What must he be feeling about being seen going through this barbaric and humiliating ritual? I imagined he was going over into Israel to do nightshift work. Each time he must have to face this procedure and one of these arrogant young soldiers.

'Can't you open the gate?' I said.

'You'll have to wait until he's been through the system,' the young soldier said. Finally the gate was opened and the Palestinian and I went through together. I longed to communicate to him my empathy and my disgust. For a moment he raised his head and I saw his face. It was deeply furrowed – the face of someone who has been in a war zone, defeated, only half-alive.

The older soldier must have seen my look. 'Soon we're going to have a better system,' he said ingratiatingly, 'where internationals go through a separate door.'

The gulf between our understanding was so great there seemed nothing to say, but I gazed steadily back at him.

'Yeah, yeah,' said the young soldier, with a kind of ironic bravado. 'We're all wrong, the Israeli army. It's all our fault.'

TWENTY

I arrived in London just too late for the opening of Tom's exhibition at the Frontline Club, but on seeing it next day with Anthony I was bowled over. It was as if I was in Rafah again – the hideously destroyed buildings with their protuberances of rusting steel girders, the bleak, litter-strewn streets. And I was stabbed with thoughts of Amjad, and of all the ravaged people we'd met there who were trying to make a life against all the odds.

Anthony had chosen the venue carefully. One of the Frontline Club's aims is to promote freedom of expression and to support those working at the sharp edge of journalism, and its members include some of the best photographers, journalists and camera-men in the world. It gives off a tremendous sense of vigour and immediacy, of leaving no stone unturned to bring back the truth. Tom, I knew, would have loved its intellectual energy; it was a place, I felt, that might well have become part of his professional life if he had lived. Now I felt incredibly proud and moved to see his pictures on the exposed brick walls.

Anthony had collated three thousand images on various discs and cartridges taken during Tom's months in the Middle East. Many of them were different versions of the same picture, and in London Anthony and Kay had struggled to sort them. Eventually they had reduced them to nine hundred, and with huge difficulty and the help of a picture editor from the *Sunday Telegraph* from these we had selected twenty-one.

Looking now at the blown-up mounted photographs of tanks bearing down on the peaceworkers I could hear the earsplitting noise of metal against metal and feel the terrifying vibrations of the revving engines. One powerful photo showed Raph walking calmly past a tank at full throttle, spewing out a cloud of poisonous fumes, almost burying him from sight.

I stood for a long time gazing at the picture of a wistful child leaning pensively against the ruined wall of his demolished home. All Tom's anger, all his shock at the thought of those children's futureless lives, were in that photograph. It was an extraordinarily humbling feeling to be looking through his eyes, almost as if searching to understand his judgement. Inside me a respect grew, and a kind of realisation that this was what he had gone to the Middle East to find.

The week after I left Israel, Pinhaus Zuaretz, the brigade commander whose name I had first heard mentioned in early January, was called to Ashkelon to give evidence, and Karin described the scene in court. She told me Zuaretz held a very senior position in the army, the equivalent probably of a British brigadier-general. It was his responsibility to ensure that soldiers were trained in the rules of engagement. And he it was, I learned from one of the foreign correspondents, who had helped reformulate the IDF's rules of engagement after the Second Intifada to permit soldiers to shoot children as young as fourteen.

Zuaretz, so Karin told me, was a man with a deceptively easy and friendly manner. He had clearly been called by the defence to bolster Taysir's testimony, to give him a character reference, as it were. And that is what he did. He praised him warmly and at length, calling him an excellent soldier. This was interesting, since we already knew that Taysir had been convicted of taking drugs while on duty. It had also emerged during the trial that he had been convicted of illegal use of a weapon after using a field near his home as a shooting range. It seemed that off-duty firearms regulations were very strict.

More strangely still, Zuaretz said that he had believed Taysir's original testimony. This I couldn't understand, since from very early on it was clear that Taysir had lied and given contradictory versions of the event. Zuaretz said he had been disappointed to discover that Taysir had lied. The picture he attempted to draw, in defiance of all the evidence, was of a soldier dealing with a crisis professionally and appropriately.

'But this is fantasy,' I said to Karin on the phone.

'It's just the way the IDF behave,' said Karin. 'Commanders always tend to back up their soldiers.'

In fact Zuaretz turned out to be a better witness for the prosecution than for the defence. When examined about whether there was a line of vision from the watchtower to where Tom was standing, at first, on the basis of the court's outdated material, he said that there was not. However, when the prosecution showed him more accurate pictures proving that there had been a line of vision, he was forced to agree.

The final expert witness called by the defence was a forensic pathologist, Dr Chen Kugel, an opinionated young army doctor with a dramatic manner who appeared in court in military uniform. When I heard this I was astonished. Could he really be said to be unbiased? The line Dr Kugel took, based on hospital reports, was that Tom could not have been in a vegetative state since he was breathing unaided and had certain basic reflexes, and so should have been treated with antibiotics. He claimed that Tom's death had not been caused by pneumonia, but by an overdose of morphine – a decision for which we, his family, and the English doctors were responsible.

I was outraged that Dr Kugel, like Dr Lazary, was attempting to break the causal link between the shooting and Tom's death, and to shift the blame on to the English doctors who had given Tom such outstanding care. It was preposterous.

Karin told me there had been a revealing exchange when the prosecution team pointed out that they had originally approached Dr Kugel for an opinion with a view to his appearing as an expert witness for the prosecution, and had shown him various medical documents. During these conversations he had expressed entirely different opinions from the ones he had just proffered in court. In the event Dr Chapman had been able to attend, and the idea of using Dr Kugel was dropped. Dr Kugel seemed furious that his fickleness had been exposed. It left me questioning a system that allowed expert witnesses to change their 'considered' professional opinions according to the side for which they were giving evidence. What view would the judges take?

A few days after the second anniversary of Tom's shooting, an Israeli military court acquitted an IDF lieutenant of the killing of the English cameraman James Miller, though there was little doubt, in my view, that he had been knowingly targeted. Evidence had been tampered with, and the soldier had apparently changed his account of the incident six times. Just what had happened with Tom – it was still the same old story. And even though the Israelis were set to pull out of Gaza in August, they would maintain their stranglehold. They would still control the borders, the territorial waters and the air space, and had even reserved the right to invade. Gaza would still be a prison, its borders hermetically sealed, its economy trampled and squeezed out of existence.

I remembered a tragic description I had read of an old man standing on the beach in Gaza with a box of oranges – his sole means of livelihood – beside him, throwing them, hopelessly, one by one into the sea. He was prevented from exporting his oranges to Israel, and rather than let them rot in his orchards, he preferred to do this. The utter waste of it all.

Yet amazingly, among our friends in Rafah, humanity still prevailed. On the anniversary of Tom's shooting I received an e-mail from the family of Dr Samir:

Dear Tom family, we will never forget the time when Tom first came at our house with Alison. He was high-spirited and so generous with his care and concern. Probably we were to him just a family that needs his support. He played with our children and

take many photos of them. He lost his life for children, and instead
of them. At this anniversary we share with you the pain and agony
of losing him. He will remain deep in our hearts. May God bless
his soul and replace this sad memory with happy one.

The trial had now been going on for almost a year. Anthony had
decided he would fly to Israel for the verdict, which was due on
27 June, and Billy was determined to go with him. Peter Carter
had been trying to obtain permission for him from the Israeli
Foreign Ministry and eventually we received the following
communication: Billy could enter Israel if the Embassy guaran-
teed that he would leave within twenty-four hours; if an Embassy
official accompanied him throughout; and if Billy provided a
letter signed by himself and a lawyer stating that he would not
attempt to enter the Gaza Strip, and that he would do nothing
illegal.

To us it seemed insulting beyond belief. There was no good
reason why Billy should be barred from Israel, and the government had made no attempt to provide one. Billy, however, wasn't
about to accept such conditions. 'The bastards!' was his reaction.
He was adamant that he was going to go, and Anthony and I were
fully behind him, though we had no idea what the outcome
would be. Anthony called me just as they boarded the aircraft and
I phoned the Foreign Office to ask them to notify the Embassy in
Tel Aviv that Billy and Anthony were on their way.

'Well,' I said to the smooth young Foreign Office duty officer
at the other end of the line, 'if they refuse to let Billy in we will let
the media know.'

'Oh, I shouldn't do that,' he said quickly. 'It won't do your
cause any good.'

I bit my tongue, but something snapped inside me. Unlike the
FCO, we didn't have to work with the Israelis on a day-to-day
basis. We were free agents. 'I think by now we've learned that, if
it hadn't been for the media, if we had simply relied on diplomatic
channels, we would never have got as far as we have,' I said.

I doubted there was any chance that when their plane touched down in Tel Aviv at three o'clock in the morning Billy might somehow be able to get through, but we did hope the Israelis might respond to the absurdity of the situation. Vain hope! Anthony phoned very early to say they had been stopped by Israeli Security and Billy had been detained at the airport.

'I told them that either Billy and I stayed together or we left together,' Anthony said, 'but they told me that was impossible. Although Billy was standing right beside me, my passport had been stamped and I was now in Israel. So I'm afraid I had no alternative but to leave him.'

Anthony was clearly furious. He had been in touch with Karin who had spoken to Billy, suggesting that she should go to court straight away on his behalf with a request that he should be able to attend the trial without conditions. Billy agreed, but the request had to go through many judicial stages, ending with the Attorney General. By the time a reply came it was too late, in any case, for Billy to reach the court in Ashkelon.

The request was turned down on the vague grounds of 'security'. This, we had been told, was common practice with the Israeli security service, Shin Bet. Very rarely do they give specific information on why an individual is being denied entry – even in matters of life and death. Though Billy had no record of lawlessness whatever, the fact that they had shot his brother to them gave him an immediate motive for revenge. The Israeli Deputy Ambassador would later say on Channel 4 News that they had denied him entry because they feared 'trouble'.

So Billy spent the day at the airport in a room with another detainee, with the Embassy keeping in touch by phone. When lunchtime came and food was brought, Billy put a mischievous note on the glass panel of the door saying 'Gone to lunch. Back in ten minutes'. This 'trouble' caused confusion among the young soldiers of Israeli Security, who are not known for their sense of humour.

*   *   *

On the afternoon of 27 June 2005, Taysir Walid Heib was convicted of manslaughter. He was also convicted of obstruction of justice, submitting false testimony, obtaining false testimony and unbecoming behaviour. The long and impressively thorough ruling found that he had lied repeatedly about events in Rafah on 11 April 2003 and that he had shot Tom with clear knowledge of the consequences. The judges stated categorically that it was Taysir's shot that had caused Tom's death – they found no evidence of medical malpractice, and they completely accepted Dr Chapman's report. There was no doubt Taysir had broken the rules of engagement and had 'brought Israel into disrepute'.

As Taysir was led from the court he tried to break loose from his guards and lashed out in fury at the crowd of foreign journalists – there were very few Israeli journalists in court. Interviewed outside the courtroom Anthony looked drained. I thought of all the exhausting months he had spent pursuing this investigation and producing his report – doing the work that the Israeli justice system should have done.

'Does this amount to justice, Mr Hurndall?' the BBC journalist James Reynolds asked him.

'It amounts to limited justice,' Anthony said. 'We're very pleased that it has got to this stage as we were told at the outset that there was no way we would get the Israelis to turn their story round. My concern is that the crime was not actually fairly laid at this soldier's door. He is a scapegoat, a pawn in a larger system. As a Bedouin he has been laid at the sacrificial altar of Israeli policy, one of very indiscriminate shooting and very little accountability. We don't feel that the underlying policy has been addressed.'

'So what is your response to the verdict?' James Reynolds asked.

'In terms of this particular soldier it is the correct verdict on the evidence that has been presented,' Anthony replied. 'It might have been appropriate to bring a murder prosecution, but we haven't seen all the evidence, though we have asked to do so repeatedly. Maybe there should have been further prosecutions, and indeed we think this goes much higher up the chain of command.'

'What is your feeling for the Israeli government today?' Reynolds asked.

'Great disappointment,' Anthony replied. 'Israel is a democratic and open society in many respects, but it has great failings which the government is failing to face up to. It has behaved irresponsibly, and been oppressive and dishonest.'

'And finally, Mr Hurndall, do you have a message for the Israeli people?' Anthony was asked.

He answered. 'I would say to them, you are a great people but there are matters that you seriously have to address, both about the way the army handles itself in Gaza and the West Bank, and the way it deals with a number of other issues. We sincerely hope as a family that you will address these so that you can find peace and security.'

On 11 August 2005, Taysir Walid Heib was sentenced to eight years in prison – the longest sentence imposed on a soldier for killing a civilian since the Second Intifada broke out in 2000, the previous maximum having been twenty-one months for 'conduct unbefitting a soldier'. The prosecution had asked for the maximum sentence for manslaughter of twenty years, but the court held back, saying that a heavier sentence would only lend credence to claims that Taysir had been made a scapegoat.

Before the judge pronounced sentence he spoke the following words:

> Sergeant Wahid Taysir caused a soul to leave this world. He spilt the blood of a young man in the bloom of youth, causing the loss of an entire world. When that young man was alive, there was no one else like him, and there will never be anyone like him again.

The Israelis immediately claimed the case as a triumph for Israeli justice. But I thought of the peaceworker Brian Avery, shot in the face by the IDF, and of the United Nations worker Iain

Hook, killed by an Israeli marksman in the Jenin refugee camp, of James Miller, and Rachel Corrie, all of whose cases had been dismissed. I thought of Amjad's dead friends, and of little Iman al-Hams, and of the 3,600 unnamed Palestinian civilians and 600 children whom Amnesty reported had been killed by the Israeli army since September 2000, not to speak of the thousands who had suffered injuries without proper access to medical care. None of these people had received any justice. This couldn't be the end of it. We must try to salvage some good from all the pain we'd suffered, that we'd seen for ourselves, fight on to bring the faceless men in charge of Israeli army policy to account. Do it for Tom.

AFTERWARDS

It is October 2006 and I am sitting looking out at the garden. The garden has been my summer project. I wanted to create a place of beauty where all Tom's family and friends could relax and be together, a place where we would all exchange stories of Tom. Jay, a friend from the choir, created a design with diagonal raised beds which I had built using old stock bricks, and I filled them with fragrant climbing roses, evergreen jasmine, lavender and so much else that there is hardly a square of earth still visible. Cream and pink honeysuckle, deep pink tea roses and several types of clematis cover the walls. I gave one corner a flavour of the Middle East, with canna lilies, oleander and grevillea, and designed a wrought-iron garden table with green and blue hand-painted Palestinian tiles brought back from Jerusalem to remind me of the American Colony Hotel.

We've all found healing in the garden. Kay, who has become an important part of our lives, has created a special corner with miniature dark pink sedums. Fred enjoys it from the balcony Billy built for him. Sophie has always loved fragrant flowers and Anthony, not known as a keen gardener, has taken an interest. Even the cat has found a favourite spot amongst the ferns behind an ornamental urn.

But now the summer is over, and I'm sitting looking out, surrounded by files of documents and press cuttings, thinking about all that has happened during the past eighteen months, since the conviction of Taysir.

The inquest into Tom's death was finally held in London, at

Camden Coroner's Court, in April 2006. It had had to wait for
the outcome of Taysir's trial. We were fortunate to be represented
by Michael Mansfield, QC, and Imran Khan. I found the dynamic
Michael Mansfield extremely warm and likeable and greatly
admired his laser-sharp brain. It was inspiring to see these two
lawyers working together, as I know they regularly do.

The jury returned a unanimous verdict of Unlawful Killing, as
it had done a few days earlier at the inquest of James Miller. On
my desk is the jury's statement:

> We the Jury unanimously agree that Mr Thomas Peter Hurndall
> was shot in Rafah in Gaza between 3.30 p.m. and 4.30 p.m. on
> 11.4.2003. He was shot intentionally with the intention to kill
> him. The Jury would like to express their dismay at the lack of
> cooperation from the Israeli authorities during this investigation.

The Israeli authorities had refused to allow the Metropolitan
Police to travel to the site of the shooting, and refused to release
vital documents for the Coroner's investigation directly to him, or
to attend the inquest. Yet even so, it had been clear to the jury
that Tom had been shot intentionally, in cold blood, within an
army culture where soldiers were not held to account for killing
civilians, where those in command were too quick to believe a
soldier's story, or turned a blind eye.

I think Anthony and I were surprised at the devastating effect
the inquest had on both of us. Reading from Tom's journals, as
I did in court, seeing the film of Tom's shooting which was
shown, hearing Anthony read from his report, brought it all
back. As Anthony said afterwards, although it was three years
now since Tom was shot, it had been impossible for us to deal
properly with what happened. We had had to put a part of
ourselves aside just in order to carry on. 'I have tried to keep
myself forensically impartial,' Anthony told a journalist, 'partly
to ensure I got to the truth but also to protect myself. The
process has put my feelings into something like deep freeze. I

thought the inquest would provide an end to it but it is just going on.'

What the inquest did, however, was to bring the case into the public eye again with huge media coverage, and to strengthen political support. The *Independent* devoted its front page to an extract from Tom's journal under the headline 'A Death Foretold'. The Labour MP Richard Burden, whose close involvement we had so much appreciated, tabled an Early Day Motion in the House of Commons, which was signed by more than a hundred MPs, expressing renewed concern over Israel's failure to investigate the cases of innocent civilians killed by the IDF, and urging Israel to comply with international law and to withdraw from all the Occupied Territories.

In July Anthony, Fred and I were in the House of Lords to hear Baroness Northover question the Attorney General, Lord Goldsmith, about the possibility of bringing prosecutions in the UK over the deaths of Tom and James Miller, as suggested by the Camden coroner. I knew it was good that Fred should hear that people still cared about his brother, and about the cause for which he had died. He sat gripped by the proceedings and wanted to stay and stay.

And we have had our own meeting with the Attorney General, who is pursuing Tom's case with the Israeli authorities to ascertain whether there should be other arrests. To this day we have received no official public apology from the Israeli authorities.

I look with anger and despair at the press cuttings describing Israel's actions in the Gaza Strip during this past summer. A Palestinian family blown up during a day out on the beach – an act denied by the IDF, though an independent ballistics expert found that 'the crater size, the shrapnel, the types of injuries, their location on the bodies' left little doubt that this family was killed by an Israeli shell. The orgy of destruction and killing in Gaza in retaliation for the kidnapping of Corporal Gilad Shalit.

The fact that thousands of Palestinians are still held without trial in 'administrative detention' in Israel is rarely mentioned, though in July 150 distinguished British Jews, including Harold Pinter, Lynne Reid Banks and Miriam Margolyes, publicly expressed their horror at 'the collective punishment of the people of Gaza', and urged the public to write to the British government and to the Israeli Embassy: 'Presenting this as an isolated hostage-taking incident ignores Israel's regular snatching of Palestinians from their homes,' they wrote. As the outstanding Israeli journalist Gideon Levy put it in *Ha'aretz*: 'We kidnapped civilians and they kidnapped a soldier, we are a state and they are a terror organisation.'

I am keen to pursue the project we have been discussing with the union to which I belonged for thirty years, the National Union of Teachers, to set up a scheme in Gaza in Tom's name to give learning support to children with disabilities. I couldn't forget the sight of the School for the Deaf in Rafah in its poor, war-torn, crumbling building, and of so many disabled people, especially children. But for the present anyway we can't get into Gaza, and the people in Gaza can't get out.

But there was good news, too. In July I received an exuberant e-mail from Amjad to say that he had passed his exams. Now he is even more desperate to come to England, but it's difficult, and I remember how much his last visit disturbed him. It's so painful for me to think about Amjad. There are days when I know I should e-mail him, but it would be cruel to get up his hopes of leaving Rafah. I suppose this is a pattern that's easy to get into – turning away from situations that are too dreadful to think about. But after what I have seen, I know I must not turn away, which is why I have written this book.

Mohammed is in London studying for a master's degree in engineering, and comes to the house often. One summer Sunday not long ago he and some friends from a Palestinian dance group were performing at a local street party. They came back for tea in the garden afterwards and I listened with amazement to the tragic stories they all had to tell. There was not one amongst them who had not lost a member of his or her family. They were all embarked on advanced courses, studying for PhDs and master's degrees. When I asked them what they planned to do afterwards, the answer was the same. 'It's terrible to be separated from our families, but we don't want to go back. We want a life. Gaza is a prison and the Israelis want us to leave.' I felt for Mohammed's mother on hearing such things.

Mohammed has taken to London. He makes us laugh with his grasp of slang, his urban body language and his street cred. He, Billy and Fred have become close. Recently Mohammed came with Anthony and me to see Fred play football for Winchester – Tom's old school, where Fred is now very happily into his second year. The sight of Mohammed in this safe and traditionally beautiful English setting, among green meadows and ancient grey school buildings, was a vivid reminder of the daily conflict and insecurity with which he had lived. After the match, Mohammed ran on to the pitch in true Palestinian style and lifted six-foot Fred right off the ground, and suddenly I had a vision of Tom picking Fred up and throwing him over his shoulder as he used to do. Fred, who's become used to the expressive ways of the Middle East, didn't mind a bit, though I expect other boys might have.

As for the rest of us, our lives are very gradually beginning to settle – but in quite a different form from before. I constantly think of snow globes, those glass toys that you shake to create a snowstorm. Eventually everything settles, as things have slowly begun to do for us. We've all changed, found new strengths and different priorities. I think we've all become more public people, more politically aware, able to speak out in a way I certainly never would before. Sophie has always been articulate, and in speaking out strongly about the Middle East and the policies of our government she has in a sense found a new platform for her abilities. She now has an interesting new job helping charities and voluntary organisations develop their communications effectively.

Billy, with his creative scientific brain, is doing a physics degree at Queen Mary's University in London. Anthony is reshaping his legal practice. For myself, this year has been a search – for Tom and for a greater understanding of the person he was. I knew that I must do this if I was ever to be whole, and able to be there for the family again.

In March this year I went back to Jerusalem. I wanted to retrace Tom's steps, to find the rooftop café where he had sat, Coke in hand, writing his journal, to visit the Church of the Holy Sepulchre, which had made such a deep impression upon him.

I was staying at the crumbling and characterful 'New' Imperial Hotel near the Jaffa Gate, and on the first morning I set off into the Old City, making my way uncertainly through the maze of alleyways with their pale, glowing, almost translucent flagstones, avoiding the carts that came rumbling towards me, trying not to get into conversation with all the shopkeepers and storeholders who wanted to stop me and show me their goods.

Within a very short time I was lost, and as I stood wondering what to do I heard a voice: 'Lady, you look sad. I am a Bedouin and I know. What are you looking for?' It was one of the shopkeepers. He came out of his shop and I explained my mission. 'I know the place you mean,' he said. 'I will take you there.'

We walked along silently together until we came to a staircase between the stalls in the Suk Aftimos. I thanked him and he laid his hand on my arm: 'Everything has a beginning and an end,' he said. 'We have a saying in Bedouin' – he pointed to his forehead – 'that it was written that your son should die. You could have talked to him, argued with him, but it would not have been different. You must look to the future, allow yourself to breathe, get on with your life.' Then he waved and was gone.

I mounted the staircase, which gave on to a wide roof terrace with tables and chairs. There were big clay pots with plants, and in a corner a stack of hookahs. It was wonderfully quiet. I went and leaned on the terrace railing and there below me in the morning

sunlight was the gold Dome of the Rock and the grey dome of
the Holy Sepulchre, just as Tom had described them. The roofs of
Old Jerusalem stretched away, red tiles, creamy domes, hundreds
of small balconies and water tanks. Here and there a dark cedar
tree poked up, and I could hear the different sounds of birds.
Tom's presence was so strong. If I turned round he would be
there, sitting at a table with his long legs stretched out, smoking a
hookah, writing in his notebook with that very peculiar concentration of his.

I thought about the Bedouin's words, which seemed to have
come from a place of deep suffering, and all that they meant. It
came to me strongly that it was precisely because Tom was aware
of death that he was so vividly and passionately alive; his journal
showed that. And that given the person he was, there was really
nothing I could have done to stop him.

Then I made my way to the Church of the Holy Sepulchre.
Standing in its great silent, dim interior, I thought about Tom,
wondered where he had walked, where he had sat. On my right
and left were side chapels, Catholic, Russian Orthodox, some
simple, some glitteringly ornate. Eventually I chose a simple little
chapel, unfrequented and slightly out of the way off one of the
transepts, and sat down on the stone seat. It seemed to be a space
without distractions, without a name, a spiritual space with no
particular allegiance and the one that was truest to Tom.

It was very quiet, and I sat and let the atmosphere of the church
seep into me. I could almost physically feel the pulls of the
different religious dogmas which we human beings use and abuse
for our own purposes. Yet somehow this building seemed to
incorporate the essence of what was good in them all. It was a
place of division, and yet of unity, a place that penetrated deep
into the soul, so powerful and serene that it had caused Tom, an
agnostic leaning towards atheism, to buy a crucifix. Within its
stillness I lit a candle for him and sat for a long time, watching its
small light burning steadily against the dark.

*   *   *

A few weeks ago I left London and drove north. Ever since Tom died I had longed to go to some wild and lonely place where I could lose myself in the power and vastness of the sea. After my last visit to Rafah, when I had been utterly demolished by the destruction I had seen, the need to be somehow cleansed by the sea had become an overwhelming urge. I had a yearning to go to Scotland, with its reassuring links to my childhood, and especially to Fingal's Cave, that mysterious place which had inspired the young Mendelssohn to write music of such haunting beauty. I wanted to scream my grief and anger to the waves and let them do my struggling for me, to encounter a force so great that it would give me a perspective, an understanding of what had happened and how it fitted into the larger scheme.

So on a calm, sunny day I arrived in Fionnphort and took a little motor boat past Iona to Staffa. As we drew nearer to the tiny island its extraordinary cliff face came into focus, gigantic grey-green basalt columns, crowned with rock of a rougher texture, with the sea foaming around the mysterious entrance to Fingal's Cave. There were only a few of us in the boat, and we climbed out and made our way gingerly along the rocky path down to the yawning black opening.

Once inside I stood in awe. The cave was like a cathedral, with great Norman pillars and internal arches, and suddenly I was back at Tom's memorial service in Westminster Cathedral. Round the edge of the cave were more clusters of basalt pillars which had been cut off by some natural cataclysm and which formed a kind of path. They looked like groups of people, very solemn and still, and as I stepped along them it seemed to me that I was walking beside all the people who had come to pay tribute to Tom, and that their love and respect for him was somehow holding me, supporting me.

At the end of the transept were more basalt columns, like the pipes of a massive organ, and I stood very still, listening to its sounds – the many-layered ethereal music of the ocean, the echoing roar, the irregular deep surges and sucking noises, the wilder explosions as the water hit the rocks.

As I looked down into the crystal water I could see that the pillars changed from grey to pink, right down to the bottom of the volcanic rock, and suddenly out of the water the small dark shape of an otter appeared, slid between the rocks and disappeared below me. I thought of all the eruptions of the earth's crust, the geological upheavals, the fragmentations that had gone to form this place. And now it was a whole, compacted together by some mighty force, and stronger than before. And I thought that perhaps, after all this life-changing upheaval that had been like some volcanic fire, my own fragmented self might be put together again, and be stronger. One day I would be able to remember Tom and celebrate his life without the intense, racking sadness I felt now, with happiness even. Some-how this ancient place gave me hope. I didn't cry out to the sea as I had thought I would. I sang. Quietly to myself, the overture to *Fingal's Cave*, which is called in Gaelic the Cave of Melody.

When we got back into the boat the wind had got up and there was a lashing rain. Holding on tight I gave in to the tossing of the boat, feeling the crash of the waves on the bow, and the whipping rain and wind on my face. I was glad the weather had changed. I wanted the elements to cleanse me, to blow through my head. Looking back at Staffa as it receded into the distance I felt certain that there must be some grand design, some force and intelligence that had shaped it – a design of which we were all a part if we could only know it.

Next day I took the ferry back to the mainland. I drove along the North West Coast and then turned inland towards Glencoe. On either side of me rose mountains of an intense emerald green which swelled into a bowl as I approached Glencoe. It had been raining and streams were gushing down the mountainsides, over the great boulders, and I longed to get out, to bury my face in the clear mountain water, to breathe the clean air, but something powerful forced me on.

Nearer to the pass the mountains began to close in. As I entered the pass, I began to feel an almost physical pressure, as if a great force was bearing down on me. Again I wanted to stop, but I somehow knew I must go on, through the narrow passage in the mountains. My face was wet with tears, and I heard a voice, which was my own, calling out 'Thomas! Thomas!' It was an anguished, involuntary cry that came from the depths of my being, like the cry of birth. I remembered the travail of Tom's birth, the moment of first holding him, vulnerable and restless, and the overwhelming feeling of wanting to protect and nurture him. Now I knew that I must let him go and return to life, that it was part of loving to be able to let go. *What will survive of us is love.* I thought of Tom's 'Rules for Life', which he'd written in his teens, and I seemed to hear his voice saying to me, *None of us deserves this life, and one single minute on this planet is an undeserved blessing.*

And I drove on through the pass until finally the mountains parted and I found myself on a plateau, with fresh green countryside opening out before me.

ACKNOWLEDGEMENTS

When I embarked on my diary while sitting beside Tom in hospital it never occurred to me that I would one day feel moved to write and publish a book about him. That I have now done so is thanks to a multitude of talented people to whom I owe a great debt.

My deepest gratitude is to Hazel Wood, who held my hand through-out the writing process. Hazel, from whom I learnt so much, has been invaluable in harnessing and giving shape to my thoughts, emotions and the events of the story.

My thanks to Victoria Millar for her sensitive and acute judgment, to Mary Morris for her diligent attention to the final details, and to so very many other hugely able and inspiring people at Bloomsbury.

I shall be eternally grateful to Andrew Nurnberg, my literary agent, for believing in and nurturing the book, for his unending encouragement and for guiding me through the unfamiliar world of publishing with great expertise.

My thanks to Colonel Tom Fitzalan Howard, former British Defence Attaché in Israel, who led me through and commented on the minefield of military and diplomatic matters with absolute integrity, breadth and patience.

My thanks to Kay Fernandes, professional photographer and research-er, whose outstanding flair, skill and painstaking care continues to fill me with awe. It was Garth Stead, as the foreign photographer present at the scene, who helped to expose the truth which British and Israeli govern-ments could not ignore.

My sincere thanks to a host of spectacularly helpful people in Palestine, Israel and the UK who guided us through the different processes and who made a difference. Many I have interviewed and, where relevant, a few people have been kind enough to check sections of the text. These include lawyers, Parliamentarians, diplomats, those involved in Tom's medical care, Union members, representatives of NGOs and aid agencies and those who were with Tom in the Middle East. Some cannot be named for their own security – subject to potential threat both from their own and other governments. To name just a few: Imran Khan, Matthew

Ryder, Danny Friedman, Michael Mansfield QC, Michel Massih QC, David Freeman, Avigdor Feldman, Karin Loevy, Kiran Bhogal, Michael Sfarad, Phil Shiner, Richard Burden MP, Jeremy Corbyn MP, Crispin Blunt MP, Sir Gerald Kaufman MP, Andrew George MP, John Austin MP, Dr Ahmad Tibi MK, Baroness Elizabeth Symons, Baroness Lindsay Northover, Baroness Jenny Tonge, Baroness Shirley Williams, Lord Navnit Dholakia, Sir Sherard and Lady Bridget Cowper-Coles, Peter Carter, Scott Simpson, Afif and Christ'l Safieh, Professor Reichental, Professor Gabriel Gurman, Netta (whose surname I never knew), Professor Keith Andrews, Professor Derick Wade, Dr C. Chapman, Dr Roy McGregor, Patti Simonson, Steve Synott, Sulieman Mleahat, Belinda Coote, Chris Doyle, Gillian Watts, Linda Ramsden, Nathan Chapman, Michelle de Mello, Phil Callan, Joseph Carr, Alison Phillips, Raphael Cohen.

There are many people in the media to whom we owe much. I am particularly indebted to the following enlightened foreign correspondents and writers upon whose extensive knowledge I depended: Lyse Doucet, Chris McGreal, Rageh Omaar and Sandra Jordan. Simon Block, playwright, helped me with his insight and tremendous wit to know Tom more deeply. Antony Wood shed light on many tricky decisions.

I'd like to thank Guy Protheroe, Director of the English Chamber Choir, and his wife Ann Manly, and my friends in the English Chamber Choir, from the bottom of my heart for the exquisite music at the 'Concert for Tom', Tom's funeral and memorial service, for their warmth and for helping me to return to music.

My warmest thanks to my dear cousin, Vari Havard-Millar, and my truly wonderful friends Patricia and Charles Brims, Jamil Bullata, Erella and Danny Danievsky, Elisabeth Eidinow, Mike Evans, Vicky Farmer, Ian and Janet Harrison, Jo Fitzalan Howard, Max Hughes, John and Catherine Jardine, Didi Al-Khalil, Ehud Krinis, Anne Perkins, Anne Ritchie, Diana and Harold Rose, Julia Singer, Anne Stoneham, Ann Sullivan, Sarah Taylor, Mike Torbe and Olivia and Patrick Whitworth for accompanying me and keeping my feet on the ground throughout this journey. I shall never forget their affection, the spirit of our conversations, our walks across Hampstead Heath, our laughter and gentle quietness.

Above all, I would like to thank Anthony for helping me to remember all manner of details, our thoughts, observations and the order of events, and for endeavouring to explain to me, repeatedly, the bewildering legal mazes. Without his meticulous report the picture would have been vastly different.

My deepest wish in writing this book is that, with the healing passage of time, Tom's dear friends and our extraordinarily courageous children, Sophie, Bill and Fred, will smile at the thought of him and always remember Tom's love for them.

SOME CURRENT NGOs AND AID AGENCIES

UK:

The Amos Trust: www.amostrust.org

The Council for the Advancement of Arab-British Understanding (CAABU): www.caabu.org

Christian Aid: www.christian-aid.org.uk

The Israeli Committee Against House Demolitions (ICAHD UK): www.icahduk.org

Jews for Justice for Palestinians (JFJFP): www.jfjfp.org

Medical Aid for Palestinians (MAP): www.map-uk.org

Palestine Solidarity Campaign (PSC): www.palestinecampaign.org

War on Want: www.waronwant.org

Palestine:

Al-Haq: www.alhaq.org

MIFTAH: www.miftah.org

Palestinian Centre for Human Rights (PCHR): www.pchrgaza.ps

Palestinian Human Rights Monitoring Group (PHRMG): www.phrmg.org

Palestinian NGOs network (PNGO): www.pngo.net

Israel:

Architects for Human Rights: www.bimkom.org

Breaking the Silence: www.shovrimshtika.org

B'Tselem: www.btselem.org

Gush Shalom: www.gush-shalom.org

Machsom Watch: www.machsomwatch.org

The Olive Tree Movement: www.o-t-m.org
Parents Circle: www.theparentscircle.com
Physicians for Human Rights: www.physiciansforhumanrights.org
Rabbis for Human Rights: www.rhr.israel.net
Yesh Din: www.yesh-din.org
Yesh Gvul: www.yesh-gvul.org

Israel and Palestine:
Combatants for Peace: www.combatantsforpeace.org
One Voice: www.blog.onevoicemovement.org
Ta'ayush: www.taayush.org

International organizations and other sources of information:
The Alternative Information Centre (AIC):
   www.alternativenews.org
Amnesty International: www.amnesty.org
Electronic Intifada: www.electronicintifada.net
Occupation Magazine: www.kibush.co.il
Open Bethlehem: www.openbethlehem.org
PLO Negotiations Affairs Department: www.nad-plo.org
United Nations Office for the Coordination of Humanitarian
   Affairs (OCHA): www.ochaonline.un.org
US Campaign to End Israeli Occupation:
   www.endtheoccupation.org

THE TOM HURNDALL EDUCATION FUND

The National Union of Teachers, along with Education Action International (Charity No: 1003323), has established a fund in memory of Tom with the aim of making provision for vulnerable, disabled children in Gaza. It wil be managed by the Canaan Institute for Education Development in Gaza.

Education Action International (TH Education Fund)
3 Dufferin Street
London EC1Y 8PD
UK

Tel: 00 44 (0)20 7426 5800

Email: info@education-action.org

A NOTE ON THE AUTHOR

Jocelyn Hurndall was born in Winchester and spent her early childhood in Mauritius, the only English-speaker in a French-speaking school. In the early 1970s she worked as kibbutz volunteer on the Israeli/Lebanese border, influenced by her father, who had worked as an engineer in Jordan before the Six Day War. In 1974 she began a career as a teacher, developing a special interest in inclusion and disability and gaining a master's degree. She eventually became Head of Learning Support in an inner-city school. She lives in North London with her family.